Facets of Indian Advertising and Consumer Behaviour

An Empirical Approach

Facets of Indian Advertising and Consumer Behaviour

An Empirical Approach

Kaleem Mohammed Khan
Department of Business Administration
Aligarh Muslim University
Aligarh

Mohammed Naved Khan
Department of Business Administration
Aligarh Muslim University
Aligarh

KANISHKA PUBLISHERS, DISTRIBUTORS
NEW DELHI 110 002

KANISHKA PUBLISHERS, DISTRIBUTORS
4697/5-21 A, Ansari Road, Daryaganj
New Delhi-110 002
Phones: 327 0497, 328 8285
Fax: 011-328 8285

First Published 2002

ISBN 81-7391-447-8

PRINTED IN INDIA

Published by Madan Sachdeva for Kanishka Publishers, Distributors, 4697/5-21 A, Ansari Road, Daryaganj, New Delhi 110 002; Lasertypeset by Baba DTP Services, Delhi, and Printed at Nice Printing Press, Delhi.

Preface

Advertising is a multi-dimensional and multifaceted business activity. Because of its persuasive powers and pervasive nature, all of us are exposed to it through multitude of mass and selective media vehicles. Because of its pervasiveness, it has been the target of criticism of researchers, feminist advocates, economists, public policy makers and social scientists. But it also has a large number of supporters in industry who are of the opinion that it is one of the most potent marketing tools in their hands.

In India, advertising has made great strides in terms of creativity, execution and technology. The Indian advertisements are comparable to that of any developed country of the world. Advertising expenditure and variety, both in rupee terms and in coverage, have increased phenomenally during the last two decades. However, as a percentage of gross domestic product (GDP) it is still low as compared to other developed countries. During this period, mass media has also undergone complete metamorphosis. Television has emerged as the most prominent and fastest growing medium for advertisement of consumer goods – FMCGs, white goods, consumer electronics and other durables.

Despite these developments, not much research of serious nature pertaining to various facets of advertising has been done in India. Special interest magazines and business & marketing magazines provide lot of factual information about advertising. These magazines also publish journalistic articles as well as opinions, views, and reactions of people associated with the advertising profession in India. However, very little research based literature on advertising is available in India. There is a strong need for a scholarly journal in which articles covering different facets of advertising and marketing may get a place. Advertising and Marketing (A&M) magazine provides this opportunity to some extent, yet, most of the articles appearing here are either journalistic in nature or reflect the experiential nature of advertising. The authors strongly feel that various facets of advertising and consumer behaviour should be researched from an empirical angle. This book is the result of this concern. But the authors would like to caution that this volume does not claim to cover all possible facets of advertising and consumer behaviour in the Indian context.

These studies were undertaken during a span of five years (1996-2000). In completing this volume, the authors received generous cooperation from various quarters. In particular, the help extended by the students of MBA, in collection of primary data, deserves special mention.

We are thankful to our colleagues in the department who served as a constant source of inspiration for undertaking these studies.

Finally, we are thankful to our families for their support and understanding. This book is dedicated to them.

Kaleem Mohammed Khan
Mohammed Naved Khan
Department of Business Administration
Faculty of Management Studies & Research
Aligarh Muslim University
Aligarh (India)

Contents

1

Facets of Indian Advertising and Consumer Behaviour: An Introduction

It is needless to say that advertising has gained profound recognition and importance all over the globe as an indispensable tool of marketing. This recognition has led to its remarkable growth–both quantitatively and qualitatively. On the negative side, advertising has been constantly criticised by economists, social thinkers, anthropologists and public policy makers for its adverse economic and social impact on the society. One thing, which is certain about advertising, is that, in spite of growing concern towards some of its social effects, both profit and non-profit organisations are increasingly being compelled to use it for furthering their objectives. Taking the Indian perspective, advertising has witnessed a tremendous growth in the last two decades. During the last ten years, the gross billing of advertising expenditure increased by more than ten folds. The booming advertising industry is projected to grow to a size of Rs. 8400 Crores by the year 2005 from just Rs. 8.6 Crores in 1976. Furthermore, The share of television in total advertising expenditure in India is expected to grow from the current share of 36 per cent to 40 per cent by the year 2010.

During this period, Indian market scene has also experienced a drastic change. The competition has become intense in consumer products and industrial goods category. In almost all the industries the complacent seller's market has given way to vigilant buyer's market. Presently, Indian industry is churning out an impressive array of products in almost every product category. In the unpredictable razor edge competitiveness of today's market, marketers regard advertising as being indispensable marketing tool. Marketers are resorting to creative advertising strategies so as to outmaneuvere competitiors in the market. In order to distinctly position their products in the specific market segments, marketers are making increasing use advertising. Al Ries and Jack Trout see positioning as a creative exercise done with an existing product. In their words "positioning starts with a product. A piece of merchandise, a service, a company, an institution or even a person .... but positioning is not what you do to your product. Positioning is what you do to the mind of the prospect. That is, you position the product in the mind of the prospect" (Al Ries and Jack Trout, *Positioning: The Battle of Your Mind,* 1982). Thus, positioning invariably requires creative advertising campaigns to distinctly position the product and this is what Indian and Global marketers are doing today.

Due to the shift from seller's to buyer's market, the consumers are in a potentially advantageous position as far as the selection of goods and services is concerned. Further, in order to survive and grow, it is imperative on the part of marketers to fully *understand* and *know* their consumers.

In the changed market scenario there is increased concern for the role of advertising in society and its necessity as business and marketing tool. In the light of above mentioned sweeping changes on the marketing front, the researchers thought it fit to conduct studies on different facets of Indian advertising and consumer behaviour. Since advertising is a multifaceted and multidimensional business activity, conducting research on its various dimensions is itself a challenge and requires a team effort. And the same is true for research in the area of consumer behaviour. Thus, the present work does not claim to cover all the facets of Indian advertising and consumer behaviour. The present volume contains fifteen research studies, all of which are empirical in nature. Conceptual issues, changing trends and relevant research methodologies specific to advertising and consumer behvaiour have been discussed. The authors feel that these studies will be of immense help to advertising practitioners in the planning of their promotional strategies on the one hand and to academicians and researchers in gaining an insight into advertising and consumer behaviour dynamics, on the other. Going a step further, we recommend a research approach where both academicians and practitioners work together so that a symbiotic relationship is established between the two. This approach may be termed as multiple orientation. Unfortunately in India there is very little interaction and co-operation between academics and practitioners.

These research studies were undertaken between 1996 to 2000. The first study "Mega Attitudes Towards Advertising: A Study of Men and Women" attempts to measure the attitudes of men and women exposed to advertising through various mass media vehicles. The basic purpose here is to gauge the feelings of those who are most probably influenced by it as consumers. The attitudes have been measured in terms of various facets of advertising. For this purpose a comprehensive scale was developed after an extensive literature search. The aspects covered in this study are as follows:

1. advertising as business tool;
2. advertising's informative role;
3. advertising and materialism;
4. influence of advertising on adults and children;
5. advertising and media; and
6. present status of Indian advertising.

On account of TV emerging as a powerful medium for advertising in the recent years, a need was felt to measure the perception of those who are exposed to commercials appearing in TV, especially at prime time. Thus, the second study deals with the perception of people towards TV advertising. The viewer's reactions have been measured in terms of five adjectives i.e. *amusing*, *irritating*, *appealing*, *convincing* and *informative*. For this purpose commercials appearing at prime time were video recorded and later screened before the sample. Their reactions were recorded in terms of the above mentioned adjectives and later they were analysed using appropriate statistical techniques.

The next study concentrates on the influence of cinema advertising on attitudinal change and consequently on purchase intentions. Despite decreased importance of cinema as a medium of entertainment and advertising, it is still popular among middle and lower income groups. This study has been undertaken to explore some specific aspects of cinema advertising. They are:

1. movie going pattern;
2. degree of attitudinal change and consequent purchase intentions;
3. optimum number of exposures to bring attitudinal change and to maintain visual interests; and
4. relative effectiveness of different formats used in advertisements.

The advertising communication sources have been researched extensively. Advertisers, quite often use different types of endorsers, to make advertising campaign effective. Of all the endorsers, using a celebrity spokesperson has always been a favourite strategy of advertisers and agencies. The study titled "Use and Effectiveness of Celebrity Endorsers in Advertising Messages" was undertaken to explore this important dimension of advertising. It was carried out in two phases. In the first phase, content analysis was done for those advertisements in which different celebrities appeared. In the second phase, the effectiveness of celebrity endorsers was measured by conducting consumer survey using a structured research instrument.

The objective of the next study titled "Audience Perception, Motivation and Recall of Humorous Appeals in Advertisements" was:

1. to gauge general and specific attitudes towards humorous advertising;
2. to find out the relationship between demographic variables and attitudes;
3. to ascertain the relative effectiveness of copy demand used for depicting humorous messages; and
4. to find out the impact of humorous appeal on brand recognition and recall vis-à-vis the serious appeal.

The next study i.e "Media Exposure, Media Effectiveness and Demographics" deals with media usage, habits and relative effectiveness of major media. This study tried to find out the media exposure patterns for four major media i.e. newspapers. magazines, T.V. and cinema. In addition, an attempt has been made to associate the relative effectiveness of these media with audience demographics.

The next study titled "Content Analysis Study of Comparative Television Commercials" is primarily based on content analysis technique. It discusses the comparative advertising as an image building strategy in the Indian context. The following issues have been addressed in this study:

1. the relative use of comparative advertising in television for different categories of products;
2. the type of comparison used;
3. the different competitive advantages stressed; and
4. the methods of comparative advertising utilised.

The successful subscription of a public issue, particularly from the new and lesser known companies, is very crucial and requires specialised kind of advertising–financial advertising. Since financial advertising requires special skills, there is a strong need to explore and investigate its impact on the potential investors. To accomplish this objective a study titled "The Role of Financial Advertising in Influencing Investment Decisions" was conducted with the following issues in mind:

1. to find out how investors search for different sources of information and how they obtain this information about the companies entering the capital market with equity issues;
2. to find out the type of companies whose equity shares are more likely to be purchased by prospective investors;
3. to measure the relative weights assigned to various information sources by the investors; and
4. to find out the relative importance attached to different characteristics of a company by the investors.

The next study i.e. "Selling Appeals, Demonstration Techniques and Basic Approaches in Audio Visuals" tries to explore the various appeals, execution styles and the bas ic tones used in various advertisements through content analysis.

The next three studies deal with the role portrayal of women in advertising. One of the most frequently levelled charges against advertising is the stereotypic portrayal of women. Researchers, public policy makers, social scientists and feminist advocates have been expressing concern over that portraying women in narrowly defined roles gives the impression to a common man that this is proper and natural. Continued portrayal of women in these narrow roles may not augur well for society because it creates misconceptions about women and encourages stereotyping. These studies are the offshoot of this concern. The first of these studies deals with the role portrayal of women in advertising and its impact on the image of companies who portray women in such stereotypic roles for promoting their brands. This study also attempts to explore the attitude of men and women, refelcted in their purchase intentions, towards those products/brands that are being promoted through stereotypic role portrayal of women. In the second study of this category, content analysis technique has been used for ascertaining the extent of role portrayal of women in TV commercials. The third study is comparative in nature. In this study the role portrayal of men and women has been studied in a cross-cultural context. The advertisements from India and US were compared in terms of role portrayal. Specifically, the basic aim of this study was to compare the role portrayal of men and women in TV advertisements of India and US. The specific objectives were:

1. to analyse the differences in role portrayal in Indian TV commercials on the pattern of a study undertaken in US;
2. to analyse and compare the role portrayals of two sexes as shown in the advertisements of both countries.

The last three studies, though not directly related with advertising, could have far reaching practical implications in devising advertising and marketing strategies. Marketers have acknowledged the role of family in general and involvement of husband-wife dyad in the purchase decision making process in particular. The first study attempts to investigates the effect of type of family on husband and wife involvement in the purchase decisions of certain selected products. The information about who influences the purchase decision within a family setup serves as the basic input in designing the marketing communication and subsequently in media selection. The penultimate study deals with one of the important emerging areas of marketing i.e. the significance of psychographics in the purchase of big-ticket items. This study tried to explore the significance of psychographics in the purchase of different brands of cars. This study has an applied research bias. Car manufacturers may use these findings in developing advertising and marketing campaigns. These types of studies may be periodically undertaken to find out the changing role of psychographics in the purchase of various' consumer products.

The last study deals with the measurement of consumer satisfaction which is a substantive domain in the field of marketing management. This study has assumed greater importance in the present scenario where the companies' survival and growth depends to a great extent on generating high amounts of consumer satisfaction. Excellent companies constantly try to monitor the satisfaction levels of their consumers and take prompt actions in case they find any form of consumer discontent. Through this study, the authors propose the use of importance performance analysis as a potent technique for measuring consumer satisfaction.

In undertaking these studies care has been taken to use appropriate research methodologies. However, there are certain limitations of these studies, which emanate from practical constraints such as paucity of time, non-accessibility of specific population segments, non-availability of perfect sampling frame, and lack of sufficient financial resources. In spite of these limitations, it is hoped that this volume will equally serve the needs of academic community, business organisations and advertising practitioners.

2

Mega Attitudes Towards Facets of Advertising: A Study of Men and Women

INTRODUCTION

Of all the marketing activities advertising is the most visible one and, therefore, it is also most controversial. The role of advertising in the business and in the society at large has been studied, analysed, defended, and criticised by large number of people representing a wide spectrum of professional groups, which include economists, sociologists, politicians, businessmen, novelists, anthropologists, psychologists and historians (Pollay, 1986) . It is generally considered that advertising as an institution leaves a formative influence in a modern society even though people do not, yet, know its exact impact. If it is not omnipotent, it is definitely, omnipresent. Given its pervasive and persuasive nature, people are continuously exposed to it through an array of mass media vehicles. There also exists somewhat general claim that advertising has the raw power to manipulate consumers. Big advertisers, having the capacity of obtaining large number of advertising exposures and using highly sophisticated and scientific techniques, can influence people's minds. The same may not be true for small or medium size organisations who do not possess that much of financial clout.

The role advertising plays in a society is a debatable one. Protagonists of advertising generally argue that it is a form of 'speech' which is analogous to news and entertainment components of mass media and that it should be kept free of governmental interference as far as possible. On the other hand, those who oppose it, often argue that government should be actively involved to protect the interests of public, to keep consumers away from being duped by the power of advertising, and to protect the interest of competitive firms whose performance or existence could be adversely effected by unfair advertising practices (Aaker, Batra and Myers, 2000).

Most of the criticism of advertising comes from those who focus on advertising's social role, whereas, most of its defence comes from those who emphasise its economic function. Summarising the negative consequences of advertising, UNESCO report concludes as follows (Singh and Gross, 1981):

> "Regarded as a form of communication, it (advertising) has been criticised for playing on emotions through stereotypes, exploiting anxieties, and employing techniques of intensive persuasion that amount to manipulation. Many social critics have stated that advertising is essentially concerned with exalting the materialistic virtues of consumption by exploiting achievement drives and emulative anxieties, employing tact of hidden manipulation, playing on emotions, maximising appeal and minimising information, trivialising, eliminating objective considerations, contriving illogical situations, and generally reducing men, women and children to the role of irrational consumers. Criticism expressed in such a way may be overstated but can not be entirely brushed aside".

If the negative influence of advertising can be summarised in the UNESCO publication, one can also present the positive consequences of advertising as described by many scholars and people associated with business. Advertising is an important institution and therefore, its costs and benefits should be evaluated in order to determine the total impact of advertising in a society. The economic consequences of advertising may be enumerated in the following as discussed by those who advocate its positive role and impact in a society.

It is considered as a useful business tool and therefore, an efficient source of information for consumers about product quality, new merchandise, new technology and prices. It also reduces distribution costs by making personal selling more effective. Historically, economists held the view that it leads to distortions in consumption expenditure and helps the bigger firms more than the medium or small firms. But this traditional view point is changing and some now believe that advertising encourages competition by lowering information costs and hence is desirable (Holton, 1980). Advertising is also supposed to encourage the development of new products. It also, as argued by some, adds (psychological) value to products leading to increased consumer satisfaction. It also increases the variety and quality of goods offered and stimulates competition in technical progress. The growth of different media is largely due to advertising because it subsidises substantially their costs (Gilligan and Crowther, 1983).

The above discussion of advertising makes it clear that it is definitely controversial and there are two schools of thought and their opinion on advertising can be seen to range on a spectrum from those having a whole-hearted belief in the efficacy of advertising as an indispensable business tool to those who strongly feel that all advertising should be dispensed with. However, the truth lies somewhere in between the two extremes of the spectrum. Therefore, the present study is an attempt to find out the attitudes of those who are exposed to advertising. For this purpose, the authors have developed a scale to capture and measure the attitudes towards different aspects of advertising using scale construction techniques in behavioural sciences and marketing disciplines (Edwards, 1957).

Present study attempts to measure the attitudes of those who are exposed to it through various mass media vehicles. The basic purpose was to gauge the feelings of those who are most probably influenced by it. The attitudes measurement towards its various facets has been carried out in the context of men and women. This has been done because there is a differential exposure of men and women with respect to various media with respect to advertising. To carry out this study a scale was developed.

SCALE DEVELOPMENT FRAMEWORK

In order to construct a reliable and valid scale, the following steps were taken:

Definition of Concept and Generation of Scale Statements

To encompass the different facets of advertising, a comprehensive literature search was carried out. This review examined the viewpoints of those who criticised the role of advertising in the society as well as of those who feel that advertising plays a positive role and is one of the major business tools. On the basis of this review of literature, a detailed list of different facets of advertising was prepared. The main aspects that were considered for the present study are listed below:

1. Advertising as a business tool
2. Advertising's informative role
3. Advertising and Materialism
4. Influence of Advertising on Adults and Children
5. Advertising and media
6. Present status of Indian advertising.

Keeping in mind these aspects a large number of statements were generated. In order to strike a balance, statements having both negative and positive connotations were prepared. At this stage it was thought proper to generate as many statements as possible in the item pool. This resulted in a battery of sixty-two statements related to various facets of advertising.

Item Analysis and Selection

To further refine the scale, sixty-two statements of the item pool were subjected to detailed item analysis. The basic purpose was to ascertain the reliability and discriminative capacity of these statements. In the development of an attitude scale researchers often use t-test to ascertain the discriminative power of the statement (Huges, 1967). However, due to certain practical difficulties a less stringent method was used for this purpose. These sixty-two statements were given to six management teachers, on account of their theoretical and practical insight in the field. They were apprised of the objectives of the study. In the light of the objectives, the teachers were requested to carefully go through these statements and critically evaluate each statement on the following guidelines:

(i) Relevance of each statement to the objectives of the study.
(ii) Discriminating ability of each statement in measuring the attitudes.
(iii) Avoiding duplication, in case more than one statement tried to measure the same thing.

The criterion for retaining any statement for the final selection was the agreement of at least five experts out of six on the three guidelines i.e. *relevance*, *discriminating power* and *duplication*. Even if four members agreed and two disagreed on any one of the guidelines, the statement in question was discarded. In this way thirty-eight statements fulfilled the norms and therefore, they were finally included in the scale.

Scaling of Items

It was thought, at this stage, that the items of this scale should not only measure the direction of attitudes towards different facets of advertising but also the intensity of their directions. Therefore, a simple dichotomous scale of attitude measurement was not considered to be useful for providing the pertinent information. After considering different types of attitude scales, choice was narrowed down to Likert type scale because of its versatility, ease of construction, ease of administration and the ability to simultaneously measure the intensity and direction of attitudes. The use of Likert type scale also allows inclusion of large number of diverse statements believed to be necessary to comprehensively measure all types of constructs. A five-point interval scale from "strongly agree" to "strongly disagree" was used to measure the response to each statement (items). The breakdown of these thirty-eight statements with respect to different facets of advertising is given below:

1. Advertising as a business tool (seven statements)
2. Advertising and information (five statements)
3. Advertising and materialism (six statements)
4. Advertising influence on adults and children (seven statements)
5. The role of advertising in media (five statements)
6. Status of Indian advertising (eight statements)

Objectives and Sample

After the scale was developed, it was administered on a group of people who are generally exposed to advertising. At the outset, the primary objective was to gauge the reactions without taking into consideration any demographic variable. Later, in order to have more meaningful comparisons, it was decided to measure these attitudes in terms of sex. The sample was selected in such a way that both the sexes were represented proportionately. The basic hypothesis was based on the premise that there should be significant attitudinal differences between these two groups i.e. males and females. Initially, it was planned to select 250 respondents from both the groups. Telephone directories of two cities Aligarh and Lucknow were used as sampling frames. Through systematic random sampling, 100 respondents were selected from Aligarh and 150 from Lucknow. This was done purposely in order to get a balanced view because both cities are unequal in population size and other demographic characteristics. Respondents were initially contacted on phone and those who gave their consent were approached for data collection. In all,182 respondents completed the questionnaire (scale). Of them, 75 were women and 107 were men. Owing to the use of telephone directories as sampling frames, the socio-economic status of the respondents may be considered at higher level than average one. In a way this sample represents medium and higher strata of society.

RESULTS

The advertising attitude scale comprising thirty eight statements was distributed to the respondents personally, and they were requested to go through each statement and then given their degree of agreement or disagreement on a scale ranging from "strongly agree" to "strongly disagree". In order to bring about consistency, scoring was done according to the nature of statement. For those statements which reflect positive feelings 5-points were assigned to "strongly agree", 4 to "moderately agree", 3 to "neither agree nor disagree, 2 to "moderately disagree" and 1 to "strongly disagree". The scoring pattern was reversed for those statements which reflected negative feelings. For example, for a negative worded statement, 1 point was assigned to "strongly agree" and so on. Higher score for positive statement meant that the respondent held positive attitude towards that advertising facet and higher score for negative statement meant otherwise i.e. negative attitude towards that facet. The mean score for each statement was calculated for two groups i.e. men and women. The results on each facet of advertising with respect to male and female respondents are discussed in the following:

Advertising as a Business Tool

In the present competitive business world, consumers have to be

Table 2.1
Advertising as Business Tool

	Statement	*Mean Scores*		
		Men	*Women*	*"t" Value*
1.	Advertising contributes very importantly to India's industrial prosperity.	4.05	3.89	0.45
2.	The Indian public would be better of without advertising.	4.08	4	0.65
3.	Advertising is O.K. for new products but for established products it is a waste of consumer's money.	3.59	3.57	0.16
4.	I wish there were more advertising than there exists now.	3.54	3.13	3.14*
5.	Advertising is the most powerful tool in the hands of business companies to sell their products.	4.08	3.83	2.85†
6.	There is no need for stringent laws by the Government in regulating advertising. However, the advertisers should device code of conduct for themselves based on ethical norms.	3.88	3.97	0.48
7.	Large companies do not allow other smaller companies to grow or survive in the market.	3.43	3.53	0.66

* = Significant at 1% level.
† = Significant at 5% level.

persuaded to purchase a specific brand from a plethora of competing brands. Advertising is considered by many, specially those who are dealing with marketing, as one of the most potent tools of consumer persuasion. This becomes all the more necessary in case of consumer products where advertising plays a dominant role in the overall promotion mix. In spite of all criticism, one can not deny the fact that advertising does play informative and persuasive role in promoting goods and services. Therefore, the role of advertising as a business tool has been encompassed and manifested into seven statements. The respondents' mean scores for these seven statements as are given in Table 2.1. The first statement in this table describes advertising as one of the important factors in India's industrial prosperity. The tone of the statement is extremely positive and therefore any one who agrees with this statement is deemed to have positive attitude towards advertising. Examining Table 2.1 one finds that majority of respondents, both male and female, strongly agreed with this statement. The mean score of male respondents was slightly higher (4.05) as compared to the female respondents (3.89). However, this difference was not statistically significant. One may safely conclude that people have positive attitude towards advertising as far as its contribution to India's industrial prosperity is concerned. The second statement has negative connotation. It states that Indian public would be better off if advertising is totally stopped. Again, both the respondents showed strong reservations against this statement. Most of them, irrespective of sex disagreed with this statement indicating that they consider advertising a necessary business tool and people will not be better off if advertising goes out of the scene. Again, both men and women exhibited similar attitudes. Some economists do agree with the slight positive role of advertising in case of new products but they feel that for established products it is a waste of consumer's hard earned money. To explore this view, the third statement was developed and it was ambivalently worded. Respondents showed mixed reaction to this statement. Nearly twenty five per cent respondents–both male and female–agreed with the statement, but majority disagreed. This indicates that majority of people think that advertising is not only essential in promoting new products but is also needed for sustaining awareness level for established products. In order to keep a particular brand in consumer's awareness and evoked set, companies have to continue their advertising effort so as to prevent the *forgetting effect* and at the same time to maintain or increase market share. The fourth statement had a highly positive connotation. This statement was developed in order to measure the attitude of people towards quantity of advertising to which they are exposed. There is a feeling among certain people that there is a surfeit of advertising and, therefore, the quantity of advertising has to be curtailed. The mean score of male and female respondents revealed that most of them were neutral. However, female respondents were more neutral as compared to their male counterpart. This was found statistically significant. Fifth statement explicitly says that advertisement is the most potent tool available to business for enhancing sales. There was strong agreement among both the groups on this statement. However, male respondents showed more agreement than female respondents. This indicates that males consider advertising as one of the most potent business tools. This is possible because majority of females in India still are housewives and they are less exposed to advertising as compared to males. In the recent years, with the popularity of TV as a major medium, women are increasingly being exposed to advertising.

Critics argue that there should be stringent laws which can prevent advertisers from indulging in unfair means and there has been a growing demand to regulate advertising within the framework of prevailing ethical norms of the society. However, others argue that there is no need for stringent laws but that there should be some sort of self regulatory mechanism in the form of code of conduct by advertisers themselves. Therefore, the sixth statement took this view point into account and elicited response of male and female respondents. Again, majority of both the groups agreed on this statement, though females were in greater agreement than their male counterparts. However, this difference was not significant. The agreement by both the groups indicated their positive attitude towards advertising. The need for a code of conduct was emphasised rather than stringent government laws. Fortunately, Advertising Standard Council of India (ASCI) has devised a code of conduct which has the consent of advertisers, ad agencies and media owners.

The last statement under this heading was related to the power of the big business houses. Generally, it is stated that big houses, on account of their large resources, resort to heavy advertising for their products and services. Thus, they are able to prevent smaller firms from growing and surviving in the market (Ferguson 1978). It is also argued that advertising makes it difficult for new entrants to enter the marketplace by erecting entry barriers and in addition, it also reduces competition by bringing about industry concentration and monopoly profits (Ferguson, 1974). Tesler (1968) studied the relationship between advertising and sales concentration in different industries and concluded that in many instances instead of finding positive relationship between advertising intensity and monopoly, there was a negative relationship i.e. an inverse association between changes in advertising intensity and changes in industry concentration. It has also been proved that in some cases smaller firms have been able to succeed or even sometimes snatch the dominant position from the market leader. In India, Nirma is the classical example in the detergent powder market where it became market leader in a short span of time, displacing Surf, a brand of the marketing giant Hindustan Lever which till then had occupied the top slot. This statement was framed to measure what people generally have in their minds regarding the exploitative role of bigger companies *vis-a-vis* the smaller companies. A substantial number of respondents belonging to both the groups felt that to a certain extent it was true. Whether this reflects reality or not is debatable, yet, people believe that large companies, because of their financial clout, do prevent the smaller firms from growing. They also create entry barriers for new firms.

Advertising and Information

In a competitive business environment, consumers do not have complete knowledge of the various products and services which they need, and therefore, they seek information from various sources including advertising. Advertising's main role is to provide information about the product, company and competitive brands to the target market. Further, it has proved to be more efficient and less costly source of information than other information sources controlled by the marketer. However, advertising does involve cost and consequently leads to higher consumer prices. Khan, Azam and Mahmood (1992) content analysed the Indian advertisements in terms of number of information cues provided in the advertisements. They found that in the midst of advertisements there was at least one informational cue that was available to the target market. They also found that in several advertisements more than one informational cue was provided. This study showed that Indian companies, because of intense competition, are now giving importance to the provision of information to the target market in order to persuade them effectively. Therefore, in order to measure the attitude of respondents on this aspect, five statements were prepared which reflect different facets of informative function of advertising. The tone of all the five statements is negative. Therefore, whoever disagrees with the statement will be considered having negative attitude towards the informative role of advertising and *vice versa*. The findings for each statement are presented in Table 2.2.

The first statement expresses the opinion that advertising merely increases the prices of the products which people have to pay without giving them any useful product/brand information. It has been criticised that by resorting to heavy advertising, the cost of a product is increased considerably and this addition in cost is transferred to

Table 2.2
Advertising and Information

S. No.	Statement	Mean Scores Men	Mean Scores Women	"t" Value
1.	Advertising merely increases the prices of products which people have to pay without giving them any useful information.	3.78	3.49	1.81
2.	Advertising does not inform the public and is not worth its cost.	4.12	3.89	1.72
3.	Majority of advertisements today give false or misleading information.	3.83	3.83	0
4.	Advertising helps people in learning about the different product characteristics and this enables them to choose the right brand with the right quality.	3.72	3.7	0.15
5.	Often advertisements give incomplete information, half truths, and are deceptive in nature.	2.69	2.96	2.48*

* = Significant at 5% level.

the consumers by charging high price. The additional cost that the consumer pays does not compensate the additional information he/she receives through advertising. Both male and female respondents slightly disagreed with the statement. This means that the respondents did realise the significance of advertising's informative role but they were also of the opinion that advertising is not fulfilling this role in a satisfactory way. In this regard, males exhibited more negative attitude than females. The same is understandable because women are comparatively less exposed to other mass media sources as compared to males. Therefore, the information women receive through advertising is more important to them as compared to men. The second statement was related to the informational utility of advertising and said "advertising does not inform the public and is not worth its cost". Again, lesser number of males agreed with this statement as compared to females. This indicates that there is a clear verdict in favour of the informative role of advertising. Critics of advertising argue that most of the information that is provided to the consumers in the advertisements is misleading or false and instead of appealing in a rational way it is mainly suggestive in nature. Therefore, this type of appeal is likely to impede rational comparison and choice. Keeping this dimension in mind, the third statement was framed and people were asked to give their verdict as to whether they agree or disagree as far as misleading information in the advertisements is concerned. Majority of males and females thought that information provided in the advertisements was not false or misleading. Only a few thought it was false or misleading. There was no significant difference between male and female respondents on this statement. Fourth statement was positive in connotation which said that "advertising helps people in learning about the different product characteristics and this enables them to choose the right brand with right quality". Proponents of advertising claim that this is what advertising is meant for. Results of this study corroborate this contention to a great extent. Both male and female respondents agreed with this statement. Very few of them disagreed (~15%). Thus, one can not deny the informational utility of advertising. The final statement under this category again carries negative connotation towards advertising. This statement says that advertisements often give incomplete information, half-truths and are deceptive in nature. Mean scores of males and females respondents revealed that they were in agreement with this statement, which to a great extent coincides with the critic's claim of exaggeration and deception in advertisements. The attitude of men and women on this statement was statistically significant ($P<.05$). Women did not feel as strongly as men. One reason for this could be attributed to the degree of persuasibility among the audience. Generally, it is considered that women can more easily be persuaded than men. Cox and Bauer (1964) also found that women who value traditional sex roles are more persuadable than women who do not accept traditional sex roles.

Advertising and Materialism

One of the social criticisms against advertising is concerned with the so-called encouragement to materialistic comforts by advertisements. People blame that there is a link between advertising and materialism. Different persons have described materialism in different ways, but in essence it means the desire to obtain tangible goods and to give undue importance to material interests (Wright, Winter and Zeigler, 1989; Aaker, Batra and Myers, 2000).

Many intellectuals consider the abundance of this trait among people to be undesirable and argue that people should be interested in fine things of life such as music poetry and painting instead of owning material comforts in the form of luxury goods. Advertising is being blamed because it is accused of promoting products that satisfy the materialistic requirements of consumers, and thus is indirectly responsible in promoting materialism. Another dimension of this criticism is that advertising increases the expectations of people through its appeal towards the acquisition of things which will gratify the people's basic and inner needs and aspirations.

Bauer and Greyser (1968) argue that, advertising being the chief means of communication tries to persuade the people through various reasons for which they might want to acquire material objects and as these reasons are within the cultural norms, advertising can not be prevented from appealing to such reasons.

Zinkhan and Prenshaw (1994) opine that advertising portrays vision of good life and serves to stimulate consumption behaviour. It is a fact that commercial messages portray materialism as a "value". We live in a materialistic culture and materialism encourages customers to *buy* and *consume*. Materialism leads to the idea that more is better. A desire foı "more" means increased sales, so advertisers often incorporate materialistic appeals in their messages. Pollay (1986) identified as many as 42 values, which are represented in both print and audio-visual media.

It is true that advertising and the products promoted through it are a part of our culture and thus, in some way contribute to materialism. However, linking advertising with fostering materialism is stretching a point too far and it is almost impossible to prove or disprove this presumed causal relationship. Though advertising has the potential to persuade the consumers yet it does not have the power to dominate other forces (family, religion, literature etc.) that largely shape the values in a society.

Keeping in mind the different dimensions of this criticism i.e. advertising and materialism, six statements were administered to the respondents for measuring their attitudes. Except for one statement (No. 2) all the statements had negative connotations. The mean scores of male and female respondents are given in Table 2.3, along with the t-values to indicate significant and insignificant differences. The first statement says that "advertising persuades people to buy products and services that they should not buy". The results indicate that neither of the sexes had positive feelings nor were they negatively inclined towards this statement. They showed more or less a neutral attitude towards this statement and it was statistically insignificant. The second statement tries to link advertising with material comforts in a positive tone. Some social thinkers argue that in order to foster materialistic comforts, advertising inculcates the habit of hard work among the people and thus enables them to purchase goods. Keeping in mind this thinking the second statement was framed. There was significant difference among male and female respondents on this statement. Females demonstrated less positive attitude as compared to males. One possible reason may be that men give more importance to material comforts in comparison to their female counterparts. However, one should be cautious in interpreting these results unless further evidence is obtained through future research.

Table 2.3
Advertising and Materialism

S. No.	Statement	Mean Scores		
		Men	Women	"t" Value
1.	Advertising persuades people to buy products and services that they should not buy.	2.97	3.04	0.49
2.	Advertising encourages people to work hard so that they can afford to purchase more and more goods and thus enjoy the life.	3.33	2.94	2.95†
3.	For too many people advertisements create needs but do not fulfill them perfectly.	2.73	2.91	1.2
4.	Advertising creates desires and wants among those who are exposed to it.	2.42	2.48	0.71
5.	Advertising encourages gross materialism	3.93	3.35	1.53
6.	Advertising is one of the major causes of inflation in the world in general and India in particular.	2.63	2.82	0.86

* = Significant at 1% level.
† = Significant at 5% level.

The third statement says that "for too many people advertisements create needs but do not fulfil them perfectly". The attitude of both the groups on this statement was found to be neutral. Though no significant differences were found between male and female respondents and there was near unanimity among both the sexes. This disagreement, to a great extent, disproves that charge by marketing critics that "marketers create needs" or "marketers get people to buy things they do not want". Kotler (2000) strongly refutes this charge by saying that marketers (which includes advertisers) do not create needs and they, along with other influences in the society, influence wants. In essence advertising tries to influence demand by communicating the various features of the products instead of creating the needs. The fourth statement was framed slightly in a different way. Instead of need creation, here it was said that advertising creates desires and wants among those who are exposed to it. There was agreement between both male and female respondents on this statements. The scores of both the sexes indicate that people do not feel that advertising creates desires and wants. In the fifth statement a direct link was proposed between advertising and materialism. People did not agree with the statement. Most of them felt that advertising does not foster materialism. This disagreement with the statement gave an indication that they did not subscribe to the criticism of intellectuals who believe that advertising fosters materialism. There may be two possible reasons for this response. Firstly, respondents may have felt that there was no association between advertising and materialism. Secondly, they might be of the opinion that materialism is not an undesirable trait. Whatever may be the reasons, people did not link advertising with materialism.

Final statement in this section also has a negative connotation and says that advertising is one of the major causes of inflation. People showed agreement with this statement, which indicates that they were aware of monetory implications of advertising and felt that because of it, advertised products are sold at a higher price, leading to inflation. This gives an idea that people have negative feelings towards the cost of advertising and consequently its association with the rate of inflation. In this connection men showed slightly higher negative attitudes as compared to women. However, this difference was not found to be statistically significant.

Advertising Influence on Adults and Children

This section deals with seven statements which have been grouped under one head i.e. influence of advertising on adults and children. Many thinkers in the field of sociology feel that advertising because of its all pervasive nature and the facility of repeating the massage over different mass media vehicles, can influence the lifestyles of people and also their behaviour. During the last three decades, many social thinkers have expressed fear that the freedom of people to make decisions of various kinds, including the freedom to select a particular brand, would be jeopardised by the manipulative *power* of advertising. They feel that advertising is so effective that it can manipulate a buyer into making a decision against his or her will or at least against his or her best interests. So, there is a general claim regarding the power of scientific advertising to persuade i.e. to make people believe things and behave in ways that are not in their own or society's best interests (Aaker, Batra and Myers, 2000). Owing to the writings and opinion of people not directly related to marketing, a feeling has been spread that advertising could identify sub-conscious motives, and by playing on these motives, it could influence the unsuspecting public. The fear that the consumer can be manipulated even at the sub-conscious level reached at its peak with the concept of subliminal perception. This concept says that if an individual is exposed to stimuli which are too weak or too brief to be consciously seen or heard, may nevertheless, be strong enough to be perceived by an individual's receptive cells. Subliminal perception created a great furore in the late 1950s when it was reported that advertisers expose consumers to subliminal messages that they were not aware of receiving. These messages purportedly were persuading people to buy goods and services without being aware of why they were motivated to do so. James Vicary (1956) in one study to show the effectiveness of so-called subliminal advertsing tested it at a drive-in-cinema in New Jersy where the words "eat popcorn" and "drink coke" were flashed during the movie after every five seconds. These phrases were flashed for 1/3000th of a second, well below the threshold level. The tests which covered a six week period, were reported to have increased Cola sales by 57 per cent and of popcorn sales by 18 per cent (Wilkie, 1986). Subsequent to these results many researchers tried to document the existence or the effectiveness of subliminal advertising. However, they failed to provide any substantial evidence (Hawkins, 1970; Caccavale, Wanty & Edel, 1981; Kelly, 1979; Saegert, 1987). Whether there exists subliminal advertising or not, there is no doubt that because of its all pervasive nature, advertising has the capacity to persuade the people through emotional appeals.

Communicating the factual information about a brand's primary functions is usually accepted as being of value to the consumer.

Table 2.4
Advertising Influences on Adults and Children

S. No.	Statement	Mean Scores: Men	Mean Scores: Women	"t" Value
1.	People do read/see/hear the advertisements, but generally they do not get influenced by them.	3.35	3.57	0.63
2.	Generally, there is a tendency on the part of the people not to believe what is said in most of the advertisements.	3.47	3.64	1.27
3.	In general, advertisements are basically created to persuade people to purchase goods and services but it also insults their intelligence in a subtle way.	3.62	3.51	0.08†
4.	Today, advertising does not appeal to reason but to emotions and tries to sell the products and services to the consumers by exploiting them emotionally.	3.07	3.12	0.45
5.	On moral grounds advertisements are harmful. They breed vulgarity, hypothesize the imagination and the will of the people.	3.43	3.41	0.45
6.	Advertising creates negative impact on the minds of the children.	3.54	3.13	1.85
7.	Today, advertising has invaded on the judgment of children and influences them in such a way that their parents are helpless in yielding to their demands.	3.39	3.04	1.36

* = Significant at 1% level.
† = Significant at 5% level.

However, when advertising utilises appeals that go beyond "reason why" the charge of manipulation via emotional appeals is raised

So this section deals with the attitudes of men and women towards this *power* of advertising in influencing their behaviour. The first statement was framed to find out whether people thought that they might get influenced if they are repeatedly exposed to advertising through various mass media vehicles. The results showed that both the sexes had a divided opinion and the attitude towards getting influenced by advertising was found to be statistically insignificant. However, among both the groups, a substantial number of respondents were of the opinion that advertising does influence them substantially. The mean scores of both the groups indicate the positive correlation between advertising and change in attitude. There is a strong feeling among certain sections of the people that advertisements generally exaggerate the claims or attributes of the advertised brands and therefore, people do not believe the claims given in the advertisements. Millman (1984) conducted a study to determine the believability of various types of advertising claims. 1,250 respondents were asked about the believability of three types of approaches – sample demonstrations, qualitative claims, and statistical claims. Of the three, only sample demonstrations reached the 'neutral' category of believability. Both qualitative and statistical claims were rated as "somewhat unbelievable". The results of the study also found that females were more positive than males towards the believability of advertising. In the present study, when the mean scores were calculated on the second statement relating to believability, they revealed that, by and large, both the groups had apprehensions on the claims of advertising and therefore did not have much faith as far as believing the advertisements was concerned. Statistically also both groups did not differ significantly, though women had much less believability than men. The third statement relates with the persuasive capability of an advertisement and the information processing capability of the audiences who are exposed to it. This statement says that while persuading people to buy goods and services, advertisements also insult the native intelligence of the people. Though nearly 30 per cent of men and 28 per cent of women did not agree with this statement, yet, majority felt that many a time advertisements are prepared in such a manner that they assume their audience are fickle minded. Again both the groups did not differ statistically. Fourth statement relates to the use of emotional appeals in advertisements. Till the mid-1970s advertisers more often used rational appeals than emotional appeals. However, from the 1980s onwards, the use of emotional appeals has increased substantially. Therefore, this statement reflects this dimension of advertising and is framed with a negative connotation. The results showed that attitudes were divided as far as exploitation of people's emotions was concerned. Fifty-two per cent of males and fifty-five per cent of females agreed with the statement. However, substantial percentage of respondents in both the groups had reservations and did not agree with the statement. The fifth statement relates with the use of sex appeal in advertising. Many psychologists believe that skilful manipulation of sexual appeals in visual images – in copy or in both – may arouse substantial desires that manifest in the purchase of goods or services. For this reasons, many advertisers use sex in their thematic appeals hoping to catch the consumer's attention or persuade him or her beneath the level of conscious awareness. Nevertheless, many people believe that the use of sexual appeals in advertising is not *good* marketing. They argue that if sex appeals are related with the type of product then they may enhance the attention as well as persuade the people in purchasing the advertised products. However, if the appeal does not match with the product it can be counterproductive. Since long, use of sex appeals has been quite common in the West. Of late, in India too the use of sex appeals is on the rise. In the light of these developments the respondents were asked to indicate their attitudes towards this dimension of advertising in the fifth statement of this section. To a great extent, there was unanimity in responses on the statement which says that advertisements breed vulgarity and hypothesise the imagination and the will of the people. Majority of respondents (70%) agreed with this statement in both the groups.

The last two statements of this section were framed keeping in mind the influence advertising exerts on the children. With the emergence of TV as one of the major media for advertising and its pervasiveness, many people, including economists, social thinkers, public policy makers and politicians, have criticised advertising in general, and television advertising in particular, for its negative influence on children. These critics believe that television advertising *corrupts* children by instilling values that are not acceptable in a society. Actually what is more likely involved is a clash between the values of children and those of their parents. In US both marketing managers and public policy makers have reacted to this criticisms of advertising, particularly advertising directed at children. The controversy surrounding this issue grew so intense in the 1970s that the Federal Trade Commission (FTC) of US was stimulated to examine television advertising directed towards children. FTC recommended the following in 1977:

- All television advertising be banned for any product which is directed to or seen by audience composed of a significant proportion of children who are too young to comprehend the selling purpose of advertising.
- Either balance television advertising for sugared food products

directed to or seen by audience composed of a significant proportion of older children with nutritional and or health disclosures funded by advertisers or ban it completely.

These proposals of FTC were hotly debated and were ultimately defeated. However, the issue remains, and parents and consumer groups are still concerned and active. In India too, since mid 1980s the advertising directed at children for various products increased tremendously, particularly on television.

In order to investigate the impact of advertising on children a number of studies were undertaken by researchers in US. In fact the controversy generated by FTC recommendations has led to the on-going stream of research on the influence of advertising directed towards children from various angles. Goldberg and Gorn (1977 and 1978) in a series of statements concluded that advertising can influence children to select the advertised product (highly sugared cereals, candy, etc.) over more nutritious products. In another experiment done by the same authors, it was found that children who viewed candy commercials picked significantly more snacks over fruits. When the candy commercials were removed from the experiment, children were tilted towards the more nutritious products such as fruits (Gorn and Goldberg, 1982).

In one study it was found that older children and those with more media exposure tend to recall more advertising slogans (Reece, 1983). Butter, Popovich, Stackhouse, and Gardner (1981) while examining the impact of the separator (i.e. audio-visual break, audio break only, visual break only, or blank screen used before and after each commercial interruption) in aiding pre-school children to discern between programmes and commercials, found that majority correctly identified the programmes and commercials and as such the form of separator was not significant Another study that looked at the impact of host selling (the use of programme characters to promote products) on the child's desire for the products, compared commercials that either offered a premium, used host selling or that had an independent announcer. This study found that children who viewed the host selling commercial selected the advertised brand significantly more than those who had viewed the announcer commercial. However, the premium commercial was superior to both of these in influencing the children to select the advertised brand (Miller and Busch, 1979). Hoy and Young (1986) examined whether the placement of an animated host selling commercial relative to the cartoon (i.e., before, in the middle, or following) had any impact on young children's ability to tell the programme from the commercial. They found that the majority of children recognised that they had seen a commercial regardless of whether or not it involved host selling and regardless of its location with respect to the programme.

One dimension of children's advertising is the constant parental concern regarding its influence in the purchase of certain products which are not good for children. This concern has its roots in the fact that a high proportion of advertising aims at children for products that contain large amounts of sugar. As a result of exposure to these types of commercials, children tend to consume more sugared products, have a greater preference for sugared foods even if they have not seen the specific product advertised and are less well informed about proper nutrition (Scammon and Christopher, 1981). Grossbert and Crosby (1984) demonstrated that parents with higher socio-economic status were concerned with the nutrition and quality (specially the high sugar content) of food advertised to children, while parents lower on the socio-economic scale were more concerned that such advertising would lead to family conflict with the child, and less concerned that it would promote bad eating habits.

Research in this area also focused on the impact of television advertising on children of different groups. Stephen and Stutts (1982) found that pre-schoolers respond to perceptual cues and do not truly understand the difference between programmes and commercials. Gorn and Florsheim (1985) found that commercials targeted to adults have great influence on children. For example, television commercials for lipstick favourably influenced nine-and-ten-year-old girl's perception of the product and brand, because they associated the product with being an adult. In another study older aged children were found to recognise more symbolism in advertising than younger children. Those who had experience with the product held strong consumption based stereotypes suggesting that personal experience is more important than media exposure (Belk, Mayer, and Driscoll, 1984). Research also indicated that children of parents who more sincerely control their children's viewing habits (and who generally were found to be of higher socio-economic level) exhibit a better understanding of the purpose and nature of advertising and make a fewer purchase requests to their parents (Wiman, 1983). A number of studies in this area point out the need to develop better measures of children's understanding of television commercials. Macklin (1987) showed that traditional verbal measures usually underestimate the child's ability to understand television commercials, while non-verbal measures, such as asking the child to point at something, indicate that young children are capable of understanding the television commercials. Banks (1980) studied the effects of television advertising on children and one of his conclusions was that "children exhibit such variations in viewing behaviour that one must conclude that they exhibit a fairly substantial degree of selectivity in what and when they choose to watch on television."

Keeping in view the research on various aspects of advertising directed towards children and the concern of parents as well as many others, two statements were framed. The first statement relates to the negative impact of advertising on children's mind. The respondents' mean scores are given in Table 2.4. There seemed to be general agreement on this statement by both men and women. Both the groups acknowledged the negative impact of advertising on the children's minds. However, men seemed to be more critical on the negative impact than women. The possible reason, one may guess, is that, still in majority of Indian families, the man is the sole breadwinner and because of this he has to meet the household expenses including the demands of children. Therefore, men might have shown more negative attitude towards the role of children's advertising. Women in majority of the Indian families are not the breadwinners. Therefore, they showed less critical attitude towards this aspect of advertising. This difference in attitude between men and women was also found statistically significant ($P<.05$).

The parent child relationship, as it relates to purchasing behaviour, can be viewed as an *influence versus yield* situation. Specifically, children attempt to influence their parents to purchase a product (to yield). It has been frequently observed that in a store or shop, children not only attempt to influence their parents in areas of their own interest, but also for products of remote interest to them. With the increase in television viewing, the average time spent by the children in viewing the television advertisements has gone up substantially. Thus, there is a strong possibility that the clout wielded by children in influencing family purchases may grow in the future. In US, a number of research studies focused on parent-child influence versus yield situation. Berey and Pollay (1978) focused exclusively on breakfast cereals and found that more involved the mother was with her child, the more likely she was not to yield to the child's preference for sugared breakfast cereals, presumably, because she considered such cereals to be nutritionally unsound. Shiffman and Kanuk (2000) reported a study which examined child-parent interaction across a number of products (including cereals) which found a significant positive relationship between the number of children's influence attempts and the yielding of their mothers. This study also found that children's attempts to influence tended to decrease somewhat with age, and mothers yielding tended to increase with the child's age. These results seem to indicate that children become more discriminating in their requests as they get older, and that parent acknowledge their children's increased judgements by acceding more readily to their purchase requests.

Keeping in mind this parent-child influence versus yield situation, which has become more relevant because of the increased amount of children's advertising, the last statement of this section was framed. This statement says "today advertising has invaded the judgement of children and influences them in such a way that the parents are helpless to yield to their demands". This statement basically tries to emphasise the negative impact of advertising in parent-child influence versus yield situation and therefore, is negatively worded. Again, the responses to this statement by majority of males and females were in the affirmative. This indicated that both the sexes were of the opinion that on account of increased exposure to advertising, their children had become more vocal and demanding. As a consequences of this, they had to yield to their demands as far as the purchase of various products was concerned. Though the women were more in agreement in terms of percentage *vis-a-vis* men but the results did not show any significant difference.

Advertising and Mass Media

One of the most frequently repeated charges against advertising is the financial relationship that exists between the advertisers and mass media. Because of this relationship, questions are raised frequently about the freedom of the mass media from advertiser's control. Implication of this criticism is that mass media are at the mercy of advertisers, who dictate editorial policy and force publishers not to place any story or article of which the advertiser disapproves. This criticism has its roots in the system of democracy. In a democratic society, any attempt to restrict the freedom of mass media, whether it comes from advertisers, religious institutions, government or any other special interest group, demands both attention and action.

The fact is that advertising provides between 60 to 70 per cent cost of newspapers and magazines. In case of commercial television channels it provides almost 100 per cent funds. The reality is that commercial television is almost wholly dependent for its survival upon revenue derived from advertisers. Even government controlled television channels such as Doordarshan also depend to a large extent on the revenue from advertising.

Table 2.5
Advertising and Media

S. No.	Statement	Mean Scores		
		Men	Women	"t" Value
1.	Advertising helps media (newspapers, magazines, TV, etc.) to become self sufficient, autonomous and makes them free from undesirable political influence.	3.52	3.6	0.52
2.	On account of advertising the prices of newspapers and magazines are low and therefore, people can afford to purchase them.	4.04	4	0.43
3.	On account of advertising on TV, the quality of TV programmes has improved substantially.	3.73	3.91	1.11
4.	Today, advertising is too pervasive on all major media and one cannot escape from it.	4	3.89	1.25
5.	Big advertisers on account of their heavy spending capacity are able to control the mass media.	2.67	3.25	4.0*

* = Significant at 1% level.

The common justification puts forward for the continuation of this relationship is that advertising revenue subsidises the press and television, thereby enabling them to provide these things to the general public at a price below the actual expenses incurred. Without the income derived from selling space to advertisers, many newspapers and magazines would be unable to exist as few people would be prepared, or indeed be able, to afford the significantly higher prices that newspaper and magazine owners would be forced to charge. Similarly, television, even government controlled one, would no longer be independent in its programmes and its functioning, but would be forced to rely on subsidies from government and other institutions. Another defence for the continuance of this relationship is that any influence that one advertiser might wish to exert is likely to be opposite to what the other advertiser may wish. Presently, large number of advertisers patronize a particular newspaper or magazine, therefore, it gives a high degree of freedom to that publisher who can afford to loose some of them in case of undue interference without fear of financial loss.

The situation is slightly different in broadcast media, and specially in television network programming. Here, unlike newspapers and magazines, the advertiser not only pays for the time his commercials are on the air, but also may pay the cost of the entertainment between his commercials. In a sense, he is at the same time both advertiser and publisher or producer. In the past, there have been instances when the advertisers have exerted some influence on the content of the programmes they have sponsored and paid for. However, as television costs have mounted, more and more advertisers have turned to spot commercials or joint sponsoring of a particular programme. As far as India is concerned, for more than 25 years Doordarshan was the only channel available to the viewers. Because of this, frequently the criticism was directed towards the excessive control of government rather than towards the advertisers. With the coming of satellite television, Doordarshan was forced to bring changes in the programme content.

Whether or not advertisers exert influence on mass media – in the editorial policy of newspapers or in the contents of the television programmes – the fact is that this arrangement will continue in the future too, unless some alternate viable arrangement is discovered. The real question from the point of view of those who are exposed to advertising from different mass media is what opinion they hold about such advertising. On account of the huge revenue that accrues from advertisers, the media owners are able to improve the quality of print media, television and radio programming, etc. Keeping this objective in mind five statements were prepared which reflect the relationship between mass media and the revenue derived from advertisers.

The first statement relates to the print media. This statement says that because of advertising, print media has become self-sufficient, autonomous and free from undesirable political influence. Results showed that there was a general agreement among both males and females. Very few respondents from either group disagreed. This indicates that people do not think that advertising is bad for the mass media. The second statement of this section says that on account of advertising the prices of newspapers and magazines are low and therefore people can afford to purchase them. On this statement, there was complete unanimity. Both men and women either strongly agreed or agreed with the theme of this statement and there was no disagreement between them.

There is a difference as far as advertising in print media and television is concerned. In case of print media, the readers can easily skip the advertisements, whereas, in case of television, the viewers can not easily escape from the advertisements which are shown either before or in between the programmes. There is a possibility of mental and physical zapping on the part of TV viewers. Generally, people get irritated when there is an interruption in their favourite television programmes because of advertising. For many people, advertising, especially television advertising, is often like a visitor who has overstayed his welcome. It rather becomes an intrusion. Greyser (1973) postulated a life cycle wherein an advertising campaign moves with repetition from a period of effectiveness and presumably audience acceptance to a period of irritation. The third statement was about the impact of advertising on the quality of television programmes. Because of intrusive nature of TV advertising, the extent of agreement for this statement was less as compared to the previous statement which was related to the print media. This does not mean that people strongly disagreed with this statement. Despite, advertising being considered as an unwanted guest, still people thought that because of advertising the quality of television programmes has improved substantially and there was no significant difference between men and women on this matter. The penultimate statement of this section tried to elicit the responses on the all pervasive nature of advertising in the mass media. The results indicated disagreement on this statement. Both males and females were of the opinion that advertising was not that pervasive. Important advertising implications of the findings are that advertisers should, on a periodic basis, measure whether there is a surfeit of advertising in the mass media or not. If it is found that advertising is considered to be excessive, then effective steps need to be taken to curtailed it or should be carried out in a more creative manner. The results of the last statement of this section were very interesting. This statement is about the power of big advertisers. Generally, it is criticised that big advertisers on account of their financial clout spend large amounts of money on promotion including advertising. This often leads to the concentration of power and ultimately in control of mass media. Here there was significant disagreement among the two groups. The male were in disagreement with the statement, whereas, sizeable proportion of females agreed. The results were highly significant ($p<.001$).

Attitudes Towards Nature of Indian Advertising

During the last three decades, the face of Indian advertising has changed drastically. These welcome changes have raised the standard of Indian advertising and brought it at par with the advertising in developed countries. Improvement in print technology, use of colour, advent of computer graphics, use of special effects, and improvement in photographic technology have revolutionized Indian advertising. Along with these changes the amount of advertising to which a consumer is exposed to has also increased tremendously. This increase in advertising might have created some negative consequences. This section deals with this aspect. To encompass the nature of Indian advertising seven statements were formulated. The results of this section are given in Table 2.6. The first statement deals with the poor *taste* exhibited in advertisements. Some critics feel that advertising is objectionable because the creative effort behind it is not in good taste. Therefore, the first statement says that majority of advertisements to which people are exposed are in bad taste. Results indicated that people were indifferent towards this statement. Apart from this people also felt that most of the advertisements were interesting. Most of them did not agree with the second statement that most of the Indian advertisements are *uninteresting*. In the third statement, the *irritation* dimension was considered. Surprisingly very few people found advertisements to be irritating. No significant difference was found between males and females. Generally, it is considered that people do not relish advertising. To test this proposition, the fourth statement was framed which says that people *enjoy* reading or seeing the advertisements. Nearly sixty-seven per cent males and sixty-four per cent females strongly agreed with this statement.

Protagonists of advertising defend it whenever it is attacked by saying that advertising is like a *mirror* and it reflects only what is present in the society. The sixth statement was framed to measure this dimension. Men agreed more than women on this statement. The results also showed significant difference between the two groups. Many people also felt that the advertising for certain types of products such as cigarettes, liquors, women undergarments, and certain types of hygiene products should be banned.

Table 2.6
Attitudes Towards Nature of Indian Advertising

S. No.	*Statement*	*Mean Scores*		*"t" Value*
		Men	*Women*	
1.	Majority of advertisements to which people are exposed to are of poor taste.	3.55	3.64	0.63
2.	Majority of advertisements to which people are exposed to are uninteresting in nature.	3.72	3.7	0.15
3.	Majority of advertisements to which people are exposed to are irritating in nature.	3.72	3.79	0.43
4.	People, generally enjoy reading or viewing the advertisements on the mass media.	3.98	3.94	0.37
5.	The quality of advertising in major media has been improved in the recent years because it is now prepared by professionals.	4.08	3.81	1.48
6.	Advertising is like a mirror. It reflects the existing cultural and moral values of the society.	3.94	3.52	2.44†
7.	Advertisements for certain types of products (cigarettes, women's undergarments and hygiene products) should be banned on the mass media.	3.68	3.06	3.42*
8.	The quality of Indian advertisements is at par with the quality of advertisements of any foreign country.	3.72	3.59	0.86

* = Significant at 1% level.
† = Significant at 5% level.

In order to find out what people had to say on this aspect the seventh statement was framed. Majority of men and women felt that advertisements for these products should be banned. However, women felt more strongly than men. The last statement says that *quality* of Indian advertising is at par with that of any foreign country. Majority of respondents agreed with this statement. It is interesting to note that in the eyes of people, Indian advertisements were of very high quality.

CONCLUSIONS

The following conclusions can be drawn from the study:

1. Most of the respondents acknowledged the importance of advertising as a business tool; wanted advertising to continue; realised the significance of advertising for the promotion of products, especially new products; did not feel the need for stringent laws to regulate it, and did not agree that big companies do not allow smaller companies to grow.
2. As far as the role of advertising in dissemination of information is concerned there was a mixed reaction. To some extent, they agreed that advertising does not misinform, yet, they also felt that it does not play very positive role in information dissemination. However, one good thing about advertising is that people did not think that it gives half truths and is deceptive in nature. However, some women believed that advertising sometimes lies.
3. As far as advertising and materialism is concerned, by and large people did agree that advertising encouraged materialism. Out of the six statements on materialism only on two statements the results showed significant differences between men and women.
4. As far as the influence of advertising on adults and children is concerned, the reactions of respondents was not uniform. Most of the people who were exposed to advertising were influenced by it. The believability of advertisement was also high and they felt that advertising did not exploit their emotions. As far as the impact of advertising on children was concerned, people showed some amount of concern. However, men were more concerned about the negative impact of advertising on children than women.
5. As far as the relationship between advertising and the media is concerned, again the respondents believed that there was nothing wrong in this arrangement. They felt that because of advertising revenues, the prices of newspapers and magazines were low, and therefore, they could afford to purchase them. They also felt that because of advertising

revenues, the quality of television programmes has also improved substantially in the recent years. The male respondents did not believe that big advertisers, because of their heavy spending, control the mass media. However, the female respondents thought otherwise.

6. As far as the attitude towards the Indian advertising is concerned, the reaction was not uniform. Majority of them agreed that some amount of advertising was in bad taste, uninteresting and irritating. It is strange to note that despite the feeling stated above, most of the people enjoyed reading or viewing the advertisements. Men more strongly agreed that advertising reflects the existing moral and cultural values of the society. Women strongly felt that advertisements for certain types of socially undesirable products should be banned. In this regard men also had more or less the same opinion but their intensity was lower than women. Both men and women thought that Indian advertisements are equal in quality and creativity to any foreign advertisement.

This study has clearly demonstrated that people were not in agreement with the charges levelled against advertising by the critics. One may conclude that advertising is not that bad as it has been projected. The people to whom most of the advertising is directed acknowledged the positive role it plays in the society in general and marketing in particular.

REFERENCES

Aaker A. David; Rajive Batra; and John G. Myers (2000), *Advertising Management,* Prentice Hall of India Pvt. Ltd., New Delhi.

Banks Seymour (1980), "Children's Television Viewing Behaviour," *Journal of Marketing,* 2, pp. 52-58.

Bauer A. Raymond and Stephen A. Greyser (1968), *Advertising in America: The Consumer View,* H.B. School, p. 368.

Beatty Sheron and Del L. Hawkins (1989), "Subliminal Stimulation : Some New Data and Interpretations," *Journal of Advertising,* 18, pp. 27-36.

Belk Russel, Robert Mayer and Amy Driscol (1984), "Children's Recognition of Consumption Symbolism in Children's Products," *Journal of Consumer Research,* 10, pp. 386-397.

Berey A. Lewis and Richard W. Pollay (1978), "The Influencing Role of the Child in Family Decision Making," *Journal of Marketing Research,* 5, pp. 70-72.

Butter G. Eliot, Popovich, R. H. Stackhouse and R. Gardener (1981), "Discrimination of Television Commercials by Preschool Children," *Journal of Advertising Research,* 21, pp. 53-56.

Caccavale G. John, Thomas C. Wanty III and Julie A. Adell (1981), "Subliminal Implants in Advertisements : An Experiment," in Andrew A. Mitchel Eds., *Advances in Consumer Research,* (Association for Consumer Research), IX, pp. 418-423.

Cox D. F. and Bauer R. A. (1964), "Self Confidence and Persusibility in Women", *Public Opinion Quarterly.* Fall, pp. 453-66.

Edwards A. Allen (1957), *Techniques of Attitude Scale Construction,* New York, pp. 20-29.

Furgusan M. James (1974), *Advertising and Competition: Theory, Measurement, Fact,* Cambridge, Mass., p. 15.

Furgusan M. James (1978), "Commentary," in David G. Tuerck, eds. *Issues in Advertising: The Economics of Persuasion,* American Enterprise Institution, Washington D.C., p. 199.

Gilligan Colin and Geffrey Crother (1983), *Advertising Management,* Heritage Publishers, New Delhi.

Goldberg E. Marvin and Gerald J. Gorn (1977), "Chilren's Reactions to Television Advertising : An Experimental Approach," *Journal of Consumer Research,* 1, pp. 69-75.

Goldberg E. Marvin and Gerald J. Gorn (1978), "Some Unintended Consequences of TV Advertising to Children," *Journal of Consumer Research,* 5, pp. 22-29.

Gorn J. Gerald and Marvin E. Goldberg (1982), "Behavioural Evidence of the Effects of Televised Food Messages on Children," *Journal of Consumer Research,* 9, pp. 200-205.

Gorn J. Gerald and Renne Florshein (1985) , "The Effect of Commercials for Adults' Products on Children," *Journal of Marketing Research,* 11, pp. 962-967.

Greyser A. Stephen (1973), "Irritation in Advertising," *Journal of Advertising Research,* 13, pp. 8-10.

Gross Bart L. Sanford and Lawrence A. Crosby (1984), "Understanding the Basis of Parental Concern and Reaction to Children's Food Advertising," *Journal of Marketing,* 48, pp. 79-92.

Hawkins L. Del (1970), "The Effects of Subliminal Stimulation on Drive Level and Brand Preference," Journal of Marketing Research, 7, pp. 322-326.

Holtan H. Richard (1980), "How Advertising Achieved Respectability Among Economists (or Anyhow, They are Heard of it)," *Advertising Age,* p. 56.

Hoy G. Mariea, Clifford Young and John C. Mowen (1986), "Animated Host-Selling Advertisements : Their Impact on Young Children's Recognition, Attitudes and Behaviour," *Journal of Public Policy and Marketing,* 5, pp. 171-184.

Huges G. D. (1967), "Selecting Scales and Information Recovery," *Journal of Marketing Research,* 4, pp. 85-87.

Khan M. Kaleem; Khalid Azam; and Mahmood (1992), "Information or Persuasion," *Asia Pacific Journal of International Marketing,* 4, pp. 48-56.

Kotler Philips (2000), *Marketing Management Analysis, Planning, Implementation, and Control,* Prentice-Hall India Pvt. Ltd. New Delhi.

Macklin M. Carol (1987), "Preschooler's Understanding of Informational Function of Television Advertising," *Journal of Consumer Research,* 14, pp. 229-239.

Miller R. Joseph and Paul Busch (1979), "Host-Selling Vs Premium TV Commercials : An Experimental Evaluation of their Influence on Children," *Journal of Marketing Research,* 16, pp. 323-332.

Pollay M. Richard (1986), "Quality of Life in the Padded Sell: Common Criticism of Advertising's Cultural Character and International Public Policies," in James H. Leigh and Claude R. Martin, Jr. Eds. *Current Issues of Research in Advertising,* Ann Arbor: University of Michigan Press, pp. 173-250.

Pollay W. Richard (1986), "The Distorted Mirror: Reflections on the Unintended Consequences of Advertising," *Journal of Marketing,* 50, pp. 18-36

Reece B. Bonnie (1983), "Chilren's Ability to Identify Retail Stores from Advertising Slogans," in Thomas C. Kinnear, Eds. *Advances in Consumer Research,* 11, pp. 320-323.

Schiffman G. Leon and Leslie L. Kanuk (2000), *Consumer Behaviour,* Prentice Hall India Pvt. Ltd., New Delhi, pp. 360-362.

Seagert Joel (1987), "Why Marketing Should Quit Giving Subliminal Advertising the Benefit of Doubt," *Psychology and Marketing,* pp. 107-120.

Singh Kusum and Bertram Gross (1981), "MacBride: The Report and the Response," *Journal of Communication,* 31, pp. 104-117.

Stephens Nancy and Mary A. Studs (1982), "Preschoolers Ability to Distinguish Between Television Programming and Commercials," *Journal of Advertising,* pp. 16-26.

Tesler L. G. (1968), "Some Aspects of the Economics of Advertising," *Journal of Business,* 15, pp. 32-34.

Wiman R. Ellen (1983), "Parental Influence and Children's Responses to Television Advertising," *Journal of Advertising,* 12, pp. 12-18.

Wright S. John; Willis S. Winter; and Sherilyn K. Zeigler (1989), *Advertising,* Tata McGraw-Hill Pub. New Delhi, pp. 36-37.

3

Viewers' Perceptions Towards Prime Time TV Commercials

INTRODUCTION

In recent years people are being increasingly exposed to advertisements that appear in major media in general and TV medium in particular. Of late, TV commercials have gained immense popularity and their share in the overall advertising budgets of major consumer goods companies has increased tremendously. Thus, increasingly, need is being felt to measure the perception of the viewers towards TV commercials. For researchers the pertinent question is why some commercials are liked and others disliked? How and in what way these commercials are received and perceived by the audience? What impact do liked and disliked commercials exert on the purchase behaviour of the consumers? Present study attempts to address the first two questions.

The answer to these questions is important because the perception of viewers towards commercials can greatly affect the extent their effectiveness. Burke and Edel (1989) found that the feelings generated by advertisements were linked to the consumer's evaluation of both advertisements and brands. Research has also showed that those commercials, which leave pleasant feelings among audiences may prove to be effective in terms of attitudinal changes and finally in positively influencing purchasing behaviour *vis-a-vis* advertised brands. Aaker and Bruzzone (1981) found that well-liked commercials prove to be more effective than those that are neither liked nor disliked. However, Shafiq (1985) found that some advertisements, which generated strong negative reactions, were found to be generate high level of attention and subsequently high level of recall too. In this context, the famous *Lalitaji* advertisement for Surf washing powder is a classic example.

In order to measure the perception of the audience towards TV commercials, three areas are particularly important to understand. Firstly, how consumers are likely to perceive the advertising message. Secondly, how their attention can be captured. Finally, what interpretations are likely to be made of various components and parts of the advertised message. These are important because negative perception process has long been recognised as the most significant barrier to effective communication.

Measuring audience perception for TV commercials has become even more important with the emergence of video technologies where the viewers have the option of mechanical *zipping*. Another reason for measuring audience perception is the question of *clutter* i.e. placing of large number of advertisements one after the other in a short span of time. Most of the TV commercials encounter this problem when they appear before or between the popular serials. Therefore, there is a strong possibility of irritation on the part of the viewers when their popular programmes are interrupted by the commercials which is in all probability considered as an intrusion. Because of these reasons, if a negative attitude develops towards the TV commercials, then the purpose of airing them will become self defeating and their effectiveness will decrease substantially. The negative feelings towards the commercials may also result in public support for stringent government regulations.

Keeping in mind the above reasons, present study was undertaken to measure the viewers' reactions towards prime-time TV commercials. The viewers' reactions were measured in terms of five adjectives i.e. *amusing, irritating, appealing, convincing* and *informative*. These adjectives have been used because they reflect both cognitive and affective feelings associated with positive and negative attitudes.

RESEARCH METHOD AND DATA BASE

In order to measure the perceptions of viewers towards prime-time TV commercials with respect to feeling and information content, all commercials appearing between December 7 to 31, 1996 were videotaped during prime time. In all 327 commercials were recorded and they form the database for this study. They were grouped under the following product categories:

- Textiles and garments
- Cosmetics and personal care products
- Medicine and health care products
- Foods/snacks and soft drinks
- Toothpaste & toiletries
- Consumer durables

After grouping the commercials under different product categories, 35 commercials were randomly picked up, taken off from the data base and recorded separately. No two commercials from the same product category were recorded sequentially.

The 35 slelcted commercials were screened on a video before the audience in home-settings. In order to measure the perception of TV viewers, a list of brands featured in these commercials was supplied to the respondents. Questions pertaining to these commercials were placed randomly in the questionnaire. After viewing the commercials the respondents were asked to rate each commercial on a five point rating scale on each of the five adjectives i.e. amusing, irritating, appealing, convincing and informative. The respondents were explained how they should rate each commercial on each of adjectives. For example, they were to allot 1 for "extremely", 2 for "very", 3 for "somewhat", 4 for "not very", and 5 for "not at all" for that adjective. This meant that if a respondent rated a particular commercial 2 on amusing, 4 on irritating, 1 on appealing, 2 on convincing, and 3 on informative, it meant that particular commercial had been considered by respondents as "very amusing", "not at all irritating", "extremely appealing", "very convincing" and "somewhat informative". Next, the scores of each respondent were added up and a mean score of each respondent was calculated for each adjective for that commercial. The mean scores for each commercial and for each adjective was calculated in terms of male and female respondents. In total 122 respondents gave their rating for the commercials. Instead of using probability sampling technique, a more convenient non-probability sampling technique was used for data collection.

Table 3.1
Aggregate Score of Commercials on Five Adjectives

Advertisements	*Amusing*	*Irritating*	*Appealing*	*Convincing*	*Informative*
Iodex	3.06	4.09	3.07	4.25	2.75
Everest Masala	3.38	4.02	3.28	4.20	3.52
Ariel	2.60	3.90	3.15	3.78	2.48
Dinesh	3.20	4.35	2.7	3.38	4.42
Gagan Oil	3.92	4.57	3.02	4.11	3.10
Vicks	3.17	4.21	3.24	3.25	2.79
Colgate	3.96	3.74	3.70	4.58	2.51
Evita	3.60	4.67	2.52	3.66	3.80
Raymonds	3.38	4.51	2.55	3.40	4.40
Oil of Ulay	3.60	4.52	2.82	3.68	2.56
Vectra	4.16	4.53	2.58	3.48	2.97
Volform Jam	2.49	4.52	3.03	3.49	4.01
Fair and Lovely	3.57	4.32	3.04	3.68	3.02
Close Up	3.67	4.52	2.75	2.88	3.97
Tata Tea	3.93	3.57	3.58	4.18	3.85
Timex Watches	3.46	4.73	2.43	2.69	3.73
Hajmola	3.02	4.38	3.10	3.82	3.58
Rin	3.71	3.75	3.43	4.22	2.91
Amity Perfume	3.28	4.47	2.73	3.24	4.19
Yamaha	3.55	4.00	2.40	2.31	3.98
Nescafe	3.37	4.68	2.21	2.84	3.40
Anacin	4.20	3.15	4.35	4.72	2.66
Maggie Sauce	1.79	4.75	2.27	2.70	3.86
Lakme Nail Polish	3.17	4.79	2.09	2.51	3.86
Gwalior Suitings	3.29	4.52	2.75	3.03	4.19
Le Sancy	2.92	4.81	2.56	3.56	2.64
Hero Puch	3.93	4.11	3.08	2.86	3.50
Cadbury's	2.56	4.56	2.24	3.31	3.78
Glycodin	4.25	3.34	3.84	4.43	2.72
BPL Sanyo	3.95	4.75	2.86	2.88	2.29
Nirma	4.14	3052	3.68	4.20	3.63
Clearsil	2.78	4.47	3.33	3.93	2.57
Sapan Dairy	3.64	4.38	2.99	3.71	2.97
Pepsodent	2.90	4.24	3.06	3.83	2.70
Graviera	3.29	4.52	2.75	3.06	4.30

RESULTS

The analysis and the results of this study have been divided into two parts. The first part deals with the mean scores of all the commercials for all the five adjectives for all respondents without segregating them into male and female categories. The second part of the results deals with the ranking of commercials on each adjective for male and female respondents. This has been done to find out the effect of sex on the perception of the respondents towards the various commercials.

Rating of TV Commercials

Table 3.1 gives the rating for all the TV commercials included in the study in aggregate terms on all the five adjectives. Only the mean scores for all adjectives of each commercial are shown in the table. However, for the purpose of deeper insight, the scores for each adjective were grouped into four categories.

All those mean scores which fell between 1 and 1.99 were considered *very high*; a mean score between 2 and 2.99 as *high*; mean score between 3 and 3.99 as *average*; and a mean score between 4 and 5 as *low* on that particular adjective for each advertisement. The results of this grouping are given in Table 3.2. Examining this table one can easily discern the magnitude of commercials which fell in any of the four categories. After perusing Table 3.2 one can find that the modal category for amusing adjective was *average* (i.e. 68.57%). It meant that most of the advertisements which the audience saw and perceived were *average* as far as amusing adjective was concerned. Nearly 17.14% of the commercials fell under the category of *high* on amusing. Only 11.43% advertisements were perceived as being *low* on amusing. Only one advertisement was perceived *very high* on amusing.

As far as the level of irritation was concerned no advertisement fell under the categories of *very high* and *high*. This is a bit strange in the sense that in one study Aaker and Bruzzone (1985) found that both the product and the copy approaches influence irritation. It is to be kept in mind that in this study, advertisements of those products which by their very nature were considered to be offensive, were not included. This category included advertisements for cigarettes, feminine hygiene, family planning/birth control products and liquors. However, the execution style of commercials can also be a cause for irritation. In our study, no commercial was perceived as *very high* or *high* on irritation. More than three fourths (80%) advertisements were found to be *very low* on irritation and one fifth (20%) of the advertisements were considered by the audience as average on irritation. By referring back to Table 3.1, one can notice that Anacin, Glycodin, Nirma, Tata Tea, Colgate, Rin and Ariel advertisements did generate some amount of irritation. Out of these seven advertisements, three were in the detergent category, two were OTC drugs, one each for tea and toothpaste.

Regarding the adjective "appealing", no advertisements was found to be in the *very high* category. But, more than half (51.43%) of the commercials, whose mean score ranged between 2 to 2.99, fell in the *high* category. This showed that people enjoyed watching these commercials and consequently they may generate positive feelings towards the advertised products. A substantial number of advertisements (54.3%) were found to be *high* on "appealing" adjective. Except for Anacin advertisement, which was *high* on irritation and *low* on appealing, nearly 45.7% of the advertisements were average on appealing.

As far as adjective "convincing" was concerned, it carries a positive connotation but it is slightly different from "amusing" and "appealing". "Convincing" advertisements can create a lot of conviction of the consumers in the advertised product. By examining Table 3.2 it is clear that most of the advertisements (77.14%) were perceived by the respondents as being either *low* or *average* on convincing. There was no commercial which was considered *very high* on "convincing" adjective. Nearly one-fourth (22.86%) of the commercials were perceived as being *high* on "convincing". The three most convincing commercials, as perceived by the respondents, were Yamaha, Lakme Nail Polish and Timex watches.

It may not be out of place to mention that advertising should be informative so that consumers can use such information in making right purchase decisions. One can not deny the fact that there is practical need to incorporate product information in commercials and effective advertisements tend to fulfil this need. In a content analysis study of Indian magazine advertisements, Khan, Azam and Mahmood (1991) found that of the 97.4 per cent of the advertisements pertaining to industrial products, 80 per cent for consumer non-durables and 74 per cent of the advertisements for consumer durables, contained one or more of the 14 possible

Table 3.2
Perception of TV Commercials on Five Adjectives

Adjectives	*Very High (1.0 to 1.99)*	*High (2.0 to 2.99)*	*Average (3.0 to 3.99)*	*Low (4.0 to 5.0)*
Amusing	1 (2.8)	6 (17.14)	24 (68.57)	4 (11.43)
Irritating	0 (0)	0 (0)	07 (20.00)	28 (80.00)
Appealing	0 (0)	18 (51.43)	16 (45.71)	1 (2.86)
Convincing	0 (0)	8 (22.86)	18 (51.43)	9 (25.71)
Informative	0 (0)	14 (40.00)	15 (42.86)	6 (17.41)

Note:- Figures in parentheses are percentages.

information cues. In another study of 524 prime-time TV commercials by Aaker and Norris (1982), it was found that TV advertising in US was perceived as informative by a substantial number of people. In order to find out what people think about Indian TV commercials, in terms of information content, this study was undertaken. Interestingly, no advertisement was perceived as *very high* on information content. While only 17.4 per cent advertisements were perceived as being *low* on information. More than 80 per cent commercials were considered as being either *high* or *average* on information. This means that advertisers apart from giving importance to creativity also provide valuable information to consumers, which may enable them to make right decisions in purchasing different products or services.

Gender Effect on Rating of Commercials

In order to measure the effect of sex, the commercials were ranked in ascending order on each adjective in terms of male and female respondents. Instead of showing the ranking all 35 commercials, only top 10 commercials were included. The purpose of this analysis was two-fold. Firstly, to find out ten outstanding advertisements on each adjective, as perceived by either sex, and secondly, to find out the differences, if any, in the perception of these commercials.

Table 3.3 lists the top ten commercials, as perceived by the respondents, on the adjective "amusing". This table separately shows the perception of male and female respondents. Maggie's advertisement which had used humour and celebrities was found to be the "most amusing" by both the sexes. Perusing this table one can also notice that of the two lists of the top ten advertisements, seven advertisements were common. Except Maggie's commercial, other six commercials were ranked differently by male and female respondents. Three advertisements i.e. the ones for Lakme Nail Polish, Nescafe and Timex watches were ranked by males within the top ten amusing advertisements. The advertisements for Iodex, Hajmola and Dinesh Suitings were ranked by females as being within top ten. However, these were not in the top ten category in case of males. As far as seven advertisements were concerned, they were more or less identically perceived by male and female respondents on amusing adjective. The three advertisements which were among the top then category on amusing adjective for males were not in the top ten category of females. The vice-versa was also true. Interestingly, some advertisements featuring products exclusively used by males were rated *high* by females on amusing. The same were not rated similarly by males. In the same way, advertisements featuring female oriented products were rated *high* by males and not by females. This demonstrates that the perception of males and females on amusing adjective was similar for seven of the top ten advertisements and dissimilar in case of three, in each category.

Table 3.3
Top Ten Amusing Commercials

Commercial	*Male Mean Score*	*Rank*	*Commercial*	*Female Mean Score*	*Rank*
Maggie Sauce	1.8	1	Maggie Sauce	1.77	1
Clearsil	2.36	2	Volform Jam	2.26	2
Ariel	2.42	3	Cadbury	2.48	3
Le Sancy	2.64	4	Ariel	2.7	4
Cadbury	2.7	5	Iodex	2.74	5
Volform Jam	2.87	6	Pepsodent	2.88	6
Lakme Nail Polish	2.93	7	Hajmola	2.95	7
Pepsodent	2.94	8	Clearsil	3.04	8
Nescafe	2.97	9	Le Sancy	3.09	9
Timex Watch	3.04	10	Dinesh Suiting	3.15	10

As discussed earlier, in aggregate terms, no commercial was found to be *very high* on irritation when the commercials were ranked in terms of top ten irritating advertisements for male and female respondents. Again, only in case of Anacin, the irritation aspect was *high* and was to be most irritating commercial both by males and females (see Table 3.4). However, this commercial generated more irritation among the males in comparison to females and this was found statistically significant too ($P<0.05$). By analysing Table 3.4 it becomes clear that on an average the irritation level of males is higher than that of females. Though, table 4 gives the top ten commercials on irritation, yet, if one analyses, in absolute terms, except for Anacin commercial, all the other commercials were either *average* or *low* on irritation. This was more pronounced in case of female audience. Thus, we can conclude that there is some association between the level of irritation and the gender of the resepondents. Findings suggest that males are more prone to irritation than females who showed greater tolerance even for those advertisements, which generated high level of irritation among males. The mean scores of top ten irritating advertisements were subjected to t-test. The differences in the scores for three advertisements viz. Anacin, Glycodin and Nirma, were found to be significant.

Table 3.4
Top Ten Irritating Commercials

Commercial	*Male Mean Score*	*Rank*	*Commercial*	*Female Mean Score*	*Rank*
Anacin	2.68	1	Anacin	3.44*	1
Glycodin	2.81	2	Rin	3.57	2
Nirma	3.13	3	Tata Tea	3.6	3
Tata Tea	3.53	4	Glycodin	3.63*	4
Pepsodent	3.68	5	Yamaha	3.64	5
Gwalior Suiting	3.83	6	Colgate	3.65	6
Colgate	3.89	7	Nirma	3.77*	7
Dinesh Suiting	3.96	8	Ariel	3.85	8
Everest Masala	4.02	9	Everest Masala	4.01	9
Rin	4.04	10	Hero Puch	4.05	10

*significant at 5% level.

Table 3.5 gives the ranking of commercials, considered to be appealing by both the sexes. Generally, it is considered, advertisements that appeal to the audience create positive impact on their attitudes. However, their impact on purchase decisions is debatable. Out of the top ten commercials given in Table 3.5, seven were common for both the sexes. Graviera Suitings, Evita and Hero Puch were among the top ten advertisements as far as the perception of males was concerned and Vectra, Raymonds and Dinesh Suitings were among the top ten appealing commercials. Analysing the differences in the perception of male and female responses one can discern that three commercials were in the category of *very high* and remaining seven were *high* in terms of females' perception. In case of males, no commercial from among the top ten fell under *very high* category. In aggregate terms, females' perception of appealing commercials was higher than males.

Table 3.5

Top Ten Appealing Commercials

Commercial	*Male Mean Score*	*Rank*	*Commercial*	*Female Mean Score*	*Rank*
Nescafe	2.17	1	Yamaha	1.33	1
Cadbury	2.18	2	Vectra	1.47	2
Le Sancy	2.19	3	Lakme	1.89	3
Maggie Sauce	2.29	4	Nescafe	2.25	4
Graviera	2.34	5	Maggie Sauce	2.28	5
Timex	2.36	6	Cadbury	2.31	6
Lakme	2.40	7	Raymonds	2.45	7
Evita	2.47	8	Timex	2.47	8
Raymonds	2.70	9	Dinesh Suitings	2.55	9
Hero Puch	2.76	10	Le Sancy	2.62	10

The fourth dimension of perception of viewers was concerned with the convincing aspect. Table 3.6 gives the top ten commercials ranked on adjective "convincing" as perceived by male and female viewers. There were some similarities as well as differences, between the perception of male and female respondents. Out of the top ten convincing advertisements, six were common to both the sexes.

Table 3.6
Top Ten Convincing Commercials

Commercial	*Male Mean Score*	*Rank*	*Commercial*	*Female Mean Score*	*Rank*
Yamaha	1.81	1	Lakme	2.46	1
Hero Puch	2.51	2	Yamaha	2.63	2
BPL-Sanyo	2.55	3	Maggie	2.68	3
Lakme	2.57	4	Timex	2.77	4
Nescafe	2.59	5	Close Up	2.83	5
Timex	2.64	6	Hajmola	2.84	6
Graviera	2.68	7	Gwalior Suitings	2.87	7
Maggie Sauce	2.74	8	Nescafe	2.94	8
Close Up	3.04	9	Vicks Drops	2.97	9
Amity Perfume	3.06	10	BPL-Sanyo	2.98	10

However, they differed in ranking. Four top convincing advertisements were different for males and females. Another important difference was that male scores for convincing advertisements were higher in aggregate terms when compared to the females scores.

Table 3.6 gives the responses of both male and female respondents on the information adjective. Both the sexes had almost the same perception as far as the information nature of advertisements was concerned. Out of top ten commercials, eight commercials were common to both men and women. Looking back at Table 3.1, we can notice that nearly 80 per cent commercials were considered either high or medium on information and only 18 per cent were considered low on information. These observations corroborate the findings of Kaleem, Azam and Mehmood (1997) on informative role of advertising. It seems that on account of increase in competition, and the availability of wide range of products, advertisers are increasingly giving more emphasis on providing informational cues to their target audience. The same is reflected in the perception of majority of respondents irrespective of sex.

CONCLUSIONS

This study revealed that viewers, by and large, have a positive predisposition towards commercials appearing on TV. As far as "amusing" aspect is concerned, most of the advertisements ranged from *high* to *average* on this adjective. This indicates that advertisers keep in mind the entertainment aspect while promoting their products and services to target audience. The quality of most of the advertisements was quite high and the execution style of various advertisements was also good. The "irritation" score of various advertisements corroborates the earlier findings as "amusing" and "irritating" are mutually exclusive. Normally, if one commercial is considered amusing then it can not be considered simultaneously as irritating. Therefore, more than three fourth of the commercials were found to be *low* on "irritation". The remaining advertisements were found *average* on irritation. No commercial was found to be *very high* or *high* on irritation. Again, most of the commercials were perceived by viewers as being either *high* or *average* on appealing. However, as far as convincing aspect was concerned, the audience felt that this quality was not as high as appealing or amusing. This can be attributed to the fact that normally people do not attach much credibility to the commercial sources of information including advertising. Advertising performs more of an *informative* function than the *legitimising* or *evaluative* function. Finally, the informative function of these commercials was viewed either *high* or *average* by almost all the viewers.

In the end one can conclude that advertising is playing a positive role in the promotion of various goods and services and people who are exposed to it are influenced substantially. However, certain aspects of advertising, such as *cluttering* and *zapping,* need to be carefully addresses.

REFERENCES

Aaker, D.A. and D. Norris, (1982), "Characteristics of Television Commercials Perceived as Information", *Journal of Advertising Research,* February, 60-68.

Aaker, D.A. and D.E. Bruzzone (1981), "Audience Reactions to Television Commercials", *Journal of Advertising Research,* October, 50-58.

Aaker, D.A. and D.E. Bruzzone (1985), "Causes of Irritation in Advertising", *Journal of Marketing,* (Spring) 47-57.

Burke, M.C. and J.A. Edell (1989), "The Impact of Feelings on Ad-based Affect and Cognition", *Journal of Marketing Research,* (February), 69-83.

Khan, K.M. K. Azam and Mahmood, "Information or Persuasion! A Content Analysis of Print Advertisement in India", *Asia Pacific International Journal of Marketing,* 1991, pp. 50-57.

4

Influence of Cinema Advertising on Attitudinal Change and Purchase Intentions

NATURE OF CINEMA ADVERTISING

In a developing country like India, cinema is considered to be the cheapest mode of entertainment as well as an effective medium for advertising consumer products – both durables and non-durables. Despite the emergence of T.V. as the fastest growing medium, cinema is still among the top four advertising media. Since the introduction of television, the size of cinema audience is on decline. Therefore, cinema is finding it increasingly difficult to attract advertising revenue. As far as cinema advertising is concerned, the expenditure on it has remained more or less static for the last two decades. If, however, the characteristics of the medium are examined in isolation, the cinema appears to be an attractive advertising proposition. Perhaps its major potential advantage is that it has an essentially captive and generally attentive audience who go to cinema for entertainment. They are likely to be in a relaxed and receptive frame of mind, and this coupled with the large size screen of the cinema, availability of colour, movement, and sound, offers significant scope to the advertisers (Gilligan & Crowther, 1983).

Though, the importance of cinema as a means of entertainment and as an advertising medium has decreased on account of television's phenomenal success, still a sizeable portion of Indian population is exposed to it – both in urban and rural areas. In a recent media survey, Operation Research Group (ORG) found that in the Hindi belt, 37.7 per cent of adults in urban areas and 10.7 per cent of adults in rural areas are exposed to cinema. Surprisingly, the exposure to cinema in rural areas is considerably higher than to press (5.4 per cent). Another interesting thing from this survey, was the exposure to this medium in terms of age. Nearly 30 per cent of the population in the age group between 15 to 24 years is regularly exposed to cinema. The exposure declines as the age rises, being lowest among those over 45 years old.

As television, *the cinema of house,* becomes more popular, going to cinema will become a habit more observed in breach. However, the 15-25 age group will still make an outing of it, while the older age group will prefer front row seats in their own homes. Therefore, in future, cinema theatres in large towns will probably be used, with a difference, for product sampling and special events. Thus, in spite of its decline, cinema advertising in India will continue to play an important role after the press and the television media.

The messages employed in cinema and television commercials are similar in format and style. However, in case of cinema their length and duration are slightly larger. The length of an average cinema commercial is about 48 feet and lasts for about 30 seconds. These commercials are screened in cinema halls before the start of the feature film and sometime during the intervals also. Cinema halls continue to be visited regularly (at least once a month) by a quarter of urban dwellers. Thus, these audiences are exposed to the cinema commercials on a regular basis and therefore there is a possibility of repetition. *Zapping* which is very common in video advertising is negligible in cinema.

The present study was undertaken to measure the attitudinal changes and consequently the purchase intentions of those who are frequently exposed to cinema advertising. It was also undertaken to ascertain the role of sex and age of cinema audience as moderating variables on attitudinal change and purchase intentions.

The measurement of attitudes is central to many marketing situations in general and advertising in particular. This is because of the fact that advertising is considered as a form of marketing communication and, therefore, like any effective communication, advertising can persuade and change attitudes of those who are exposed to it over a period of time. An individual is considered as an information processing machine who when confronted with new information, tries to absorb and deal with it as effectively as possible and alter his behaviour accordingly (McGuire, 1978). Attitudes are important in marketing decision making because of the assumed relationship between attitudes and behaviour. It is generally presumed that attitudes are forerunner of behaviour or that attitudes represent a series of sequential components which lead to behaviour (Lavidge & Steiner, 1961).

The purpose of advertising is to bring about some response from the target market and in this connection cinema advertising is no exception. The response may be at the cognitive, affective or behavioural level. The cognitive component refers to the respondent's awareness or the knowledge about some object or phenomenon. This is sometimes called the belief component of attitude. The affective component refers to the respondent's liking and preference towards an object or phenomenon, sometimes called the feeling component. The behavioural component refers to the respondent's intention-to-buy and actual purchase behaviour. The intention-to-buy stage refers to the respondent's predisposition to action prior to the actual purchase. Researches have shown that there is a correlation between purchase intentions and actual purchase behaviour. Sometimes this correlation is high and sometimes it is low (Fishbein, 1967). Two factors can intervene between purchase intentions and the purchase behaviour. These are attitudes of others and unanticipated situational factors (Sheth, 1974). Keeping in mind the importance of attitudinal change and purchase intentions, the present study tries to explore the influence of cinema advertising on those who are exposed to it. More specifically the following research objectives were considered:

- To find out the movie going pattern in terms of sex and age.
- To ascertain the degree of attitudinal change and consequent purchase intentions for different categories of products for those who are exposed to cinema advertising.
- To know the optimum number of exposures of a cinema advertisement needed to change the attitudes and influence purchasing behaviour.
- To find out the optimum number of exposures required to maintain the visual interest.
- To ascertain the relative effectiveness of different formats used in cinema commercials.

METHODOLOGY

Considering the above mentioned objectives a structured questionnaire was prepared covering the different facets of cinema advertisements. To gauge the attitudinal change and consequently the purchase intentions of the respondents, a list of those products was prepared whose advertisements are generally shown in the cinema theatres. These products were classified into three categories. Category I comprised of those products which are purchased frequently, consumed in short span of time and sold through intensive distribution i.e. consumer non-durables. Category II comprised less frequently purchased goods. They were considered to be of semi-durable nature. Category III comprised of those products which are purchased least frequently and consumers spend a great deal of time and effort before taking purchase decision i.e. durables. In all, seventeen products were selected; seven in non-durables, five each in semi-durables and durables categories.

The survey was intended to cover the educated and informed population of Aligarh, a B class city of Uttar Pradesh. In order to give due representation to all sections of the society, respondents were selected from different professions such as teaching, services, fields of engineering, medicine, and business. In addition, housewives and students were also considered. A total of 400 questionnaires were distributed and out of which 250 responses were received. In order to minimise bias and fatigue on the part of the respondents, the questionnaire was kept brief, questions were undisguised and unambiguous and were straight forward. A complete random sample was not possible. Therefore, a purposive cum convenience sampling technique was used. The questionnaires were personally administered through the students of MBA who were familiar with the objectives of the study. The data were compiled, tabulated, and analysed on the basis of two moderating variables i.e. sex and age. Because the data were in the form of nominal scale, therefore, chi-square analysis was performed whenever necessary.

ANALYSIS AND INTERPRETATION

Pattern of Movie Going

Before ascertaining the possibility of attitudinal change and consequent purchase intentions it was thought proper to find the movie going pattern of respondents in terms of sex and age. Therefore, at the outset the respondents were asked to give their frequency of going to movies. Four alternatives were provided to them i.e. who go to movie *occasionally* (ranging from one month to one year), *once in a month, once in a fortnight* and *once in a week.* The responses are arranged in terms of sex and age for the movie going pattern in Tables 4.1 and 4.2 respectively. In aggregate terms, more than one fourth (29.3 per cent) were found to be occasional movie goers,

Table 4.1
Movie Going Pattern and Sex

	Sex	
Frequency	*Men %*	*Women %*
Occasionally	37.1	23.3
Monthly	19.8	29.7
Fortnightly	19.8	22.2
Weekly	23.3	14.8
Total	100	100

23 per cent went once a month, 20.7 percent once in a fortnight and 26.7 per cent once in a week. As far as distribution of respondents with respect to sex was concerned, males more often went to movies

Table 4.2
Movie Going Pattern and Age

	Age			
Frequency	*15-22 years %age*	*23-30 years %age*	*31-38 years %age*	*39-45 years %age*
Occasionally	23.3	29.9	64.2	11.1
Monthly	15	28.4	7.2	66.7
Fortnightly	23.3	19.4	21.4	11.1
Weekly	38.4	22.3	7.2	11.1
Total	100	100	100	100

than females. It was found that nearly one fourth (23.3 per cent) males went to movies *once in a week*, whereas, the percentage for women was only 15 per cent. Women were found to go for movies more often *once in a month.* When the movie going pattern was analysed in terms of age, some interesting findings emerged. Irrespective of sex, it was found that younger people were more habitual cinema goers than elders. In case of those who were in the age group between 15-22 years, i.e. 38.4 per cent went to movies *once in a week*. This percentage dropped to 22.3 per cent in the age group of 23-30 years. It further dropped to 7.2 per cent and 11.1 per cent in the 31-38 and 39-46 years categories respectively. This strongly indicates that age has strong relationship with the movie going habits. This was further corroborated when the data were subjected to statistical analysis.

Attitudinal Change and Purchase Intentions

Advertising as a form of marketing communication is intended to persuade the target market. In the process of persuation it has to first bring about change in the attitude, which may eventually lead to purchase intentions for the advertised products and services. Apart from persuation, advertising also performs the function of providing information or reminding the consumers about the qualities and features of the products (Bogart, Steward & Orenstein, 1970). Therefore, in order to measure the attitudinal change, if any, and purchase intentions of cinema audience, the respondents were asked to indicate their attitudinal change for seventeen products.

For each product class they were provided with three alternatives, namely, positive attitudinal change, no change in attitude and negative attitudinal change. The responses were arranged according to three product categories and are presented in Table 4.3. Examining this table one can find that cinema advertisements brought substantial positive attitudinal change in all the product groups among both men and women. The percentage of respondents whose attitudes were changed in the negative direction was very low (~10%) for both males and females. However, a sizeable number of both men and women remained unaffected by the cinema advertisements. In case of semi-durable goods, women indicated more positive attitudinal change (75.5%) than their male counterparts (63.2%).

This clearly demonstrated that cinema advertisements did bring about attitudinal change and this was more pronounced in the case of semi-durable goods. The percentage of those who developed negative attitudes after getting exposed to cinema advertisements among women was less as compared to men. However, when chi-square analysis was performed to find out whether these differences are statistically significant or not, no significance was found.

Table 4.3
Product Categories and Attitudinal Change

Product categories	*Attitudes*					
	Positive Change		*No Change*		*Negative Change*	
	Men%	*Women%*	*Men%*	*Women%*	*Men%*	*Women%*
Non-durables	52.9	48.1	35.6	42.6	11.5	9.3
Semi-durables	63.2	75.5	28.4	18.9	8.4	5.6
Durables	55.8	51.9	30.5	40.7	13.7	7.4

Positive attitudinal change, as stated earlier, can lead to purchase intentions and finally to purchase behaviour. Therefore, in order to measure whether the positive attitudinal change brought about by cinema advertising had any impact on the purchasing intention for different product classes, the respondents were further asked to indicate their purchase intentions if they happen to need these products. Their responses are arranged in Table 4.4. This table shows

Table 4.4
Comparison of Attitudinal Change and Purchase Intentions in Men and Women

Product Categories	*Sex*					
	Men			*Women*		
	Positive Attitudinal Change	*Purchase intention*	*% increase or decrease*	*Positive Attitudinal Change*	*Purchase intention*	*% increase or decrease*
Non-durables	52.9	46.3	-6.6	48.1	50	1.9
Semi-durables	63.2	57.7	-5.5	75.5	66.7	-8.8
Durables	55.8	35.1	-20.7	51.9	40.3	-11.6

that the degree of positive purchase intentions was more in case of women than men. The comparison of positive attitudinal change and purchase intentions of men and women indicates that for non-durables the percentage increase in positive purchase intentions was 1.9 per cent in case of women, whereas, there was a decrease of 6.6 per cent in case of men. In the same manner, for semi-durable and durable categories, women showed higher degree of purchase intentions than men. For women it was 66.7 per cent and 57 per cent for semi-durables and durables, whereas, for men it was 57.7 per cent and 35.1 per cent respectively. This difference between men and women was found statistically significant. This may lead to the conclusion that women are more amenable to persuation than men. These findings are in tune with another study which found that women are more persuasible than men (Janis & Field, 1958).

Optimal Level of Exposure and Purchase Intentions

Attitudinal change, and consequently the formation of purchase intentions are not possible in a single exposure to an advertisement. Most media decisions require judgements on the part of the advertisers as to the optimum number of exposures that may lead to intended change in attitude. Repetition of persuasive messages generally proves to be beneficial. The benefits of repetition in advertising are two fold. Firstly, it minimizes forgetting effect and secondly, it reinforces the attitudinal change. Therefore, repetition can build a continuity of impression in the minds of prospective purchasers and strengthen a predisposition to think and act favourably towards the advertised brand (Gilligan & Crowther, 1983). One study has demonstrated that repetition of advertising message leads to sustenance of brand awareness (Steward, 1964). Another study by Light (1983) found a significant positive relation between repetition and awareness.

Krugman (1975) suggests that insights into repetition can be gained by considering the difference between the first, second and third exposure. According to him the first exposure elicits a *what is it* type of cognitive response. The audience tries to understand the nature of the communication and, if possible, categorises it as being of no further interest. The second exposure to the same advertisement, if not blocked out, produces several responses. One, particularly in television and/or cinema advertising, is a continuation of the *what is it* response. The first exposure may not have been adequate to gain an understanding of what it was. Another response may be evaluative. The audience member will attempt to determine if it is relevant and convincing. So, the message will be evaluated. The third exposure is basically a reminder in case the audience member has not yet acted on message. In a classic study of repetition effects, Zielske (1959) found that continuous repetition at equal interval for a specific period lead to higher recall of the message. The experimental study of Ray and Sawyer (1971) measured the impact of repetition on brand recall, attitudinal change and purchase intentions for two set of products i.e. convenience goods and shopping goods. Overall the results produced significant repetition effects with respect to recall. One interesting finding of this study was that there was a significant difference for both recall and purchase intention for the product classification of convenience versus shopping goods. The above studies highlight the significance of multiple exposure of advertising messages for creating and sustaining attitudinal change leading to purchase intentions and behaviour.

Therefore, in order to find out the optimal exposure level for cinema advertisements, the respondents were asked to recall the approximate number of time they had been exposed to an advertisement before they were convinced to purchase the product. Later, their responses were categorised into four frequency distributions. The responses in terms of sex and age differences are given in Tables 4.5 and 4.6. Out of the total respondents (both sexes)around 50 per cent recalled that they were convinced to purchase the advertised product after being exposed to the message between one to five times; 25 per cent recalled the frequency was between six to ten exposures; for 12 per cent of the respondents, the frequency ranged between eleven to fifteen exposures and for 13 per cent of the respondents, the frequency was sixteen to twenty exposures. In Table 4.5 the same has been shown in segregated form in terms of males and females. Further, no statistical significance was found as far as both the sexes were concerned.

Table 4.5
Exposure and Purchase Intentions (Sex-wise)

	Sex	
	Men	*Women*
Frequency	%	%
1 to 5	43.8	55.6
6 to 10	28.1	22.2
11 to 15	13.5	11.1
16 to 20	14.6	11.1
Total	100	100

Frequency of exposure and its relation to purchase intention was studied with respect to age groups also. In first group, those between the ages of 15 to 22 were included. The second group included those between 23 to 30 years of age. Third group comprised respondents who were between 31 to 38 years and finally fourth group included those who were more than 38 years old. The results are presented in Table 4.6. Age-wise analysis indicated that except for 39-46 age group, majority of the respondents in other age groups opted for category one i.e. exposure of between one to five times. The age-wise analysis revealed one very interesting finding in relation to frequency of exposures and purchase intentions. It was observed that with the increasing age of respondents the number of exposures required for forming purchase intention also rose. Nearly one half (44%) of those who were in the age bracket of 39-46 years required exposure ranging between eleven to twenty times. Whereas, in case of those who were in the age bracket of 15-22 years, only 18 per cent required this much of advertising exposure. This has a major marketing implication. If an advertising campaign has to be directed to the higher age group, the number of exposures required for forming purchase intentions should be higher in number i.e. more repetition is needed for convincing the older audience.

Table 4.6
Exposures and Purchase Intentions (Age-wise)

	Age			
Frequency of Exposures	*15-22 years %age*	*23-30 years %age*	*31-38 years %age*	*39-46 years %age*
1 to 5	50	49	50	22.3
6 to 10	31.6	22.3	14.3	33.3
11 to 15	15	10.4	14.3	11.1
16 to 20	3.4	18.3	21.4	33.3
Total	100	100	100	100

Optimal Level of Exposure and Visual Interest

It is a general feeling among the advertising professionals and theorists that the value of successive exposures will eventually diminish, at least within some time framework. If the number of exposures is excessive, the audience can become annoyed and the impact of future exposures may actually be negative i.e. the advertising becomes counter productive (Aaker, Batra & Myers, 2001; Calder and Sternthal, 1980; Belch, 1982). Therefore, the respondents were asked to state their option about the optimal number of exposures to an advertisement beyond which they may loose interest. It is interesting to note that women loose interest in advertisements earlier as compared to men. More than half (55.6%) of the women told that they loose interest between one to five number of exposures of the same advertisement, whereas, 38.5 per cent of men loose interest between one to five number of exposures of the same advertisement. This difference between men and women was found statistically significant (Table 4.7).

Table 4.7
Exposure and Visual Interest (Sex-wise)

	Sex	
No. of Exposures	*Men %*	*Women%*
1 to 5	38.5	57.4
6 to 10	39.6	27.8
11 to 15	15.6	5.6
16 to 20	6.3	9.2
Total	100	100

Effectiveness of Different Formats

In cinema advertising four types of formats are used. These formats are *musical, narrative/demonstrative, melodramatic* and *humorous*. Researchers are of the view that for different types of products no single format will be superior or effective. Keeping this in mind, the respondents were asked to rank these four formats in terms of their effectiveness for three categories of products. The results are tabulated in Table 4.8.

For non-durable products, no single format emerged as the best one. Twenty-eight per cent respondents gave *musical* first rank, 21.3 per cent ranked *narrative* as first, 19.3 per cent ranked *melodramatic* first and 31.4 percent ranked *humorous* as first. Goodness of fit test has shown that there is no significant association between the type of products and the type of format used. In the same way no single format emerged as the best in semi-durable products category also. However, in the durable products category, *melodramatic* format was found to be least effective as compared to other three formats. The ranking of different formats was quite diffused in all the product categories. For details see Table 4.8.

Table 4.8
Ranking of Formats for Different Product Categories

Ranking in Products		*Type of Formats*			
		Musicals	*Narrative*	*Melodramic*	*Humorous*
Non-durables	I %	28	21	19.3	31.4
	II %	28.7	30.6	26.7	14
	III %	21.3	28	31.3	19.4
	IV %	22	20	22.7	35.3
Semi-durables	I %	22	32	21.3	24.7
	II %	30	27.3	26.7	16
	III %	26	25.3	28.7	20
	IV %	22	15.3	23.3	39.4
Durables	I %	30	30	14	26
	II %	28.7	21.3	36	14
	III %	26	30.7	23.3	20
	IV %	15.3	18	26.7	40

In order to take all the rankings into consideration, a weightage system was evolved. The first rank was given 4 points, second 3 points, third 2 points and fourth rank was allotted1 point. The ranking scores for each format were added and then divided by the number of respondents to arrive at weighted mean. In non-durable products category, *musical* commercials scored highest points (2.9) followed by *narrative* (2.6), *melodramatic* (2.5) and *humorous* (2.0). In case of semi-durable product category, *narrative* format scored highest points (2.8) followed by *musical* (2.6), *melodramatic* (2.4) and *humorous* (2.2). In durable product category, again *musical* format scored highest points (2.8), second, third and fourth place went to *narrative* (2.7), *melodramatic* (2.3) and *humorous* (2.2) formats respectively. There is not much significant difference among *musical, narrative* and *melodramatic* formats for all three groups of products. However, *humorous* format for all types of products was considered to be least effective as can be seen from Table 4.9.

Table 4.9
Weightage of Formats for Different Product Categories

Formats	*Product Categories*		
	Non-durables Weightage Points	*Semi-durables Weightage Points*	*Durables Weightage Points*
Musicals	2.9	2.6	2.8
Narrative	2.6	2.8	2.7
Melodramic	2.5	2.4	2.3
Humorous	2	2.2	2.2

CONCLUSIONS

This study revealed that there is a definite attitudinal change which can lead to purchase intention in both the sexes when they are exposed to cinema advertising. Women were found to be more amenable to positive attitudinal changes than men, particularly, in semi-durable product category. One can draw the conclusion, with some reservation, that for semi-durable goods, cinema advertising is more effective than for non-durable and durable products. One of the possible reasons may be that non-durable products because of their very nature allow people to form opinion or attitudes on the basis of prior purchase experience. As far as durables are concerned, they are purchased very infrequently or purchased once in a life time, and people engage in extensive problem solving (Howard & Sheth, 1969). For extensive problem solving situations, personal sources of information or word-of-mouth communication assumes greater importance than commercial sources of information which includes advertising.

Women were easily convinced than their male counterparts after certain amount of advertising exposure. It is also interesting to note that there seems to be some relationship between age and persuasibility. Older people require more number of exposures to advertising communication to get convinced as compared to younger ones.

In maintaining visual interest in the message, women were found to loose interest quite early just after comparatively lesser number of exposures than men. This finding has certain marketing and advertising implications. Campaign planners should change the theme of the commercial, or an aspect of it, after it has run for certain period in order to maintain visual interest.

Finally, the analysis regarding the superiority of one format over the other indicated that the respondents' preferences were scattered for all categories of products. However, *musical* and *narrative* type of commercials had a slight edge over *melodramatic* and *humorous* formats.

REFERENCES

Aaker A. David Rajeeve Batra and John G. Myers, *Advertising Management,* (Prentice Hall of India Pvt. Ltd.: (New Delhi), 2001.

Belch E. G., "The Effects of Television Commercial Repetition on Cognitive Response and Message Acceptance", *Journal of Consumer Research,* Vol. 9, pp. 56-65, June 1982.

Bogart L. Tolley, B. Steward and Frank Orenstein, "What One Little Ad. Can Do", *Journal of Advertising Research,* August 1970, pp. 35-39.

Clader B. and B. Sternthal, "Television Commercial Wearout: Information Processing Perspective", *Journal of Marketing Research,* Vol. 17, pp. 173-186, May 1980.

Fishbein Martin, "Attitudes and Prediction of Behaviour" in *Readings in Attitudinal Theory and Measurement,* ed. Fishbein Martin (John Wiley and Sons: New York), 1967.

Gilligan Collin and Geoffrey Crowther, *Advertising Management,* (Heritage Publishers, New Delhi), 1983.

Howard A. John and Jagdish N. Sheth, *The Theory of Buyer Behaviour,* (John Wiley and Sons: New York), 1969.

Janis I.L. and P.B. Field, "Sex Differences and Personality Factors Related to Personality", in *Personality and Personality,* ed. Hovland C. and I. Janis (Yale University Press: New Haven), 1958.

Krugman Herbert E., "What Makes Advertising Effective", *Harvard Business Review,* April 1975, pp. 96-103.

Lavidge, R.J., and Gary, A. Steiner, "A Model for Predictive Measurements of Advertising Effectiveness", *Journal of Marketing,* Oct. 1961, pp. 61-68.

Light Lawrence M., "An Experimental Study of the Effects of Repeated Persuasive Communication Upon Awareness and Attitudes",

Unpublished dissertation, Ohio State University cited in *Advertising Management,* by Gilligan and Crowther, *op. cit.*

McGuire William J., "An Information-Processing Model of Advertising Effectiveness" in Davis L.H. and Alvin, J., Silk eds., *Behavioural and Management Science in Marketing,* (Ronald Press: New York), 1978.

Ray L. Michael and Allen G. Sawyer, "Repetition in Media Models: A Laboratory Technique", *Journal of Marketing Research,* 8 February 1971, pp. 20-29.

Sheth Jagdish N., "An Investigation of Relationships among Evaluative Beliefs, Affect, Behavioural Intention and Behaviour", in *Consumer Behaviour: Theory and Application,* ed. Farley John V., John A. Howard, and L. Winston Ring, (Allyn and Bacon: Boston), 1974.

Stewart, J.B., "Repetitive Advertising in Newspapers : A Study of Two New Products", *Harvard Business School Bulletin,* 1964.

Zielske A. Herbert, "The Remembering and Forgetting of Advertising", *Journal of Marketing,* 23 March 1959, pp. 239-243.

5

Use and Effectiveness of Celebrity Endorsers in Advertising Messages

INTRODUCTION

In advertising communication, *source effect* has been researched extensively. The source of a message in an advertising communication system is where the message originates. There are two types of sources in advertising:

(i) the company that is interested in communicating certain information to the target market regarding its products and services;

(ii) the spokesperson i.e. model or personality which is used to convey the message.

Most of the research attention in advertising and social psychology has been focused on the individual, spokesperson or endorser as a source component.

In an attempt to communicate the merits of their product or brand, advertisers have often chosen to use endorsement as a promotional strategy. The basic reason behind this practice is the belief that a communicator's character has a significant influence on the persuasiveness of the message (Ohanian, 1990). Endorsers for a product/brand can be of many types. They may include a typical consumer, the product class expert(s), the company executive(s) or a celebrity (Fredman and Friedman, 1979). Of all these endorsers, using a celebrity spokesperson has always been a favourite strategy of advertisers and agencies. The use of a celebrity in endorsing a product is prevalent all over the world. However, extensive data is available mainly on American celebrities. A decade ago, one in three television commercials used celebrity endorsement. However, this advertising approach appears to be on the increase across all media types (Sherman, 1995).

According to Friedman, Terminy and Washington (1977), a celebrity is a person who is widely known to the public for accomplishments in domains unrelated to the product class. Celebrities, particularly, movie stars, T.V. stars and sports heroes provide a popular type of reference group appeal. Advertisers spend enormous amounts of money to have celebrities promote their products in the expectation that the target market will react positively to the celebrity's association with their product or brand (Schiffman and Kanuk, 2000).

Celebrities are generally considered to be highly dynamic with attractive and engaging personal qualities. People may also trust the advice provided by some famous persons and in certain cases celebrities may even be perceived as competent to discuss the product (Atkins and Martin, 1983). Assael (1984), suggests from a theoretical perspective, that celebrities are effective endorsers because of their symbolic aspirational reference group association. Reference groups provide point of comparison through which the consumer may evaluate attitudes and behaviour. Although he/she may not be a celebrity, or even become one, the typical consumer may still symbolically aspire to identify with this group by purchasing the product recommended by the celebrity. Kainen, Azhari and Kragh (1975) present several reasons why a famous endorser may be influential. Firstly, celebrities attract attention to the advertisement in the cluttered stream of messages. Secondly, they are perceived as more entertaining. Thirdly, they are also perceived as being more trustworthy because of apparent lack of self-interest. This final element is due to the widespread attribution that major stars do not really work for the endorsement fee but are really motivated by a genuine affection for the product.

The selection of an appropriate spokesperson for a product or a service is an important, yet, difficult decision. The dilemma for the advertisers is whether an effective and credible spokesperson is someone who is attractive, trustworthy, an expert or a combination of all these three traits. A number of empirical investigations have examined the effectiveness of using a celebrity to enhance the persuasiveness of messages. Studies have measured the process by which a communicator's perceived attractiveness, trustworthiness and expertise impacts on immediate and delayed attitudinal change and persuasion (Baker and Churchill, 1977). Generally, it is assumed that *what is beautiful is good*. Therefore, advertisers have often chosen celebrities on the basis of their physical attractiveness in order to capitalise from the dual affects of celebrity status and physical appeal (Kamins, 1990). One point of view is that the type of endorsers may interact with the type of product being advertised. Friedman and Friedman (1977) hypothesised that celebrity would be more effective for products with high psychological and social risks, involving such elements as good taste, self image and opinions of others. Expert endorser was seen as most appropriate for products associated with high financial performance or physical risks, while the typical consumer was considered to be the best source for low risk products.

Dimensions of Credibility in Celebrities

Of all the positive characteristics that a celebrity might contribute to a firm's advertising programme, celebrity's credibility with the audience is the most important. A predominant question before the researchers was to find out the factors which underlie a source credibility. Some research studies in the field of speech communication have utilised factor analytical techniques to uncover the perceptual structure of source credibility. Instead of a clear definition, however, these studies have confused the issue by resorting to different sets of dimensions of source credibility. Although, these studies were designed to measure the same constructs, there is no consistency among the authors as to the number and types of dimension the source credibility comprises. However, three factors, most often identified with credibility are *expertise*, *trustworthiness* and *likeability*. However, there is no consensus in this regard too.

Source credibility is a term commonly used to imply a communicator's positive characteristics that affect the receiver's acceptance of a message. Understanding and defining source credibility in the advertising context is often confusing because of the many different operationalisations that appeared in the literature. Research on the effectiveness of celebrity endorsers revolves around two models. First, the source credibility model, and second the source attractiveness model (Ohanian, 1990). They analysed the factors leading to the perceived credibility of the communicator and concluded that two factors – expertise and trustworthiness –underscore the concept of source credibility. According to them, expertise is "the extent to which a communicator is perceived to be a source of valid assertions", and trustworthiness as the degree of confidence in the communicators intent to communicate the assertions (Hovland, James and Kelly, 1953).

The source attractiveness model has its antecedents in the social psychological research and is a component of the "source valence" model of Mcguire (1985). The attractiveness model contends that the effectiveness of a message depends on source's "familiarity", "likeability", "similarity" and "attractiveness" to the respondents. The attractiveness dimension has received substantial amount of research attention in recent years. The decision to use attractiveness further got a fillip by the fact that it has become important factor on account of increased use of celebrities as endorsers for products, services and/or social causes (Caballero, Lumkin and Maddel, 1989).

Expertise is one of the important dimensions of source credibility. Most of the research on source credibility has focused on the expertise and trustworthiness of the communicator (Hass, 1981). Sometimes this dimension is also referred to as "authoritativeness", "competence", "expertness" or "qualification". Whatever term is used, expertise refers to the degree of knowledge, the celebrity or spokesperson possesses regarding the product advertised. Expertise refers to the extent to which the source of communication is perceived to be able of making correct assertions by virtue of having relevant skills (Hoveland, James and Kelly, 1953). Maddux and Rogers (1980) investigated source expertise in persuasive communication and are of the opinion that source expertise has positive impact on attitudinal change. In another study Crisci and Kassinove (1973) studied the effect of perceived level of communicator's expertise and the strength of advice on behavioural parental compliance. The results of this study indicated that respondent's compliance with the source's recommendations directly varied with the perceived level of expertise and the strength of advice. Homer and Kahle (1990) investigated the role of source expertise, time of source identification and involvement in persuasion in an experiment on advertising effectiveness. Their findings suggest that the source expertise information was processed more as a central persuasion cue than as peripheral information.

Trustworthiness refers to the degree to which an audience perceives the communicator and considers the assertions to be valid. The trust paradigm in communication is the listener's degree of confidence in, and level of acceptance of, the speaker and the message. A number of studies have supported the effect of trustworthiness on attitudinal change. In one study the impact of source trustworthiness on the persuability of the communication was investigated. The results showed that when the communicator was perceived to be highly trustworthy, an opinionated message was more effective then a non-opinionated communication in bringing attitudinal change. However, when trustworthiness was low, this relationship was not found significant (Miller and Basehart, 1969).

McGinnies and Ward (1980) investigated the trustworthiness and expertise as factors in source credibility and found that a source which is perceived to be both an expert and trustworthy generates the most opinion change. In fact, the trustworthy communicator was persuasive, whether an expert or not. Stemthal, Dholakia and Levitt (1978) reported that the moderately credible source was more persuasive than a highly credible communicator when subjects had an initially favourable disposition and the communicator was identified at the start of the message. The authors suggest that less credible source motivated recipients to produce more support arguments in an effort to ensure that their position was fairly represented, whereas, subjects felt highly credible sources did not need this bolstering. A highly credible source has been found to induce greater persuasion when recipients adamantly oppose the communicator's position, but less credible sources are more influential when individuals have a favourable disposition (Dean, Austin and Watts, 1971)

Attractiveness is considered to be the third element of source credibility. Many researchers in academia and business suggest that physical attractiveness is an important cue in individual's initial judgement of another person. They suggest a contingency approach to the study of source attractiveness and its effect on product and advertisement evaluation (Joseph, 1982). One hypothesis is that the physical attractiveness of a celebrity endorser may only enhance both product and ad-based evaluations, if the characteristics of the product *match-up* with an image conveyed by the celebrity. This *match-up* hypothesis, in general, suggests that the message conveyed by the image of the celebrity and the product should coincide in effective advertisements, which indicates a need for congruence between product image and celebrity image on attractiveness. It suggests that the visual imagery contained in the advertisement conveys information over and above the information contained in explicit verbal argument (Rossiter and Percy, 1980). In another study on physical attractiveness of celebrity endorsers, Kahle and Homer (1985), suggested that when a celebrity's physical attractiveness is congruent with the presence and degree to which the product advertised enhances attractiveness (i.e. attractive celebrity linked with an attractiveness related product), the *match-up* hypothesis would predict a positive impact upon product and advertisement evaluations. However, if there is incongruence between the product and the celebrity, the attractiveness evaluations will decline. In a follow-up study in which Kamins (1990) investigated the *match-up* hypothesis of celebrities, it was found that in an attractiveness related products, use of physically attractive celebrity was observed to significantly enhance measures of spokesperson credibility and positive attitude towards an advertisement relative to use of physically unattractive celebrity. Alternatively, physically attractive celebrity was found to have no effect as spokesperson for various products which were themselves low on attractiveness dimension.

Despite the vast quantity of literature addressing physical attractiveness, the verdict of experts in still not unanimous and it is a unresolved issue. A review of literature in this area indicates that the construct of attractiveness is not unidimensional and that there are myriad definitions used to operationalise attractiveness. With the increased use of celebrities in advertising, there is a need for a valid instrument, which can measure the credibility of celebrity endorsers. In other forms of persuasive communication, advertisers' primary goal is to persuade their audience and to induce in them an attitudinal change towards their offering. In this regard, credibility is a particularly important aspect of source because a receiver is much more inclined to accept and internalise the argument of a credible source than a less credible one. The persuasive effect of high credibility sources, however, does not remain intact over time. Though, a high credibility source is initially more influential than a low credibility source, research has found that both the positive and negative credibility effects of communication sources tend to disappear after some weeks. This phenomenon has been termed the *sleeper-effect*. Recent studies support the fact that over a period of time, people dissociate themselves from the source. A credible source, thus, has the potential to register a strong and lasting belief and be a very significant part of an advertising message.

Indian Scene

The use of celebrities as product endorsers is not a new phenomenon in India. Hindustan Lever is the pioneer in this regard. It has consistently been using film stars for its "Lux" brand toilet soap. With the the complexion of competition, the marketing tools, including advertising are being increasingly used with greater sophistication. With the increase in the amount and quantity of advertisements the use of celebrities has become quite prevalent in recent years. It seems that Indian advertising agencies have developed fascination for celebrities. With the advent of TV as a medium of advertising the agencies have been following the doctorine "names make news – big names make bigger news". Despite the increased use of celebrities in advertisements, there is no serious study in the Indian context which has investigated either the different dimensions of celebrity endorsers or the effectiveness of using celebrities in advertisements.

However, in one issue of A & M, a cross section of views from different professionals belonging to both advertising and marketing fields were taken regarding the use and effectiveness of celebrity endorsers (Munish and Chaudhry, 1991). According to advertising professionals there are two types of situations in which testimonial advertisements can be effective. Lifestyle products, where the person epitomises that particular kind of lifestyle – as in Gwalior suitings, Raymonds, Vimal – and where the consumer is not too sure of the product or service and seeks assurance through testimonials by some type of endorsers. But the match between endorsers and product should be perfect. Some professionals are against the use of celebrity testimonials as according to them this should be used as a last resort. Some others feel that any testimonial advertisement is effective only when it is congruent with the product. They opine that testimonial advertisements definitely boost product sales. One of the biggest advantages of testimonial advertisements is that they ensure a high recall for the product. According to Paul Nayyar, celebrity endorsement is used to achieve two ends – to get your products noticed and to show that it is tried and tested.

Thus, the opinions regarding the use of celebrity endorsers for product promotion vary on a continuum ranging from wholehearted support for celebrities to their use as a last resort. But there seems to be near consensus among the professionals regarding the need for congruence between the celebrity used and the product/brand advertised if the purpose is to create a real impact on target audience.

THE SCOPE AND OBJECTIVES OF THE STUDY

The ultimate objective of this study was to analyse the use and effectiveness of celebrity endorsers in TV commercials for various product categories.

This study has been conducted in two phases:

Phase I

The content analysis of different commercials appearing on TV.

The detailed objectives of the first phase are as follows:

(a) To find out the extent of usage of celebrities in TV commercials i.e. percentage of advertisements containing celebrities.

(b) To find out the extent of usage of celebrities in TV commercials according to product categories.

(c) To find out the percentage of male and female celebrities used in advertisements in different product categories.

(d) To find out the dominance of a particular type of celebrity i.e. TV personalities, film stars, sports heroes or others in commercials for different product categories.

(e) To find out how the celebrities are used i.e. as testimonial/endorser, actor or spokesperson for different product categories.

(f) To find out the frequency of particular copy appeal (humorous/non-humorous) used in TV commercials featuring celebrities.

Phase II

Conducting of a survey through structured questionnaire for gauging the effectiveness of celebrity endorsers in TV commercials.

The main objective of this phase of the study was to find out the effectiveness of celebrities on the respondents.

The detailed objectives were:

- *(a)* To study the effectiveness of advertisements featuring celebrities *vis-a-vis* male and female respondents.
- *(b)* To find out the weightage given to various types of celebrities i.e. TV personalities, film stars and sports heroes by the sample population.
- *(c)* To find out which celebrity – male or female has more effect on the sample.
- *(d)* To find out the impact of celebrities in advertisements on:
  - *(i)* credibility
  - *(ii)* attractiveness
  - *(iii)* convincibility
- *(e)* To find out the trustworthiness capability of celebrities in TV commercials.

RESEARCH DESIGN

As mentioned earlier, the research was carried out in two phases. The detailed procedure of research design is discussed below.

Procedure for Content Analysis of TV Commercials

The instrument used for content analysis was a proforma containing questions on various aspects of celebrities (Refer to Fig. 5.1). The procedure has been divided into following stages:

1. Stage-I : Preparation of contents of the proforma.
2. Stage-II : Recording of the advertisements.
3. Stage-III : Selection of sample of TV commercials.

Stage-I: Preparation of Contents of Proforma

In the initial phase of this study, the proforma was prepared with questions relating to each and every aspect to be studied. The proforma also contained questions that generated additional information like the name of the brand being advertised and the product category. Then the proforma contains questions regarding use of celebrity i.e. whether celebrities were used in the advertisements or not and whether these were male/female or both. Another question was about the type of celebrity used. This included the identification of celebrity in advertisement as film star, TV personality, sports personality or any other.

Next question was about the use of celebrities in different ways in advertisements. A firm that decides to employ a celebrity to promote its product has a choice of using the celebrity to give a *testimonial*, to give an *endorsement*, as an *actor* in a commercial, or as a company *spokesperson*. These promotional roles differ as follows:

(i) If the celebrity has personally used the product or service and is in a position to attest to its quality, then he or she may give a *testimonial* citing its benefits.

(ii) Almost similar to it is *endorsement* where a celebrity may or may not be an expert with regard to a product/service but may lend his or her name and physical appearance to an advertisement.

(iii) A celebrity may be asked to present the product or service as a part of a *character enactment,* rather than as a personal testimonial or endorsement.

(iv) A celebrity who represents a brand or company over an extended period of time, often in print and TV advertisements as well as in personal appearances, is usually called a company *spokesperson.*

Next question was about the number of celebrities used in each advertisement. The last question contained information about types of copy appeal used in the advertisements. This included classifying advertisements on the basis of humorous or non-humorous appeals. The proforma included 8 questions in all.

Stage-II: Recording of Advertisements

The second phase included the recording of advertisements. Here all the advertisements which appeared in various TV channels during prime time were recorded on a video cassette. In this way a total of 450 commercials were recorded.

Stage-III: Sample Selection and Content Analysis

The last phase was of selecting the sample for content analysis. All the 450 advertisements were viewed and repetitions were deleted. Thus, a sample of 250 advertisements was finally selected for content analysis. Then, the content analysis was performed by two trained coders in terms of use of celebrity endorsers. The content analysis for each advertisement was performed separately and each advertisement was viewed 2 or 3 times for accurate assimilation of information.

Procedure For Analysis of Questionnaire

The second phase of the study included questionnaire analysis. This was carried out in the following manner:

Stage-I : Formulation of questionnaire
Stage-II : Selection of Sample
Stage-III : Administering the questionnaire and analysing it.

Stage-I: Formulation of Questionnaire

In the first phase of this study, the questionnaire for measuring the effectiveness of celebrities was prepared. Initially, the scanning of literature on testimonial advertising gave various variables on which it could be tested. These variables were:

- credibility/trustworthiness
- attractiveness
- convincibility

Of all the positive characteristics that a celebrity might contribute to a firm's advertising, credibility with the consumer audience is most important. The credibility of the celebrity means, the audiences' perception of both the celebrity's knowledge about the product and trustworthiness, means how honest the celebrity is about what he or she knows about the product. The attractiveness factor here means how much attention attracting capability does the celebrity has or can the celebrity attract the attention of audience. Similarly is the convincibility factor. Here the ability of celebrity to convince the viewers was tested.

The questionnaire included seven questions:

(i) The first question was about the opinion of respondents regarding the effectiveness of celebrities in the advertisements.
(ii) The second question was about the weightage given to various types of celebrities on a five point scale.
(iii) The third question was about the relative effectiveness of male and female celebrities.
(iv) The fourth question was about the impact of celebrity on the credibility of advertisement.
(v) The fifth question was related to the trustworthiness of of celebrities *vis-a-vis* non-celebrities.

(vi) The sixth question was related to the amount of attention that celebrities attract vis-a-vis non-celebrities.

(vii) The last question was related with the convincibility of celebrities *vis-a-vis* non-celebrities.

Stage-II: Selection of Sample

The prepared questionnaire was to be administered on a sample of 250 student resepondents out of which 50 per cent were males and 50 per cent females. The students were selected on a random basis. The composition of students was taken in such a way that it should be a representative sample. Students were taken because they are usually more exposed to advertisements and on account of their ongoing socialisation process, they may be more vulnerable to the influence of celebrities as compared to other population groups. Using students as respondents is not a new thing in social psychology and consumer research, although, it may sometimes raise the question of external validity. In spite of this concern, students are popular subjects for experimental and survey research.

Stage-III: Administration of Questionnaire

After selecting the sample, the questionnaire was questionnaire was administered to the predecided number of male and female students. Due care was taken to administer the questionnaire on the students belonging to various disciplines and professional courses.

ANALYSIS

The analysis of the data collected can be divided into two parts:

I. Proforma analysis
II. Questionnaire analysis

PROFORMA ANALYSIS

Product Categorisation

The analysis of proforma was performed with initial categorisation of the advertisements into different product categories. Thus, products appearing in all the 250 advertisements were placed into the following 10 categories:

1. Toiletries (soaps, detergents, toothpaste)–35 (13.6%)
2. Drinks and eatables (tea, coffee, softdrinks and others)–17(6.8%)

Figure 5.1: Content Analysis Proforma for the use of celebrities in T.V. Commericals

1. Advertisement No.
2. Brand
3. Product Category
4. Celebrity used Yes ( ) No ( )
5. Sex of celebrity:
   Male ( ) Female ( ) Both ( )
6. Type of celebrity used:
   (i) Film star ( )
   (ii) T.V. personality ( )
   (iii) Sports personality ( )
   (iv) Any other ( )
7. How celebrities are used
   (i) Testimonial/Endorser ( )
   (ii) Actor ( )
   (iii) Spokesperson ( )
8. No. of celebrities used:
   One ( ) Two ( ) Three ( )
9. Types of copy appeals used:
   (i) Humorous ( )
   (ii) Non-humorous ( )

3. Medicine and health products–34(12.8%)
4. Personal apearance products (cosmetics, clothing and footwear)–57(23.2%)
5. Home products and home appliances–53(21.2%)
6. Services–3(1.2%)
7. Paints and home furnishings–15(6%)
8. Automobiles and vehicles–7(2.8%)
9. Chocolates and biscuits–16(6.8%)
10. Miscellaneous items (watches, mosquito repellent and gadgets as well as office equipments–19(8.4%)

After initial categorisation these were clubbed into five broad categories. These are as follows:

1. Medicine and Toiletries

This product category included OTC drugs, i.e. painkillers balms, headache tablets, health drinks, toothpastes, detergents and soaps.

The reason for this clubbing together is their chemical nature. The total number of advertisements in this category was 69, which amounted to 24.8%.

2. Drinks and Confectionary Products

Here the products included all kinds of softdrinks i.e. hot as well as cold, beverages like coffee and tea, and confectionary items like biscuits, chocolates etc. Total number of advertisements in this product category was 31(13.6%).

3. Personal Appearance Products

All the cosmetic items like feminine hygiene products, clothing and footwear were taken up. Total number of advertisements was 57(23.2%).

4. Home Products, Appliances and Furnishings

This category included items like edible oil, spices, ghee, etc. Other items like sewing machines, vehicles, pressure cooker, suitcases, bulbs, and paints were also included. Total number of advertisements in this product category was 72(30%).

5. Miscellaneous

Items included in this category were all sorts of services, products having tobacco, and office equipment like filing cabinets etc. Number of advertisements falling in this category was 19 (8.4%).

After this initial phase of product categorisation the subsequent analysis was carried out with respect to the variables contained in the content analysis proforma (see Figure 5.1).

Use of Celebrities and Type of Products

Table 5.1 deals with the frequency of celebrities used in advertisements for various product categories. Out of the 250 advertisements analysed, 126 (50.4%) advertisements had celebrities used as endorser or actor or spokesperson. The rest 124 (49.6%) advertisements had no celebrities. In all the product categories, the use of celebrities was frequent except in the miscellaneous product category where non-celebrity advertisements were more in number. Maximum number of celebrities were being used in personal appearance products, home appliances, medicine and toiletries. However, chi-square analysis revealed no significant relationship among the various product categories' advertisements as far as the relative use of celebrities was concerned.

This showed that the use of celebrities is not product specific (chi-square = 2.38, df = 4, p> 0.5).

Table 5.1
Use of Celebrities and Type of Products

		Celebrity used		*Celebrity not used*		*Total*
S.No.	*Category*	*No.*	*%*	*No.*	*%*	
1.	Medicine and Toiletries	37	53.63	32	46.37	69
2.	Drinks and Confectionary	14	42.42	19	57.57	31
3	Personal Appearance	33	57.89	24	42.1	57
4.	Home Products, appliances and furnishings	38	52.77	34	47.22	72
5.	Miscellaneous	4	21.05	15	78.94	19
	Total	126	50.4	124	49.6	250

Note: Calculated value of χ^2=2.38, df = 4, p>0.5.

Table 5.2
Number of Celebrities Used in TV Commercial

		One celebrity		*Two Celebrities*		*Three Celebrities*		*Total*
S.No.	*Category*	*No.*	*%*	*No.*	*%*	*No.*	*%*	
1.	Medicine and Toiletries	31	83.78	4	10.81	2	5.40	37
2.	Drinks and Confectionary	10	71.43	4	28.57	0	0.00	14
3.	Personal Appearance	26	78.79	5	15.15	2	6.06	33
4.	Home Products, appliances and furnishings	30	78.95	6	15.78	2	5.30	38
5.	Misc.	4	100	0	0.00	0	0.00	4
	Total	101	80.16	19	15.08	6	4.80	126

Another aspect of use of celebrity is the number of celebrities used in each commercial. Table 5.2 shows that generally one celebrity was used most frequently used in TV commercials (80.16%) and use of two (15.08%) or three (4.80%) celebrities was found in advertisements in all the product categories. Thus, the use of one two or three celebrities across the product category was more or less same and therefore, no statistical significance was found. This indicates that across all the product categories, one celebrity was being used. The use of two or more celebrities in the advertisements was found to be very low. This is understandable because of high cost associated in the use of celebrities, especially film stars.

Sex of Celebrities and Type of Products

From Table 5.3 it is clear that female celebrities are more frequently used in all the product categories except drinks and confectionary products. In this analysis 122 advertisements from four different product categories featuring celebrities were taken up. The fifth category of miscellaneous items was excluded from further analysis because of near absence of the use of celebrities in the advertisements. Further analysis revealed that the use of female celebrities was most prevalent in the personal appearance products (75.75%) followed by medicines and toiletries (67.56%) and then home products, appliances

Table 5.3
Sex of Celebrities and Type of Products

		Male		*Female*		*Both*		*Total*
S.No.	*Category*	*No.*	*%*	*No.*	*%*	*No.*	*%*	
1.	Medicine and Toiletries	10	27.02	25	67.56	2	5.4	37
2.	Drinks and Confectionary	7	50	5	35.71	2	14.28	14
3.	Personal Appearance	5	15.15	25	75.75	3	9.09	33
4.	Home Products, appliances and furnishings	10	26.31	20	52.63	8	21.05	38
	Total	32	26.23	75	61.48	15	12.29	122

Note: calculated value of χ^2=20.58, df = 6, P<0.0.

and furnishings (52.63%). The only exception in the use of female celebrities was in relation to drinks and confectionary products where male celebrities were being used more frequently. One interesting findings is that in case of home products, appliances and furnishings, nearly one-fifth of the advetisements used both male and female celebrities. In drinks and confectionary products, though the use of female celebrities was less as compared to male celebrities, yet, in nearly 15% of the advertisements, both male and female celebrities were used. In order to find out whether there exist any significant differences in the use of male and female celebrities across the product categories, chi-square analysis was performed and the results showed significant differences (χ^2 = 20.58, df = 6, P <.05).

Type of Celebrities and Type of Product

Table 5.4 reveals that film stars were being frequently used as celebrity endorsers. Other celebrities being featured were sports heroes, TV personalities, models, politicians, etc. Maximum advertisements had film stars (43.44%), followed by TV personalities (34.42%); others (18.85%). Least used clebrities belonged to sports category (7.37%).

Table 5.4
Type of Celebrity and Type of Products

	Film		*T.V.*		*Sports*		*Others*		*Total*
Category	*No.*	*%*	*No.*	*%*	*No.*	*%*	*No.*	*%*	
Medicine and Toiletries	18	48.64	14	37.83	1	2.7	4	10.81	37
Drinks and Confectionary	7	50	2	14.28	2	14.28	3	21.40	14
Personal Appearance	13	39.39	9	27.27	4	12.12	6	18.18	33
Home Products, appliances and furnishings	15	39.47	11	44.73	2	5.26	4	10.52	38
Total	53	43.44	42	34.42	9	07.37	23	18.85	122

Note: calculated value of χ^2=19.24, df=9, P<0.05.

Drinks and confectionary items had maximum number of film stars closely followed by medicines and toiletries. In case of home products, appliances and furnishings, the modal category of celebrities belonged to TV. Interestingly, sports personalities were being sparingly used as compared to celebrities belonging to TV and the film world. Chi-square analysis showed significant differences in the use of different types of celebrities across different product categories (chi-square=19.24, df = 9, P <.05).

How Celebrities are Used?

Table 5.5 shows that maximum number of advertisements used celebrities as *actors* (54.09%) followed by as *testimonial/endorsers* (41.82%). and then as *spokesperson* (4.09%). Product category-wise analysis revealed that in case of medicines and toiletries, the celebrities were being most frequently used as *endorsers* (56.76%) followed by as *actors* (37.83%) and then as *spokespersons* (5.40%). In the remaining three product categories, celebrities were used as *actors* quite frequently. In aggregate terms, only 4.09% of advertisements had celebrities being used as *spokesperson.* However, their use as *spokesperson* was marginally higher in drinks and confectionary products. However, chi-square analysis revealed that the relationship between the manner in which the celebrity was being used and the product category was was not significant (chi-square = 9.7977, df = 6, P <.005).

Table 5.5
How Celebrities are Used?

	Testimonial/ endorser		*Actor*		*Spokesperson*		*Total*
Category	*No.*	*%*	*No.*	*%*	*No.*	*%*	
Medicine and Toiletries	21	56.76	14	37.83	2	5.4	37
Drinks and Confectionary	4	28.57	8	57.14	2	14.28	14
Personal Appearance	13	39.39	19	57.75	1	3.03	33
Home Products, appliances and furnishings	13	34.21	25	65.78	0	0	38
Total	51	41.82	66	54.09	5	4.09	122

Note: calculated value of χ^2 = 9.7977, df = 6, P<0.5.

Types of Copy Appeals and Celebrity Endorsers

Table 5.6 shows the relationship between the types of copy appeals – humorous and non-humorous – used in the celebrity advertisements. Use non-humorous appeals was noticed in 86.06 per cent of the advertisements while only 13.93 per cent advertisements used humorous appeals. It is strange that humorous appeal pattern was not at all being used in case of personal appearance products. Humorous appeals were being most frequently used in drinks and confectionary products (35.7%) followed by home products (23.68%).

From this analysis one can discern a clear trend in favour of use of non humorous copy appeals. Chi-square analysis also revealed that the relationship was significant (chi-square = 10.34, df = 3, P <.025).

Table 5.6
Types of Copy Appeals and Celebrity Endorsers

	Humorous		*Non-humorous*		*Total*
Category	*No.*	*%*	*No.*	*%*	
Medicine and Toiletries	3	8.1	34	91.3	37
Drinks and Confectionary	5	35.71	9	64.28	14
Personal Appearance	0	0	33	100	33
Home Products, appliances and furnishings	9	23.68	29	76.31	38
Total	17	13.93	105	86.06	122

Note: calculated value of χ^2 = 10.34, df = 3, P<0.025.

Questionnaire Analysis

The questionnaire was analysed to evaluate the effectiveness of celebrities in commercials on student population.

The questionnaire analysis is described in terms of ranking, relative weightage and effectivness of different dimensions of celebrity endorsers.

Effectiveness of Celebrities: Ranking

Here the respondent were asked to rank the celebrities in terms of their effectiveness. The findings have been segregated in terms of male and female respondents in Table 5.7(a). It is clear that similar results were obtained from both male and female respondents. TV personalities were ranked III, sports stars were placed II and quiet obviously film stars topped the list. This clearly demonstrates that both male and female respondents consider film stars as being most effective. Sports heroes came second in terms of preference. Yet, in terms of their mean importance they were not far behind film stars. Both male and female respondents considered TV personalities to be least effective.

Table 5.7 (a)
Effectivness of Celebrities: Ranking

Types of Celebrities	*Male*		*Female*	
	Mean	*Rank*	*Mean*	*Rank*
T.V.	2.7	III	2.36	III
Film	1.56	I	1.68	I
Sports	1.76	II	1.96	II

Table 5.7 (b)
Effectivness of Celebrities: Detailed Ranking

Celebrities	*Rank*	*Male*		*Female*	
		No.	*%*	*No.*	*%*
T.V.	I	05	04	20	16
	II	25	20	40	32
	III	95	76	65	52
Film	I	65	52	65	52
	II	50	40	35	28
	III	10	08	25	20
Sports	I	55	44	40	32
	II	50	40	50	40
	III	20	16	35	28

Table 5.7(b) shows the detailed ranking of different celebrities by male and female respondents in terms of their respective effectiveness. Table 5.7(c) shows the statistical analysis of the relative weightage given to various types of celebrities. The t-test shows that there exists significant difference in the perception of male and female respondents for TV and sports celebrities. No significant difference was found as far as film stars were concerned. This indicates that film stars were considered as most effective by both male and female respondents.

Table 5.7 (c)
Relative Weightage Given to Various Types of Celebrities

Types of celebrities	*Female*		*Male*		
	Mean	*S.D.*	*Mean*	*S.D.*	*t-values*
T.V.	2.36	0.74	2.7	0.53	4.15*
Movie	1.68	0.79	1.56	0.64	1.404
Sports	1.96	0.77	1.72	0.72	2.533*

Note: *= significant at 5% level of significance.

Effectiveness of Different Dimensions of Celebrity Endorsers

Table 5.8 deals with the analysis of effectiveness of different dimensions of endorsers. This has been carried out with the formulation of five statements. These statements were related with the superiority of male versus female celebrities, credibility, trustworthiness, attention getting capability and convincibility of celebrities versus non-celebrities. Respondents were asked to give their degree of agreement or disagreement on a five point scale for each statement.

From this table it can be discerned that male students rated attention attracting capability of celebrities as being higher (mean 3.97) than female students (mean 3.80). Female students ranked higher the credibility aspect of celebrities *vis-a-vis* male students. However, t-value did not show any significant difference. For trustworthiness, both male and female respondents had the same perception. Both male and female students rated convincibility factor associated with celebrities quite high. Yet, female respondents' perception with respect to convincibility was higher than male students. The same was corroborated by t-value which was significant.

On the question of superiority of male versus female celebrities, male respondents gave higher rating to the male celebrities. Significant differences were found to exist on this factor. One can surmise that the gender factor might have affected the rating.

Table 5.8
Effectiveness of Different Dimensions of Celebrity Endorsers

Type of celebrity	*Male*		*Female*		*t-value*
	Mean	*S.D.*	*Mean*	*S.D.*	
Male celebrities more effective than female	3.08	1.2	2.6	1.26	3.08a
Use of celebrity increases ad. credibility	3.8	1.33	3.92	0.84	0.86
Celebrities are more trustworthy	2.64	1.32	2.64	1.09	0
Celebrity attracts more attention	3.97	1.04	3.8	1.26	1.16
Celebrities are more convincing	3.2	0.94	3.64	1.2	3.21*-

Note: The statements were tested on 5 point scale ranging from "Strongly Agree" to "Strongly Disagree".
*= significant at .01 % level of significance.

CONCLUSIONS

Conclusions from Proforma Analysis

The results obtained from the content analysis proforma can be summarised as follows:

1. Around 50% of the advertisements featured some type of celebrity. So it can be concluded that Indian advertisements have been using celebrities to a large extent. The chi-square anaysis proved that the use of celebrities was not product specific.
2. In most of the advertisements only one celebrity is being used. The use of two or more celebrities is uncommon.
3. Female celebrities are being used more frequently than male celebrities. Here the use of celebrities, in terms of sex, was found to be product specific.
3. As far as the use of different types of celebrities is concerned, film stars are being used quite frequently in TV commercials. The use of different types of celebrities is related to product category.

4. Most of the advertisements of home products, appliances and furnishings use celebrities as *actors*. But the relationship between type of product and how the celebrity is being used was found to be insignificant.
5. From this analysis it may be concluded that non-humorous appeals are used more in the advertisements featuring celebrities irrespective of product category.

Conclusions from Questionnaire Analysis

1. There was a general agreement on the effectiveness of celebrity advertisements amongst both male and female students. A very low percentage of students had negative opinion towards celebrity advertisements.
2. Both male and female students gave similar weightage to different types of celebrities. Their rankings were as follows:

Type of Celebrity	*Rank*
Film	I
Sports	II
T.V.	III

3. The results from t-test revealed that there was no significant difference in the relative weightage for film stars among male and female students. Though sports heroes were given second rank by both types of respondents, yet, there was a significant difference among both the groups. The same is true for TV personalities. Surprisingly, TV stars were favoured more by female students than their male counterparts.
4. Celebrity advertisements attract more attention of female students.
5. Male students attach greater credibility to celebrities than female students.
6. The responses of male students were more positive for male celebrities than female celebrities.
7. Both male and female responses were similar for trustworthiness factor of celebrities.
8. Convincibility dimension of celebrities was rated higher by female students. The same was corroborated through t-test.

REFERENCES

Assael, Henry (1984), *Consumer Behaviour and Market Action,* (Boston, M.A., Kent Publishing Company).

Atkin, Charles & Martin Block (1983), "Effectiveness of Celebrity Endorsers", *Journal of Advertising Research,* No. 1, pp. 57-61.

Baker, Michael J. and Gilbert A. Churchill (1977), "The Impact of Physically Attractive Models on Advertising Evaluation", *Journal of Marketing Research,* No. 14, pp. 538-555, Madden (1989).

Caballero, Marjorie, James R. Lumpkin and Charles S., "Using Physical Attractiveness as an Advertising Tool: An Empirical Test of Attraction Phenomenon", *Journal of Advertising Research,* No. 29, pp. 16-22

Crisci, Richard and Howard Kassinove (1973), "Effects of Perceived Expertise Strength of Advice and Environmental Setting on Parental Compliance" *Social Psychology Journal,* No. 89, pp. 245-250.

Dean Robert, John Austin and William Watts (1971), "Forewarming Effects in Persuasion: Field and Class Room Experiments", *Journal of Personality and Social Psychology.*

Friedman, Hershey and Linda Friedman (1979),"Endorser effectiveness by Product Type", *Journal of Advertising Research,* No. 19, pp. 63-71.

Friedman, Hershey, S. Terminy and Robert Washington (1977), "The Effectiveness of Advertisements Utilising Four Types of Endorsers", *Journal of Advertising,* No. 6, pp. 22-2.

Hass R.G. (1981), "Effects of Source Characteristics on Cognitive Responses and Persuasion" in *Cognitive Responses in Persuasion,* R. Patty, T. Ostron & D. Brock, eds. (New Jersey—Erlbaum).

Homer, M. Pamela and Lynn R. Kahle (1990), "Source Expertise, Time of Source, Identification and Involvement in Persuasion: An Elaboration Processing Perspective", *Journal of Advertising,* No. 1, pp. 30-39.

Hovland Carl I., Irwing K. Janes and Harold H. Kelley (1953), *Comunication and Persuation,* (New Haven, C.T.—Yale University Press).

Hovland Janes and Kelly, *op.cit.*

Hovland, Carl I., Arthus A. Lumsdaine and Ferd D. Schefield (1949), *Experiments in Mass Communication,* (New York Viley).

Joseph W. Benoy (1982), "The Credibility of Physically Attractive Communicators: A Review", *Journal of Advertising,* No. 11, pp. 15-24

Kahle, Lynn R. and Pamel M. Homer (1985), "Physical Attractiveness of the Celebrity Endorser: Social Adaptation Perspective", Consumer Research, No. 11, pp. 954-961.

Kamen, Joseph, Abdul Azhari and Judith Kragh (1975), "What a Spokesman does for a sponsor", *Journal of Advertising Research,* No. 16 pp. 17-24.

Kamins A. Michael (1990), "An Investigation into the 'Match-up' Hypothesis in Celebrity Advertising: When Beauty May be Only Skin Deep", *Journal of Advertising,* No. 1, pp. 4-13.

Maddux, James E. and Ronald W. Rogers (1980), "Effects of Source Expertness, Physical Attractiveness and Supporting Arguments on Persuasion: A Case of Brains Over Beauty", *Journal of Personality and Social Psychology,* No. 39, pp. 235-244.

Mcginnies, Elliot and C. Ward (1980) "Better Liked Than Right: Trustworthiness and Expertise as Factors in Credibility", *Personality and Social Psychology Bulletin,* No. 6(2), pp. 467-472.

Mcguire William J. (1985), "Attitudes and Attitude Change", in *Handbook of Social Psychology,* Vol. 2, Gardner, Lindzey and Elliot Aronson, Eds. (New York Random House).

Miller, Gerald P. and Joln Basehart (1969) "Source Trustworthiness Opinionated Statements and Response to Persuasive Communication", *Speech Monograph*–36, p. 127.

Munish, Mukul and Sonya Chaudhry (1991), "Reflected Glory", *Advertising and Marketing Issue,* Feb. pp. 20-25.

Ohanian, Roobina (1990), "Construction and Validation of a Scale to Measure Celebrity Endorsers perceived expertise, trustworthiness and atttactiveness", *Journal of Advertising,* No. 3, pp. 39-52.

Park, Whan, G. V. Parker Lessing (1977), "Students and House Wives: Differences in Susceptibilitv to Reference Group Influence", *Journal of Consumer Research,* No. 4, pp. 102-110.

Rossiter, John R. and Larry Percy, (1980), "Attitude Change Through Visual Imagery in Advertisement", *Journal of Advertising,* No. 9, pp. 10-16.

Schifftnan, Leon G. and L.L. Kanuk (2000), *Consumer Behaviour,* 6th ed. (New Delhi, Prentice Hall of India, Pvt. Ltd).

Sherman, Stratford P. (1985), "When You Wish Upon a Star", *Fortune,* No. 13 8, pp. 66-73.

Strenthal, Brian, R.R. Dholakia and Clark Levitt (1978), "The Persuasive Effect of Source Credibility: Tests of Cognitive Response", *Journal of Consumer Research,* No. 4, pp. 252-260.

6

Audience Perception, Motivation and Recall of Humorous Appeals in Advertisements

INTRODUCTION

Many advertisers over the years have used some form of humour probably because they believe that it attracts more attention and creates liking for the advertised product. Besides, the atmosphere created by humorous appeal brightens the stark surroundings of occasional disillusionment which frustrate our lives. The evidence, however, has not established that a humorous message is necessarily more affective than a straightforward version of the same message. Advertisers hold diverse set of opinions about the persuasive effects of humour. The approach to the use of humorous appeals in advertising has been changing in recent years. David Ogilvy (1964) in his book *Confessions of an Advertising Man* observed, "people are amused by clowns, they don't buy from them..... so, many people in advertising are compulsive entertainers who seek applause rather than sales." Twenty years later, in *Ogilvy on Advertising,* he admits that a humorous commercial, apart from providing entertainment, helps in positioning and selling a product (1985). He maintained, however, that it is both elusive and fragile, and must be therefore, delivered by someone who knows how to be funny. However, one should not take it for granted that in using humour, advertisers can do away with the presentation of facts about the products. Moreover, the use of humour does not imply that the advertisers can make exaggerated claims and mislead the audience/consumers. Humour should be accompanied by facts about the product or service being advertised. In advertising, humour is basically used as a technique for holding and attracting the attention of the audience. The TV commercials for *50:50* biscuits, *Sprite* (featuring Lisa Ray), *Limca,* and *Pepsi* soft drinks are good examples of the use of humour for holding audience attention. Apart from this, humour in advertising acts as a kind of *shock absorber*, which helps in bearing the jerks caused by differential existing between the assumption and perception of reality.

In short, humour in advertising means the use of soft and sensible copy with an amusing illustration and a frank message in a relaxed and free atmosphere. The humour used should be subtle, because it is said that *the lighter the touch the heavier will be the wallop.*

Survey of Literature

No direct references were available for this type of study in India. However, survey of literature revealed certain studies that have been conducted abroad on humour in advertising.

A study by Lynch and Hartman (1968) suggested that there are eight kinds of humour in advertising. The study employed factor analysis, using ratings from 24 respondents on different types of jokes and humorous advertisements. Advertising humour was found to relate with *general knowledge, sophistication, sensitivity, simplicity, visualisation, cuteness, staging* and *abstraction*. Advertisements designated as most humorous on general knowledge, for example, did not require special knowledge of the reader but presented reader in an obvious manner. Advertisements rated high on the sophistication dimension required topical knowledge and awareness of on-going activities. Staging advertisements showed people as characters on stage with the humour evolving from a put-on phoney situation. Each of the subsequent dimensions provided insight into a different form of advertising humour.

Advertisers seem to agree that humour as a strategy enhances audience attention, at least, while they view the advertisement for the first few times. However, there seems to be considerable debate as to the degree of message comprehension afforded by humorous advertisements (Levit, 1970). Advertisers who support the use of humour feel that it increases the probability that the consumer will accept the message (Harold, 1963). However, even the proponents of using humour as a creative strategy caution that the humorous appeal must be relevant, perceived as being funny and directed at the product rather than the potential user, if it is to facilitate communication acceptance (Hoppe, 1969; Philips, 1973). Harpner (1963) advocates that humour can be effective if used as a means and not as an end itself.

Sternthal and Craig (1973) reviewed the humorous literature in the context of marketing mass communication. They suggested that advertisers hold a diverse set of opinions about the persuasive effects of humour and that the available humour experimentation does little to clarify this situation. Although, several studies indicate that humour is persuasive, they have failed to exhibit that humour is more effective than a serious version of the same appeal. They suggested that the persuasive effect of humour may be attributable to its distracting quality, although this has not been tested directly. Finally, they have advised the advertisers for the effective use of humour with the following conclusions:

- Humorous messages attract attention.
- Humorous messages may detrimentally affect comprehension.
- Humour may distract the audience, yielding a reduction in counter argumentation and an increase in persuation.
- Humorous appeals appear to be persuasive, but the persuasive effect is, at best, no greater than that of serious appeals.
- Humour tends to enhance source credibility.
- Audience characteristics may confound the effect of humour.
- A humorous context may increase liking for the source and create a positive mood. This may increase the persuasive effect of the message.
- To the extent that the humorous context functions as a positive reinforcer, a persuasive communication placed in such a context may be more effective.

In a rather extensive study of the use of humour in advertising, Barry (1979) suggested that humour is a phenomenon that has existed since the beginning of man and it has been almost that long that man has tried to rationally explain humour. And the more one attempts to explain humour, the more complex it becomes. There are endless devices for humour, humour is verbal and silent, joyful and warm, hostile and evil. In the end it is too qualitative to be classified. And advertising experts surely do not agree on its use or misuse.

Some marketers use humorous appeals in the belief that humour will increase the acceptance and persuasiveness of their advertising communications. However, the marketers are shy of using humour because they feel their product may become an object of ridicule, that consumers will laugh *at* them rather than *with* them. More recently, in the US, a number of research studies have tried to enumerate the advantages and disadvantages of humorous advertising appeals (Madden & Weinberger, 1984; Duncan & Nelson 1985; Gelb & Zincon, 1986; Higgins, 1995). In another study a review was made about the impact of humour in advertising and certain conclusions were drawn (Weinberger & Gulas, 1992). These conclusions partially corroborate the conclusions drawn by Sternthal and Craig (1973) more than two decades earlier. These are given below:

- Humour attracts attention.
- Humour does not harm comprehension. (In some cases it may even help the comprehension).
- Humour does not enhance the source credibility.
- Humour is not more effective at increasing persuation.
- Humour increases the *liking*.
- Humour that is relevant to the product is superior to humour unrelated to the product.
- Audience characteristics such as gender, ethnicity, age, may effect the response to humorous advertising appeals.
- The type of the product effects the suitability of a humorous treatment.
- With existing products, humour is more effective as compared to the new products.
- Effectiveness of humour varies with the involvement level of the consumers. It is more appropriate for low involvement than for high involvement products.

Due to the many qualifying factors on the effectiveness of humour it will be wise on the part of the marketers to use humour in a selective manner keeping in mind the type of products and the characteristics of the target market Before being placed in media, humorous appeals should be pretested. In the ultimate analysis, it is imperative that before using a humorous appeal, advertisers must understand objectives and audience needs. Only in this way humour, as any other appeal, can be used effectively.

OBJECTIVES OF THE STUDY

The main purpose of this study was to measure the overall effectiveness of humorous advertising. More specifically, the detailed objectives were:

- To find out the respondents' general, as well as specific attitudes towards humorous advertising.
- To find out whether demographic and socio-economic factors like sex, age, social background, income levels and profession have any influence on the respondents attitude towards humour in advertising.
- To study the effectiveness of copy elements i.e. headline, illustration and body copy (text), used in humorous appeal.
- To find out the effect of humour in advertising, on the recall of brand names, i.e. whether advertisements with humorous appeal show higher recall rate than not employing it.

RESEARCH METHODOLOGY

The study is designed on the assumption that all advertisements try to exploit consumers' psychology. To test the effectiveness of humorous advertisements, this study, therefore makes use of psychological measures involving consumer's attitude, motivational level, recall and recognition.

On the basis of broad objectives and the hypothesis formulated a questionnaire was prepared comprising all the attributes related with consumers' behaviour. The responses were then quantitatively tested to evaluate the relative effectiveness of humorous advertisements appearing in different media.

Sampling Plan

The area covered by the present study was confined to the city of Lucknow – capital of the state of Uttar Pradesh. It was intentionally decided to select Lucknow because it has the presence of all types of socio-economic groups.

The sample consisted of 100 respondents. Purposive sampling technique was used for selecting the respondents. To keep the sample uniform and representative, it was kept in mind that selected persons should be regular readers or viewers of the advertisements appearing in print and electronic media. Questionnaire and personal interview techniques were followed to collect the information.

Formulation of Questionnaire

The information was collected on the basis of a structured questionnaire. The questionnaire was pre-tested on a random sample of ten persons within the university campus. On the basis of pilot survey modifications were incorporated in the questionnnaire. A brief description about the nature of information sought through the questionnaire is as follows:

- General information regarding respondents, viz., sex, rural/urban background, age, income, level and profession.
- Respondents' general and specific attitude towards the use of humorous advertisements.
- Respondents' opinion regarding the effectiveness of various copy elements using humour.
- Information regarding the impact of humour on consumers with respect to various product categories.

The questionnaire also involves a test for the recall capability of respondents. For the present study two types of recall tests were used:

(i) aided-recall test, and
(ii) recognition-recall test.

In the aided recall test, the respondents were shown both humorous and non-humorous advertisements. Subsequently they were asked to tick 20 brand names that featured in the screened advertisements from a given list containing 30 brand names. In the recognition recall test, the respondents were shown another portfolio of similar advertisements in which brand names or any other clues were removed. The correct/incorrect recalls were duly entered in the questionnaire. 'Don't know' answers were also noted.

Special attention was given to the selection of advertisements for 'recall testing'. It was decided to select only those advertisements which were multi-coloured and appeared on the full page of selected magazines. The idea behind selecting full page multi-coloured advertisements would have the same effect on the respondents in terms of catching or holding attention. Uniformity in size of advertisements was also maintained for the same reason. All the advertisements were selected from English language magazines.

Methodology

The responses, recorded on a structured questionnaire at the place of interview, were tabulated for understanding the general profile of respondents and their attitudes towards humorous advertisements. The data was further classified and tabulated to find the effect of various socio-economic and demographic variables on the general and specific attitude of respondents towards humorous advertisements. Moreover, the motivational level and the recall capability of respondents were also recorded. To test the significance of the hypothesis framed, chi-square text and binomial test were applied.

To test the general and specific attitude of respondents towards humorous advertisements, binomial test was used. Since the sample was larger than 25, the binomial distribution tended towards normal distribution. Respondents' degree of 'agreement' or 'favourableness' was measured by binomial test after ignoring the 'don't know' or 'indifferent' answers.

To test the impact of socio-economic and demographic variables on the general and specific attitude of respondents, their motivational level and recall capability, chi-square test of significance was used.

ANALYSIS AND DISCUSSION

Analysis of General Attitude

Attitudes represent a predisposition to form certain opinions. It is, in fact, a frame of reference that influences the individual's views or opinions on various topics and finally his behaviour. Attitudes are formed through experience, which means they are learned. Personality of an individual and his socio-economic background will therefore definitely have an effect on his attitude. Attitudes cannot be weighed on a scale like a commodity because they are intangible. Yet, they can be measured. There are two general methods of measuring attitudes – attitude scales and opinion surveys. For the purpose of measuring the general attitude, the present study used a balanced five-point attitude scale. The respondents were asked to give their opinion regarding the degree of favourableness towards humorous advertisements as shown in Table 6.1.

Table 6.1
Distribution of Respondents According to their Attitude Towards Humorous Advertisements

Degree of Attitudes	*No. of respondents*	*Intensity of feelings on two point scale*	*No. of respondents*
Strongly Agree	5	Favourable	50
Agree	45		
Indifferent	20		
Disagree	30	Unfavourable	30
Strongly Disagree	0		

Note: One-Tailed Test: Significance level = .05, p=0.625, q=0.375.

The table shows that 45 per cent of the respondents showed favourable attitude and about 5 percent were strongly in favour of humour in advertisements. Only 30 per cent respondents were not in favour of humorous advertisements. While 20 per cent respondents were indifferent towards the use of humour in advertising.

The general attitude of respondents towards humorous advertisements was tested by applying the binomial test. The hypothesis framed in this case was: "There is no difference in the probability of respondents' general attitude (favourable or unfavourable) towards humorous advertising".

The five-point scale was reduced to a two point scale after the ignoring the 'indifferent' answers. Thus, two categories, viz., favourable and unfavourable, finally emerged for applying the binomial test.

The binomial test of significance showed that Z value (0.949) was less than the value of Z at 5% level of significance i.e. 1.64. Hence, the hypothesis was accepted, and it can be concluded that there was no difference in the probability of respondents' general attitude (favourable or unfavourable) towards humorous advertising.

Sex and General Attitudes

The information regarding the general attitude of respondents was related to their sex in order to test the null hypothesis – *there is no effect of the respondents' sex on their attitude towards humorous advertising.*

Table 6.2 (a) shows sex wise distribution of respondents' general attitude towards humour in advertising on a three point scale.

This table shows shows that 65 per cent of the males and and 45 per cent of the females were in favour of humorous advertisements. While 15 per cent of the males and 25 percent of the females were indifferent towards such advertisements. When these statistics were tested with the help of chi-square, it showed that calculated χ^2 (3.82) to be much less than tabulated χ^2 (5.99) at 5 per cent level of significance for 2 degrees of freedom. The contingency coefficient of 0.19 also supported the above findings. The impact of sex on the respondents' attitude is therefore insignificant. Hence, the null hypothesis is accepted and it can be concluded that respondents' sex has no influence on attitude towards humorous advertisements.

Table 6.2(a)

Effect of Respondent's Sex on Attitude Towards Humorous Advertisements

Sex	*Attitude*							
	Unfavourable		*Indifferent*		*Favourable*		*Total*	χ^2
	F	*%*	*F*	*%*	*F*	*%*		
Male	12 (14.7)	17.91	10 (12.1)	14.92	45 (40.2)	67.76	67	
Female	10 (07.2)	10.3	8 (05.9)	24.24	15 (19.8)	45.45	33	3.82*
Total	22		18		60		100	

Figures in parenthesis are expected frequencies.
*=Insignificant.

Age and General Attitude

Respondents' age and their general attitude towards humorous advertising were tabulated to test the null hypothesis – *there is no effect of respondents' age on their attitude towards humorous advertisements.*

Table 6.2 (b)
Effect of Respondent's Age on Attitude Towards Humorous Advertisements

Age (yrs)	*Attitude*						*Total*	χ^2
	Unfavourable		*Indifferent*		*Favourable*			
	F	*%*	*F*	*%*	*F*	*%*		
Young (<30)	10 (20.16)	14	22 (18.72)	30	40 (33.12)	56	72	28.54*
Middle (>30)	18 (07.84)	64	04 (07.28)	14	6 (12.88)	22	28	
Total	28		26		46		100	

Figures in parentheses are expected frequencies.
*= Significant at 0.001, c=0.47.

Table 6.2(b) shows that 56 per cent young and 22 per cent middle aged people were in favour of humour in advertising. While 30 per cent of the young and 14 per cent of the middle aged were indifferent in their attitude. The chi-square test showed that the calculated value of χ^2 (28.54) was much higher than table value (5.99) at 5 per cent level of significance and 2 degrees of freedom. Thus, the null hypothesis was rejected. A high contingency coefficient (c=0.47) indicated that there was a strong association between the age and the attitude of respondents. Hence, it can be concluded that respondents' age has a significant effect on their attitude towards humorous advertisements.

Analysis of Specific Attitudes

In this section, an analysis was carried out of specific attitudes of the respondents towards such aspects of advertising as whether they consider humorous advertising to be persuasive, comprehensive, convincing, motivating or exaggerative and of poor taste *vis-à-vis* non-humorous advertisements.

For this purpose, eight statements relating to these aspects were developed and the respondents were asked to express their degree of agreement or disagreement to each of these statement.

For measuring the degree of agreement, Likert's five-point scale ranging from strongly agreey to strongly disagreey was used. Thus, the intensity of feeling of respondents towards humorous advertising was obtained. The information so obtained was analysed to find out the extent and intensity of agreement or disagreement with a particular statement. The binomial test was applied to test the null hypothesis according to which *there is no significant difference between the respondents agreeing or disagreeing with the statement.* Just as in testing the general attitude, here also the five point scale was reduced to a two point scale after ignoring the 'don't know' answers. Thus, two categories – those who agreed and those who disagreed – finally emerged for applying the binomial test.

Statement A: Humorous advertisements attract more attention than non-humorous advertisement.

Table 6.3 gives the distribution of respondents in terms of their degree of agreement or disagreement with the above statement. The table also shows that 81 per cent of the respondents agreed with the above statement and only 19 per cent disagreed. The binomial test showed that Z value (6.2) was more than table value (1.64) at 5 per cent level of significance. Hence, the null hypothesis was rejected. Thus, we may conclude that humorous advertisements attract more attention than non-humorous ones.

Table 6.3
Respondent's Intensity of Feelings with Reference to Statement "A"

Attitude	*No. of respondents*	*Intensity of feelings on two point scale*	*No. of respondents*
Strongly Agree	30	Favourable	81
Agree	51		
Indifferent	0		
Disagree	8	Unfavourable	19
Strongly Disagree	11		

Note: p=0.5, q=0.5 at 5% level of significance.

Statement B: The persuasive effect of humorous appeals is greater than that of serious appeals.

Table 6.4 shows the distribution of respondents according to their feelings towards the statement B.

Table 6.4
Respondent's Intensity of Feelings with Reference to Statement "B"

Attitude	*No. of respondents*	*Intensity of feelings on two point scale*	*No. of respondents*
Strongly Agree	21	Favourable	77
Agree	56		
Indifferent	6		
Disagree	11	Unfavourable	17
Strongly Disagree	6		

Note: p=0.05 (one-tailed test), q=0.5, Z=6.

The table shows that 77 per cent of the respondents agreed with the statement whereas 17 per cent disagreed with it. When binomial test was applied it was found that Z value (6) was greater than table value (1.64) at 5% level of significance. Hence, the null hypothesis was rejected.

Statement C: Humorous advertisements are easy to understand than serious advertisements.

The opinion of the respondents on the above statement was measured and tested. The null hypothesis in this case was that *there is no difference in the probability of the respondents agreeing or disagreeing with this statement*. Table 6.5 shows the distribution of respondents according to the strength of their feelings for statement C.

An analysis of the above data showed that 70 per cent of the respondents agreed and only 20 per cent disagreed. Binomial test showed that Z value (7) is greater than table value (1.64), so the null hypothesis was rejected. Thus, we may conclude that humorous advertisements are easy to understand than non humorous advertisements.

Table 6.5
Respondent's Intensity of Feelings with Reference to Statement "C"

Attitude	*No. of respondents*	*Intensity of feelings on two point scale*	*No. of respondents*
Strongly Agree	28	Favourable	70
Agree	42		
Indifferent	10		
Disagree	18	Unfavourable	20
Strongly Disagree	2		

Note: p=0.05 (one-tailed test), Z=7.

Statement D: Humorous advertisements are more convincing than non-humorous advertisements.

The null hypothesis in this case was that *probability of respondents agreeing and disagreeing to this statement is equal.* Table 6.6 shows, the distribution of the respondents according to the intensity of their feelings in this respect.

Analysis showed that 65 per cent respondents agreed while 25 per cent disagreed. When this was binomially tested it was found that Z value (4) exceeded table value (1.64) at 5% level of significance. Hence, the null hypothesis was rejected and it can be safely concluded that majority of the respondents disagreed with the above statement.

Statement E: Humorous advertisements help in the retention of brand names more than non-humorous ones.

The null hypothesis in this case was that *the respondents agreeing or disagreeing on this statement are equally divided.* Table 6.7 shows the distribution of respondents according to their degree of agreement or disagreement with the statement.

Table 6.6
Respondent's Intensity of Feelings with Reference to Statement "D"

Attitude	*No. of respondents*	*Intensity of feelings on two point scale*	*No. of respondents*
Strongly Agree	31	Favourable	65
Agree	34		
Indifferent	10		
Disagree	21	Unfavourable	25
Strongly Disagree	4		

Note: p=0.05 (one-tailed test), Z=4.

Table 6.7
Respondent's Intensity of Feelings with Reference to Statement "E"

Attitude	*No. of respondents*	*Intensity of feelings on two point scale*	*No. of respondents*
Strongly Agree	13	Favourable	48
Agree	35		
Indifferent	7		
Disagree	33	Unfavourable	45
Strongly Disagree	12		

Note: p=0.05 (one-tailed test), Z=0.4.

It was found that 48 per cent respondents agreed with the statement while 45 per cent disagreed and 7 percent were indifferent. While 13 per cent respondents strongly agreed, 35 per cent agreed, 12 per cent strongly disagreed and 33 per cent disagreed with the statement E. The calculated Z value (0.4) was less than table value (1.64) at the 5 per cent level of significance. Hence, the null hypothesis was accepted. Thus, the respondents were equally divided in their opinion as to whether humorous advertisements help in the retention of brand names more than the serious ones.

Statement F: In humorous advertisements the degree of exaggeration is greater than in non-humorous advertisements.

The null hypothesis was *that there is no difference in the opinon of the respondents regarding the degree of exaggeration in humorous advertisements vis-a-vis non-humorous advertisements*. The distribution of responses is shown in Table 6.8 which shows that 55 per cent respondents agreed with the statement while 45 per cent disagreed. Of them 5 per cent strongly agreed, 50 per cent agreed, 31 per cent disagreed and 14 per cent strongly disagreed with the statement. Statistical analysis revealed that Z value (1) was less than the table value (1.64) at 5% level of significance and therefore the null hypothesis was accepted. It can be concluded that respondents are equally divided in their opinion regarding the degree of exaggeration. Hence, it cannot be claimed that in humorous advertisements the degree of exaggeration is greater than in the serious advertisements.

Table 6.8
Respondents Intensity of Feelings with Reference to Statement "F"

Attitude	*No. of respondents*	*Intensity of feelings on two point scale*	*No. of respondents*
Strongly Agree	5	Favourable	55
Agree	50		
Indifferent	0		
Disagree	31	Unfavourable	45
Strongly Disagree	14		

Note: p=0.05 (one-tailed test), Z=1.

Analysis of Copy Elements Using Humour

Perhaps the most vital as well as the most difficult part of advertising is the creation and production of a copy. The term copy refers to the audio-visuals elements in an advertising message. In print media, such as magazines or newspapers, copy includes not only the text (body copy) but also the headlines and illustrations. In the broadcast media, such as radio, television or cinema, copy includes not only word to be spoken but also music and sound, demonstration techniques, movement of the characters. However, the scope of this study is confined to print media.

Generally, in print media, humour is depicted through either headlines, text, or illustration or through any combination of these three. The layout of these elements should be such that it should provide leverage to the copy appeal for attracting and holding the interest of the reader. Otherwise, the effort and the expense involved would be wasted. To test the effectiveness of these copy elements, respondents were asked to give their opinion regarding the same.

The responses are given in Table 6.9. It shows the distribution of responses regarding the degree of effectiveness of various copy elements. Further, this information was statistically tested by applying chi-square test on the null hypothesis in order to show that there is no difference in the effectiveness of copy elements.

An analysis of the data revealed that 36 per cent of the respondents considered humour in headline to be very effective. 18 per cent considered it to be somewhat effective and 4 percent felt that humour in headline was not at all effective. On the other hand, 9 per cent of the respondents considered humour in text to be very much effective, while 30 per cent felt that it was somewhat effective and 72 per cent felt that it was not at all effective. In case of humour in illustration 27 per cent feel that it was very much effective, 30 per cent were of the opinion that it was somewhat effective and 4 per cent said it was not at all effective. Regarding overall humour, 28 per cent were of the opinion that it was very much effective, 22 per cent felt that it was somewhat effective and 20 per cent were of the opinion that it was not at all effective. When this information was statistically tested with the help of chi-square test, it was found that the table χ^2 value (12.59) was less than calculated χ^2 value (99.61) at 5 per cent level of significance and 6 degrees of freedom. Hence, the difference in the opinion of respondents regarding the degree of effectiveness of copy elements is highly significant. It was also supported by a relatively high contingency coefficient value of 0.44. The null hypothesis was therefore rejected and it can be concluded that there is a highly significant difference in the effectiveness of copy elements. Majority of the respondents considered humour in headline and illustration to be very effective, while, majority of the respondents did not consider humour in text to be effective. On the issue of effectiveness of humour in all the elements of advertisement, opinions were equally divided. The opinions ranged from *very much effective* to *somewhat effective*. Hence, it can be safely concluded that humorous headlines and illustration can be used very effectively. However, the use of humorous text should be made when the whole advertisement copy is to be made humorous. The above findings clearly indicate that readers' attention and interest in an advertisement can be sought by making use of humorous headlines and illustrations.

Table 6.9
Respondents' Attitude towards the Effectiveness of Various Copy Elements

Degree of effectiveness	*Humour in Headlines*		*Humour in Text*		*Humour in Illustration*		*Overall Humour*		*Total*	χ^2
	F	*%*	*F*	*%*	*F*	*%*	*F*	*%*		
Very much effective	68 (45.5)	36	15 (45.5)	9	48 (45.5)	27	51 (45.5)	28	182	
Some what effective	30 (42.5)	18	50 (42.5)	30	50 (42.2)	30	40 (42.5)	22	170	99.62*
Not at all effective	02 (12.)	4	35 (12.)	72	02 (12.0)	4	09 (12.0)	20	48	
Total	100		100		100		100		400	

Note: Figures in parenthesis are expected frequencies.
* = significant at 0.001, χ^2= 99.62.

Analysis of Humorous Advertisements and their Effect on Recall

Much of the response of audience in advertising is delayed one. In order to bridge the time lag between the comprehension and perception of the advertisement on the one hand and the lasting impression and final purchase of the product on the other, lasting impressions must be made so as to influence the behaviour at the point of sale. Therefore, the memorability of an advertisement is considered as an appropriate index of its effectiveness. To measure the memorability of an advertisement certain recognition and recall tests are used which indicate the ability of an advertisement to stand out and of its intended message to be understood. Recall, in fact, refers to the "ad post-testing" or the "follow-up test" conducted after exposure of the respondent to a particular advertisement.

For the purpose of this study two types of recall tests were used– aided recall test and recognition recall test. On the basis of these tests a comparative study was made, using both "humorous and non-humorous advertisements". The respondents were asked to recall the brand names of the advertised products and the responses were listed as 'correct', 'incorrect' and 'don't know'. In order to eliminate the 'halo effect', recall test was conducted prior to recognition test.

In order to ascertain the effect of humorous advertisements on recall of brand names, two hypothesis stating that there is no difference in the recall scores of humorous and non-humorous advertisements were developed. Related scores were measured and then statistically analysed with the help of chi-square test of significance.

Table 6.10
Distribution of Respondents' Recall Scores

			Correct	*Don't know*	*Incorrect*	*Total*
Non-humorous	Aided recall	Score	375	84	41	500
		%	75	16.8	8.2	100
	Recognition recall	Score	390	34	76	500
		%	78	6.8	15.2	100
Humorous	Aided recall	Score	445	30	25	500
		%	87	8	5	100
	Recognition recall	Score	470	20	10	500
		%	94	4	2	100

Total number of recalls of brand names, using humorous and non-humorous advertisements were 2400. This refers to both aided recall scores and recognition-recall scores. In all, there were 20 advertisements (10 humorous and 10 non-humorous) which were shown to each respondent twice; once for recording aided-recall scores and then for recording recognition scores. The total recall scores were recorded and tabulated as shown in Table 6.10.

Analysis of the above data reveals that in case of non-humorous advertisements, 75 per cent recalled correctly for 'aided-recall'. For 'recognition-recall', the correct scores were about 78 per cent. The same test conducted for humorous advertisements showed in the case of aided-recall the correct scores were about 87 per cent, which increased to 94 per cent for recognition recall. This clearly showed a marked difference in the number of correctly recalled advertisements in the case of their being humorous or non-humorous.

As many as 8.2 per cent 'aided-recalls' and 15.20 per cent 'recognition-recalls' were incorrect in the case of non-humorous advertisements. The corresponding number for humorous advertisement was far less at 5 per cent incorrect aided-recalls and 2 per cent incorrect recognition-recalls. Thus, it shows that less number of humorous advertisements were recalled incorrectly.

In case of non-humorous advertisements, 16.8 per cent aided-recalls and 6.8 per cent recognition-recalls were 'don't know' and this came down to 6 per cent on aided-recalls and 4 percent recognition-recalls in the case of humorous advertisements. This showed that more respondents tended to remember those advertisements which had humorous approach.

These differences were statistically tested for their significance by applying chi-square test for aided and recognition-recalls separately.

Test of Significance for Aided-recalls

In this case respondents were given a portfolio of 20 advertisements and were given 15 minutes to go through these advertisements. After which they were asked to tick mark the brand names they remembered on a given list having 30 brand names. Correct and incorrect scores were recorded and tabulated as shown in Table 6.11.

Table 6.11
Distribution of the Respondents Aided Recall Scores

Recalls	*Non-humorous Ads Score*	*Humorous Ads. Score*	*Total*	χ^2
Correct	552 (535.84)	918 (934.2)	1470	
Incorrect	83 (99.15)	189 (172.9)	272	4.9*
Total	635	1107		1742

Note: Figures in parenthesis are expected frequencies.
* = Significant at 0.05.

The statistical analysis showed that the calculated value of chi-square (4.90) exceeded the table chi-square value (3.84), indicating the rejection of null hypothesis. However, contingency coefficient shows a very low degree of association between the correct-incorrect recalls and their respective differences for humorous and non-humorous advertisements. But the difference was significant and therefore we can conclude that there is a definite effect of the use of humorous advertisements on aided-recalls by the respondents. Advertisements with non-humorous appeals had slightly less number of correct recalls than those which made use of humorous appeals.

Test of Significance for Recognition-recall

For recognition-recall, the respondents were first given the portfolio with 20 advertisement and were given 15 minutes to go through these advertisements. Subsequently, they were given a similar portfolio, but this time the brand names or other clues were rubbed out. They were asked to recognise the advertisements and recall the brand names. The pattern of their recall scores was tabulated and is shown in Table 6.12.

When chi-square test was applied, it showed that the calculated χ^2 value (19.09) exceeds the table χ^2 (3.84) at 5 percent level of significance and 1 degree of freedom. Therefore, the difference in the recall scores of respondents related to humorous and non-humorous advertisements was significant. This finding was further supported by the contingency coefficient value of 0.40. Hence, it can be concluded that the impact of humorous advertisements on the recall capability of respondents was highly significant when compared to non-humorous advertisements.

Table 6.12
Distribution of the Respondents' Recognition Recall Scores

Recalls	*Non-humorous Ads Score*	*Humorous Ads. Score*	*Total*	χ^2
Correct	562 (567.6)	1002 (1036.4)	1564	
Incorrect	79 (43.6)	257 (223.6)	336	19.09[a]
Total	641	1259	1900	

Note: Figures in parenthesis are expected frequencies.

* = Significant at 0.005.

The analysis of the recall scores reveals that humour has a definite effect on the recall capability of respondents, a majority of whom could recall correctly the brand names of products advertised humorously. Moreover, the correct recognition-recall scores of humorous advertisements showed a 6.70 per cent increase over the correct aided-recall scores of humorous advertisements. The study therefore shows a positive trend in respondents' recall capability of humour advertisements *vis-à-vis* non-humorous advertisements.

CONCLUSIONS

This study was undertaken to obtain an idea about the effectiveness of humorous advertisements and to get an insight into their possible effect on consumers' attitude, motivational level and recall capability. The study was considered important because of the increasing use of such advertisements in marketing, particularly of consumer goods of all types. Very little is known about the effectiveness of such advertisements in India. Hence, an attempt was made to know more about it through this study. It is expected that the study would be of much practical significance for Indian marketers.

Our research has revealed that majority of the respondents (50%) favoured the use of humorous advertisements. The study showed that only age and profession influenced respondents' attitude, while sex and income-level did not. It was found that the students and professionals, especially from the younger age-group, held a positive attitude towards humorous advertisements.

Analysis of specific attitudes towards various aspects of humorous advertisements revealed that almost all the respondents agreed that humorous advertisements attract more attention than non- humorous ones and are easy to understand. However, they disagreed with the claims that humorous advertisements are more convincing and lead to more purchasing decisions than non-humorous advertisements. Opinions regarding the persuasiveness, retention of brand names, and exaggeration in humorous advertisements were equally divided. When the impact of socio-economic and demographic factors on the specific attitudes of respondents were evaluated, it was found that the opinions were not influenced by sex. The attitudes regarding the 'attractiveness' of humorous advertisements were influenced by respondents' profession only. In case of 'convincibility', respondents' age was the influencing factor.

The study further revealed that majority of the respondents considered humorous illustration to be most effective.

As the study was conducted with the major objective of knowing the recall effectiveness of humorous advertisement, it was found that the use of humour in advertising definitely had an effect on the recall capability of respondents, as majority of them could correctly remember the brand names of products featured in such advertisements. The number of correct recalls in the case of non-humorous advertisements was relatively less.

Implications for Marketing

Consumer behaviour is rather complex and is affected by many factors. Thus buying decisions and habits are influenced by consumer's attitudes, predispositions, motives, needs, expectations, likes and dislikes, etc. Besides these, several socio-economic factors also effect their behaviour. Advertising is one of the very potent tools in the hands of business organisations through which they try to influence the decision process of consumers. Advertising researches have shown that a person comes across hundreds of advertisements daily. The advertisers therefore make use of various appeals and techniques to make their advertisements stand apart from other advertisements and also try to create lasting impressions. Humour is one of the techniques of attracting audiences and holding their interest.

The study aimed at finding whether humorous advertisements created a lasting impression and held the interest of consumers or not. The main objective of the study was, however, to provide clues to the advertisers about the usefulness of humour in advertising.

The study suggests two main implications in the area of marketing strategy formulation. Firsltly, one may use the humorous advertisements only for attracting and holding audience attention, and secondly, more serious advertisements may be used in the later stages to create the desired impact.

Findings have demonstrated that the general attitude of respondents towards humorous advertisements is favourable. On the other hand, their specific attitudes show that they hold a negative attitude regarding the claims that humorous advertisements are more persuasive, convincing and lead to more purchasing decisions than non-humorous advertisements. However, they agree that humorous advertisements attract more attention, are easy to understand and create lasting impressions. This is supported by the 'aided' and 'recognition' recall scores, which showed that majority of the respondents were able to correctly recall the brand names of humorously advertised products. The analysis also showed that majority of the advertisements made use of either illustrations or headlines and that both of these copy elements were considered to be very effective. On the other hand, the study suggests that humorous text should be used sparingly.

Another marketing implication emanates from the finding that most of the humorous advertisements for various products and services were for consumer non-durable items and services. The study revealed that the impact of humorous advertisements on respondents' motivational level was more for non-durable products like cold drinks and eatables. It is a common fact that services and non-durable products involve repeat purchase. This means that at the point of sale, consumers should be aware of various brands in order to reduce their dissonance and to spend their money more judiciously. The findings of the present study have shown that humorous advertisements hold consumers' interest and create lasting impressions, which may influence their behaviour at the point of sale. Therefore, it would be more prudent to use humour in advertising for consumer non-durable products and services.

A corollary of these marketing implications suggests that humorous advertisements play a very significant role in the first two stages of consumer purchase behaviour – awareness and knowledge. As humorous advertisements were found to attract more attention and help in greater retention of brand names than non-humorous advertisements, they may prove to be very effective in creating brand awareness and disseminating brand knowledge. Humorous advertisements may also help in the sale of products by influencing consumer purchase behaviour at the point of sale, because of their memorability.

The second corollary to marketing suggests that as humorous advertisement may prove to be more effective in creating brand awareness and knowledge, they can be effectively used during the *introduction stage* of a product's life cycle. Later on, for generating liking, preference and conviction for specific brand, serious appeals can be used. However, to maintain the interest in the campaign and to assist consumers to retain the brand name, humorous advertisements should be intermittently used.

The advertisers must therefore define clearly the nature of the product, its target-market and the stage of its life cycle, before making use of humorous appeals. Identification of the target-market becomes necessary because the study has shown that respondents from middle and older age-groups were less convinced than young respondents who held a more favourable attitude towards the use of humorous advertisements.

Directions for Future Research

Due to paucity of serious literature in the Indian context, certain aspects of humour in advertising could not be clearly defined. First of all, a more precise and clear definition of humour in advertising is necessary. Based on the study by Lynch and Hartman (1968), types of humour in Indian advertising should be identified and related to factors like, general knowledge, sophistication, sensitivity, simplicity, visualisation, cuteness, staging and abstraction.

The present study has given some idea about the role of humorous advertisements in the consumers' purchasing stages of awareness, knowledge, liking preference and conviction. However, there is a need for a comprehensive study which may investigate the extent to which humour effects attitudes, retention and actual purchase behaviour in the context of India.

REFERENCES

Duncan P. Calvin and James E. Nelson (1985), 'Effects of Humour in a Radio Advertising Experiment', *Journal of Advertising,* pp. 33-39

Gelb D. Betsy and George M. Zinkhan (1986), "Humour and Advertising Effectiveness After Repeated Exposure to a Radio Commercial", *Journal of Advertising,* 15, pp. 15-20.

Harold D., *Humour in Advertising and How to Make it Pay,* (New York: McGraw Hill, 1963).

Harpner H., *Modern Advertising: Principles and Practice,* New York: McGraw Hill, 1963).

Higgins Kevin (1985), "Humour Takes the 'Ho-Hum' Out of Radio", *Marketing News,* p. 23.

Hoppe P., "Humour in Advertising", *IPA Forum,* Vol. 28, January 1969, pp. 18-21. 7. K. Phillips, "When a Funny Commercial is Good, Its Great" *Broadcasting* 74, May 1973, p. 26.

Leavit, "A Multidimensional Set of Rating Scales for Television Commercials", *Journal of Applied Psychology,* 54, August 1970, pp. 427-29.

Madden J. Thomas and Marc G. Weinberger (1984), "Humour in Advertising: A Practitioner's View", *Journal of Advertising Research,* 24, pp. 23-29.

Mervin D. Lynch and Richard C. Hartman, "Dimensions of Humour in Advertising", *Journal of Advertising Research,* 8 December 1968, pp. 39-45.

Ogilvy David, *Confessions of An Advertising Man* (New York: Atheneum, 1964).

Ogilvy David, *Ogilvy on Advertising* (New York: Vintage Books, 1985).

Sternthal B. and C. Samuel Craig, "Humour in Advertising", *Journal of Marketing,* October 1973, pp. 12-18.

Thomas E. Barry, "A Study of Humour and Its Implications for Advertising", Unpublished Masters Thesis, Southern Illinois University, Carbondale, Illinois (June 1967) cited in Robert L. Anderson and Thomas E. Barry, *Advertising Management: Text and Cases,* (Columbus, Ohio: Bell and Howell, 1979).

Weinberger G. Marc and Charles S. Gulas (1992), "The Impact of Humour in Advertising: A Review," *Journal of Advertising,* 21, pp. 35-59.

7

Media Exposure, Media Effectiveness and Demographics

THE ROLE OF MEDIA IN ADVERTISING

An advertising message cannot contribute to the success of an advertising or marketing campaign until the target audience is exposed to it. The delivery of message is performed by the advertising media.

Every advertising medium has unique characteristics. Thus, different groups and segments of population are defferentially exposed to advertisements through media. We cannot say that any particular medium is superior to others in absolute terms, though a particular medium may be more suitable for a specific purpose than others. Thus, for some purposes one medium may show superiority, for other purposes the same medium may be entirely inappropriate. Because of this reason, media planners often use a mix of media for successful launch of their advertising campaign. The sole objective of this exercise is to extract maximum benefit from available funds.

During the last few years media decisions have been influenced by a significant changes in the media and the markets. The changes are complexity of media, technological changes, changes complexion of markets and an increase in the advertising expenditure.

Major changes have occurred in almost all types of media. The country has witnessed commercialisation of Doordarshan and AIR, the coming of satellite TV, a decelaration in newspaper circulation and an amazing growth in the variety of special interest magazines. Satellite channels have made it possible for the marketers to send their messages to selected target audience.

Technological changes have also occurred in print and TV media. The improvements in ink and reproduction processes in print medium, and advancement in colour reproduction technology have all influenced print media decisions. On the other hand introduction of colour television offers a greater scope for realism in presentation. Apart from this, computer graphics and special effects have brought about dramatic changes in electronic media.

The Indian market too has undergone a sea change in terms of increase in income level, the continuing trend towards urbanisation, more working women than before, and increase in literacy levels. These developments have brought about changes in reading, viewing, and listening patterns of the Indian population which have important implications for the advertising industry in terms of allocation of funds.

Sweeping changes owing to globalisation and liberalisation have profoundly effected the Indian industry in the last few years. Indian industry is now churning out an incredible array of products and services. In this unpredictable era of razor edge competition, most manufacturers have come to realize the importance of advertising in marketing.

In the last few years the country has witnessed the emergence of television as a powerful advertising medium. The advertisers have realised its massive reach. The expenditure on advertising on television in increased by leaps and bounds. It is generally felt that television advertising has made a dent in the volume of print advertising. As the experience of west shows, the importance of print media will not diminish under the impact of television.

The increase in television advertising is to be viewed as a warning for the print media and cinema.The print media and cinema have to reorganise and recognise the fact that Television has made a considerable dent in their target audiences.

PURPOSE AND OBJECTIVES

The advent of television in this country and its going commercial have changed the advertising patterns. Prior to TV, the major advertising media were newspapers, magazines, cinema and radio.

Hoardings and posters were the other media that were commonly used. Television, with its vast reach and round the clock transmission, has forced the advertisers to allocate more funds for this medium. The telecast of sports and other special events has given advertisers more scope for reaching the Indian audience.

These changes have highlighted the need for a comparative study of print and audio visual media. Therefore, the authors selected four major media, i.e. newspapers, magazines, television and cinema for the present study.

The objective underlying this study and selection of only four types of media was that television advertising has directly affected newspaper, magazine and cinema advertising. The specific objectives of this study were:

- To determine the relative frequency of media usage in relation to sex, educational qualification and occupation.
- To determine the reading habits and the time devoted to newspaper reading among the different sections of the population.
- To determine the reading habits of magazines and amount of time spent on it by different segments of the population.
- To determine the cinema going habits and its frequency among various groups of population.
- To determine the TV viewing habits and its duration among the different groups of population.
- To determine which of the four media (newspapers, magazines, television, cinema), according to the respondents, gives more details about various products.
- To determine the relative attention attracting potential of different media (newspapers, magazines, television, cinema).

METHODOLOGY

A survey of 200 persons was conducted in the cities of Hyderabad, Lucknow and Aligarh. These cities were selected to get a balanced view from a cross section of people to make the study more representative. Magazines and journals were used to supplement the primary data collected from the sample.

The questionnaire comprised open ended, dichotomous and multiple choice questions.

Limitations of Study

1. The sample size was not as large as desired for a detailed study.
2. As convenience sample was chosen, errors associated with it are bound to occur.
3. The respondents from three cities were included in the sample, whereas for an indepth study, more number of cities should have been included to make the sample more representative.
4. Posters, hoardings etc. were not included in the study as the advertising expenditure on these media is very low as compared to newspapers and magazines. Moreover, the study laid stress on only four major media viz. television, cinema, newspapers and magazines.

ANALYSIS AND INTERPRETATION

Exposure to Newspapers

The data collected for the pattern of newspaper readership are arranged in the Table 7.1 with respect to the different demographic variables. It is interesting to note that newspaper reading is equally popular among all the groups. Taken from gender point of view, no significant differences were found, though males had a slightly higher percentage. Qualification-wise also, no statistical significance was found, though undergraduate percentage was marginally lower than that of graduates and post-graduates. In case of occupation, housewives had lower readership percentage (78.5%) as compared to other occupations. However, the differences were not statistically significant.

The second aspect regarding newspaper readership investigation was the time the respondents spent in reading. In order to investigate this aspect, the respondents were asked to indicate the time they spend in newspaper reading. Later, on the duration was divided into four categories. Then the results were arranged with respect to different demographic variables (Table 7.2).

As the table 7.2 indicates there exist significant differences in the time devoted to newspaper reading. Sex, qualification and occupation-wise too, the results showed significant differences as

Table 7.1
Newspaper Readership Profile

Variable	*Read Daily* *No.*	*%*	*Do not read daily* *No.*	*%*	*Total*	χ^2
Sex						
Male	115	90.5	12	9.5	127	1.44*
Female	62	85	11	15	73	
Qualification						
Under graduate	63	85	11	15	74	
Graduate	60	91	6	9	66	1.33*
Post Graduate	54	90	6	10	60	
Occupation						
Students	103	87	15	13	118	
Professionals	52	96	2	4	54	3.94*
Housewives	22	78.5	6	21.5	28	

* = Not significant at 5% level of significance.

Table 7.2
Duration of Newspaper Reading and Demographic Variables

Variable	*15 mt.* *%*	*15-30mt.* *%*	*30-45 mt.* *%*	*> 45 mt.* *%*	*Total* *%*	χ^2
Sex						
Male	25	44	20	11	100	11.61*
Female	45	39	5	11	100	
Qualification						
Under graduate	40	40	12	8	100	
Graduate	15	53	22	10	100	15.84*
Post Graduate	30	35	20	15	100	
Profession						
Students	35	40	17	8	100	
Professionals	37	37	9	17	100	21.5*
Housewives	9	68	14	9	100	

* = Significant at 5% level of significance.

is evident from the χ^2 values. We found that modal duration in case of females, undergraduates and post-graduates was 15 minutes. For males, graduates and students it ranged from 15 to 30 minutes. Longer duration readership was low because may be the people do not devote much time to newspaper reading as it is considered to be a daily affair. It is quite clear that maximum number of people spend less than 30 minutes for newspaper reading. This duration is also significant in the sense that it is quite sufficient for news reading as well as reading or looking at advertisements in them.

Table 7.3
Magazine Readership and Demographics

Variable		*Read regularly*		*Do not read regularly*		*Total*	χ^2
		No.	*%*	*No.*	*%*		
Sex							
	Male	85	67	42	33	127	.184*
	Female	51	70	22	30	73	
Qualification							
	Under graduate	51	69	23	31	74	
	Graduate	44	67	22	33	66	.251*
	Post Graduate	41	68	19	32	60	
Occupation							
	Students	82	69	36	31	118	
	Professionals	32	59	22	44	54	3.94*
	House Wives	22	79	6	21	28	

*= Not significant at 5% level of significance.

Exposure to Magazines

The next research question was directed towards the magazine readership. The researchers explained to the respondents that purchasing at least one magazine a month would qualify them as regular reader. The responses for this question are tabulated in the table 7.3 with respect to demographics. According to this table one can clearly say that again demographics did not affect magazine readership. By further analyzing this table, one can find that majority of respondents read magazines regularly. The female readership was slightly more than that of males. Housewives were more avid readers as compared to other professions. This is again understandable because this segment of population has more leisure time at its disposal. Professional had lowest readership percentage perhaps due to their preoccupation with their respective professions. The results clearly show that demographic variables do not have any effect on magazines readership. The same was proved statistically too.

Table 7.4

Cinema Going Frequency and Demographics

Variable		*Once a Week*		*Once a fortnight*		*Once a month*		*Total*	χ^2
		No.	*%*	*No.*	*%*	*No.*	*%*		
Sex									
	Male	38	34	22	20	52	46	112	16.29*
	Female	9	15	4	7	47	78	60	
Qualification									
	Under graduate	20	31	10	16	35	54	65	
	Graduate	22	37	9	15	29	48	60	10.38*
	Post Graduate	5	11	7	15	35	74	47	
Occupation									
	Students	37	35	19	18	51	47	107	
	Professionals	5	11	7	16	33	73	45	11.82*
	Housewives	5	25	2	10	13	65	20	

* = Significant at 5% level of significance.

Exposure to Cinema

In India, cinema is a very popular and economical means of entertainment. Therefore, it finds favour with different strata of society. However, with the advent of TV, the popularity of cinema has been waning. The respondents were asked to indicate the frequency of their cinema visits and the results are tabulated in Table 7.4.

These results are quite revealing. Males seem to be more fond of movies than females. The frequency of seeing a movie once in a week by males was 34 per cent, whereas, for women it was only 15 per cent. More than three fourth of females see movies once in a month. If we take the qualifications into consideration it is interesting to note that graduates and undergraduates watch movies more frequently than post-graduates. Again in terms of occupation students surpassed all, followed by housewives and retired persons.

This indicates that there exists differential exposure to cinema among the different segments of the population and this was found significant among all the demographic variables.

Exposure to TV

To find exposure to TV, the respondents were asked whether they watch TV daily or not and then they had to specify approximately how much time they spend on television viewing. The responses are given in Tables 7.5 & 7.6.

Table 7.5 exhibits the TV viewing behaviour of the respondents. It is clear from the table that all segments of the population watch TV. In all the groups we found that TV viewership was quite prevalent. No significant differences were found in TV viewing pattern of the respondents.

Table 7.5
TV Viewership and Demographics

Variable	*Watch TV daily*		*Do not watch TV daily*		*Total*	χ^2
	No.	*%*	*No.*	*%*		
Sex						
Male	108	85	19	15	127	2.82*
Female	68	92	05	08	73	
Qualifications						
Under graduate	60	80	14	20	74	
Graduate	53	81	13	19	66	2.7*
Post Graduate	48	84	12	16	60	
Occupation						
Students	99	84	19	16	118	
Professionals	44	80	10	20	54	5.67*
Housewives	25	94	03	06	28	

*= Insignificant at 5% level of significance.

It is surprising that of those who watched TV daily, with the exception of professionals, nearly three fourth spent one hour or more on it. Housewives and retired persons, because of spending more time in their homes, were more prone to TV viewing than the other segments of the population. However, chi-square statistics has not shown any significance in the TV viewing habits of different demographic groups.

Table 7.6
TV Viewing and Demographics

Variable	*1/2 hour*		*1 hour*		*2 Hours*		*> 2 hours*		*Total*	χ^2
	No.	*%*	*No.*	*%*	*No.*	*%*	*No.*	*%*		
Sex										
Male	25	30	38	46	12	14	8	10	83	5.29*
Female	15	27	31	55	2	4	8	15	56	
Qualification										
Under graduate	14	30	24	51	3	6	6	13	47	
Graduate	14	30	10	41	3	7	5	11	46	5.01*
Post Graduate	12	26	26	57	3	7	5	13	46	
Occupation										
Students	23	29	35	45	9	12	11	14	78	
Professionals	13	31	22	52	4	10	3	7	42	4.53*
Housewives	4	21	14	74	1	5	2	10	19	

* = Insignificant at 5% level of significance.

Information Contents and Media

Another dimension of this study was to investigate the extent of information content *vis-à-vis* the advertised products in different media i.e. newspapers, magazines, cinema and TV. To ascertain this fact, the respondents were asked to rank the four media in terms of information content of advertisements. These responses were tabulated in terms of demographic characteristics and are arranged in Table 7.7.

From the point of view of providing information to the prospective customers, surprisingly, TV outclassed all other media. In all the segments almost one half of the respondents felt that TV provided maximum information followed by magazines, newspapers and cinema. It is quite surprising that generally same advertisements appear both in TV and cinema but in the latter case the duration of commercials is generally of longer than in the former. This indicates that TV commercials are perceived as more informative than commercials placed in cinema. This trend was confirmed by all demographic groups and no significant differences were found (see Table 7.7). This has great significance for the advertisers. Information related to products and services

Table 7.7
Information Contents of Media and Demographics

Variable	*TV* No.	%	*Magazines* No.	%	*Newspapers* No.	%	*Cinema* No.	%	*Total*	χ^2
Sex										
Male	64	50	32	25	25	20	6	5	127	1.23*
Female	41	56	16	22	14	19	2	3	73	
Qualifications										
Under graduate	40	54	14	19	19	24	2	3	74	
Graduate	32	48	19	29	13	20	2	3	66	5.34*
Post Graduate	33	55	15	25	8	13	4	7	60	
Occupation										
Students	65	55	28	24	20	17	5	4	118	
Professionals	26	48	15	28	11	20	2	4	54	6.24*
Housewives	14	50	5	18	8	29	1	3	28	

*= Insignificant at 5% level of significance.

enhances the capacity of consumer in making better purchase decisions. Therefore, the perception of TV commercials as being more informative may prove to be effective in the long run.

Media Attractiveness

Table 7.8 illustrates the ranking of respondents with respect to the attractiveness of major media. When asked to rate the relative

Table 7.8
Media Attractiveness and Demographics

Variable	*TV* No.	%	*Magazines* No.	%	*Newspapers* No.	%	*Cinema* No.	%	*Total*	χ^2
Sex										
Male	83	65	19	15	16	12	9	8	127	.839*
Female	46	64	9	13	11	15	7	8	73	
Qualifications										
Under graduate	43	58	11	14	13	18	7	10	74	
Graduate	44	65	10	16	9	14	3	5	66	4.63*
Post Graduate	42	69	7	12	5	8	6	9	60	
Occupation										
Students	76	67	15	12	15	12	12	9	118	
Professionals	40	72	8	15	5	8	3	5	54	9.26*
House Wives	15	52	5	18	7	27	1	3	28	

*= Insignificant at 5% level of significance.

attractiveness, majority went for TV. Goodness of fit test further demonstrated that TV was considered the most attractive media by all segments of the population. Thus, TV was considered both an informative and attractive media. This may be having a reinforcing and magnifying effect on the minds of the TV audience.

CONCLUSION AND IMPLICATIONS

1. *(a)* The exposure to newspaper was almost the same irrespective of the sex of the respondents. Nearly same proportion of males and females read newspaper daily. Similar trend was found in other demographic groups also.

   (b) The results indicate that males devote more time to newspaper reading than females and therefore they are more likely to notice the advertisements Assuming that respondents who read newspapers for more than 15 minutes are bound to notice advertisements as compared to females. In the case of qualification, graduates (85%) are more likely to see advertisements when compared to undergraduates (60%) and post-graduates (57%). In case of occupation, housewives and government servants/retired persons (91%) are more likely to notice advertisements than professionals (82%) and students (65%).

2. Magazines are read by almost the same percentage of respondents irrespective of sex. Therefore, this media has greater potential for advertisements of household consumer goods.

3. *(a)* The cinema viewing habits of males and females were not found to be similar. This is a powerful media due to its distinct audio-visual characteristics, and further the audience are generally in a more receptive state of mind. Thus, advertisements are bound to be noticed. The percentage of respondents with different educational qualifications had little variances as far as movie going habit was concerned.

   (b) The effectiveness of cinema advertising depends on the frequency of visits by the audience to the cinema.

Thus, a persons who goes out to movies at least once a week is bound to be more effected by advertisements than a person who watches movies once a fortnight or once a month. But, as the movie going habit is on the decline this media may lose its attractiveness to the advertisers in future.

4. *(a)* TV emerged as the most powerful media both in terms of information content and attractiveness.

   (b) As the TV viewing habit and the time spent in watching, irrespective of sex, is on the rise, repetition of advertisements may prove to be very effective. Thus, products/services aiming at either of the sex can be placed in this media. But the advertisement aimed at professionals may not find its audience in this media as a majority of them watch TV for very less time.

5. TV emerged as the most popular media among males and females followed by magazines and cinema in providing information content.

8

A Content Analysis Study of Comparative Television Commercials

INTRODUCTION

In the era of globalization and liberalization, the consumers are faced with wide variety of products and services that can fulfill their particular needs and wants. Under this scenario, it has become essential for manufacturers of goods and services to use advertising as one of the major marketing tools to direct persuasive communications toward the target market.

In order to make the people buy the product, advertising has to create a distinct image of the brand in the minds of the consumers. This is necessary because consumers tend to make use of existing images to reduce their mental workload and actively avoid reanalyzing the message in the advertisement that they are exposed to. Therefore, an advertising message competes for space in consumer's mind, which is incessantly being showered with messages–both of commercial and non-commercial in nature.

Basically advertising can be used to build and reinforce a particular image of a specific brand against competing brands in the consumer's perceptual space. For this purpose advertisers use a number of creative techniques and different types of appeals. The relative effectiveness of these techniques and appeals depends to a great extent on the nature of competition, type of product, stage of product life cycle, type of image to be developed for a particular product and objective behind the particular advertising campaign. Advertising objectives can be classified as to whether their aim is to inform, persuade or remind. Persuasive advertising becomes important in the competitive stage, where a company's objective is to build selective demand for a particular brand. The comparative advertising is one of the image building strategies used in the category of persuasive advertising, which seeks to establish the superiority of one brand through specific comparison with one or more competing brands in the product class.

Definition of Comparative Advertising

According to Wilkie and Farris (1975) comparative advertising is a form of advertising that incorporates the two-sided approach. It is usually defined as advertising that:

1. compares two or more specifically named or recognizably presented brands of the same generic product or service class, and
2. makes such a comparison in terms of one or more specific product or service attributes.

Another definition of comparative advertising is given by McDougall (1977), which is more expressive. According to him, any advertisement that compares, implicitly or explicitly, two or more products and states or implies that information has been obtained or a test has been conducted on a competitive basis, or that states or implies a particular market standing in relation to other similar products, whether the other products are named or not.

According to this definition comparison can be done explicitly or implicitly. The explicit or strict comparative advertisement is one in which the competing brands or brands may be explicitly shown, and/or named *vis-à-vis* the advertised brand. Whereas the implied comparative advertisement is the one in which the advertised brand is compared to an ordinary brand 'X' or to all other brands, or even without any given 'X' brand.

A Brief Scenario of Comparative Advertising

It is interesting to note that even in US, prior to 1970s, comparative advertising was not used. In the intervening years, however, advertisers have experimented with this approach. One estimate is that as of 1977, in US from 7 to 25 per cent of advertising in major media was comparative in nature (McDougall, 1977). Also a study based on content analysis of television commercials in 1975, revealed that approximately 17 per cent advertisements were comparative in broad sense and 3 per cent were strictly comparative advertisements (Brown and Jackson, 1977). A similar study was conducted on magazine advertisements (Jackson, Brown and Harman, 1979), which revealed that about 1.2 per cent of the total advertisements were strictly comparative and 7 per cent were implicit comparisons. In US, comparative advertising has been widely used in such product categories as deodorants, fast food, toothpastes, tyres and automobiles.

Comparative advertising has been gaining usage and aggressiveness among advertisers in India too. Recent years have witnessed a host of products being compared both explicitly and implicitly on the basis of price, quality and other features. The reason being, firstly, the increase in number of products, especially consumer non-durables, thereby, trigerring an increase in competition leading to development of advertising consciousness among consumers. Secondly, the concept of advertising has undergone a revolutionary change with increase in professional approach, supplemented by market research, forcing dramatic improvement in the quality of advertising.

Instances of product categories where this strategy has been widely used include detergents, butter, photocopiers, mosquito repellents, two wheelers, cars, TVs, etc. One can witness more use of direct comparative advertising in the recent years particularly in case of various brands of cars (ex. Matiz), TVs (ex. Akai, Thompson, TCL, and Philips), and motorcycles (ex. Hero Honda versus TVS-Suzuki). The Nirma versus Surf campaigns for detergent powder and soap bars are examples of indirect comparative advertising.

Comparative advertising has been lauded for being more aggressive and factual in its approach. Many advertisers and consumer advocates have viewed the use of comparative advertising in recent years as a tool to educate consumers while also providing a means for creative marketing strategies (Jackson, Brown and Harman, 1979).

Several studies have examined the various aspects of comparative advertising effectiveness in relation to non-comparative advertising. They have indicated that the impact of comparative message is governed either positively or negatively by a variety of intervening factors such as advertising theme (Golden, 1979), market position of an advertised brand (Shimp and Dyer, 1978; Golden, 1979), claim substantiation (Golden, 1979), as well as prior loyalty to brands involved in comparative messages (Golden, 1979).

Wilkie and Farris (1975) were the first to hypothesise that comparative advertisements lead to increase in brand comprehension by giving consumers information in a format that provides higher potential for learning and clearer focused perceptions. They had suggested the following logical explanations in favour of comparative advertising:

Increased Attention and Recall

Comparative advertising compels the audience to pay closer attention to the advertisements due to selective exposure, selective attention and selective retention.

Increased Comprehension of Claims

Comparative advertising provides a consumer with wide variety of knowledge about the product in the process of differentiating it with other products, this increases his learning.

Greater Tendency to Yield to Claim

Comparative advertising makes possible to change consumer's perception of brands and thus help in claim substantiation.

Comparative advertising has been advocated by many other researchers also. Hackleman and Jain (1979) found the comparative format to be more effective than the non-comparative format for some shopping goods. In another study Shimp and Dyer (1979) found comparative advertising more effective for unknown brands or for brands with a relatively small market share.

Despite these opinions, most studies have not been supportive comparative advertising. For instance according to Levine (1976), some consumers find the comparative advertising more confusing and less believable. Wilson (1976) reports a study in which comparative advertising was found to be more offensive and less informative than non-comparative advertising. Also the issue of claim believability has been subject to doubt by Bodewyn and Marton (1978).

It is also considered that comparative advertising might cause information overload in recipients and lead to an effective blocking of advertisements. Since, information overload tends to occur in the presence of excessive amounts of attribute information, it would follow that too much information may reduce subject's attention and become dysfunctional. Information overload has, therefore, been another issue of importance in comparative advertising (Goodwin and Etgar, 1980). Thus, it has been found that comparative advertisement results in significantly more counter arguments and source derogation's and may result in negative attitudes to an advertised brand.

Most of the recent studies suggest that comparative messages are often thought to be more confusing and less believable than non-comparative advertisements, but their message and claim recall is greater (Jackson, Brown and Harman, 1979).

In general, studies have found that comparative advertisements are capable of exerting more positive effects on brand attitudes, purchase intentions, and purchase that non-comparative advertisements; however, comparative advertisements have also been found to reduce persuation (Rose, Miniard, Barone, Manning and Till, 1993). In another study, Muehling *et al.* (1990), using an information processing perspective on comparative advertsing, found that comparative advertisements elicited higher level of processing activity, had better recall, and were perceived as more relevant than non-comparative advertisements. Comparative advertisements were also found to outperform non-comparative advertisements when the advertised brand had a low market share or was unknown (Rose, Miniard, Barone, Manning and Till, 1994).

In contrast, in the Indian context, there is a paucity of literature on comparative advertising. N. Kinra and VSP Prasad (1990) investigated the communicative effectiveness of explicit comparative advertising *vis-à-vis* non-comparative advertising effectiveness and implied brand 'X' advertising which does not explicitly name any competitor brand. The study was based on a sample of purchase managers of photocopiers, drawn from 129 Indian organizations. Their analysis revealed that explicit comparative advertising is not as rewarding to new and unknown brands as non-comparative advertisements might be within the Indian cultural milieu.

The studies mentioned above have shown mixed emperical evidences. Some studies demonstrated the superiority of advertisements whereas others have not shown any significant difference in the effectiveness of both formats of advertising i.e. comparative and non-comparative. Yet, many advertsing practioners extoll the benefits of comparative advertsing. However, research evidence has suggeted a number of potential problems which should be addressed before launching an advertsing camapign based on comparative messages by the advertisers. These problems are given below.

1. Comparative advertisements have not been proved to be significantly more effective in increasing brand awareness.

2. Comparative advertisements may result in information overload for at least some consumer groups.

3. Comparative advertisements may encourage consumer's involvement and, as a consequence, lead to more counter arguments against the message. This can generate a so-called "boomerang" effect and depress brand attitudes ratther than generate more favourable ones. However, use of two-sided Comparative advertisements appear to reudce such counter arguments.

4. The effect of comparative advertisements may be influenced by various sources, audience, and situational conditions. For example, those loyal to the advertised brands may tend to respond more favourably than others. Also, some evidence suggests that such advertisements may be more effective for the brand that is not the present market leader (Bitta *et al.*, 1993).

Therefore, the real question is not whether competitive advertising is more or less effective, but rather under what conditions is it effective? Basically, the attributes chosen as the basis for comparison must be carefully researched and the claims made must be capable of substantiation.

OBJECTIVES OF THE STUDY

Although, a substantial number of studies have been conducted regarding the effectiveness of comparative advertising in other countries, only little research exists in the Indian context. Therefore, the present study is an attempt to determine the frequency and the nature of comparative advertising, with reference to TV commercials in India.

The main objectives of the study were:

1. To find out the extent of comparative advertising in one of the major advertising media i.e. television.
2. To find out the frequency of comparative advertising in television commercials with respect to type of product.
3. To find out the nature of comparative advertising i.e. implicit and explicit.
4. To find out the extent to which comparative advertising is done with respect to duration of the television advertisement.
5. To find out the extent to which a particular comparative advantage is being stressed in the comparative advertisements with respect to type of products.
6. To find out the extent to which a particular number of brands being compared against the advertised brand, and with respect to type of product.
7. To find out the extent to which a particular method of comparative advertising presentation was being used for depicting comparison with respect to a particular comparative advantage stressed and type of product.

METHODOLOGY

Selection of Television Commercials

For the present study, the data has been generated from the commercials that were telecast on various TV channels including Doordarshan over a two-week period in the month of February 1996. All the commercials during this period were recorded on videocassette. Care was taken to avoid duplications and some of the advertisements such as that for Indian tourism, conferences and exhibitions etc. were excluded, as they were irrelevant for the present study.

Data Collection Procedure

Data were collected from these advertisements through the use of a content analysis (see exhibit 1). This proforma was designed to collect maximum information regarding each advertisement required for the study. In all, 400 TV commercials were assessed. In developing the database the following definitions were used:

(a) *Comparative Advertisements:* Any advertisement/commercial that compares, implicitly or explicitly, two or more competing brands and states or implies that information has been obtained or a test has been conducted on a comparative basis, or that states or implies a particular market standing in relation to other similar products, whether the other products are named or not.

(b) *Explicit/Strictly Comparative Advertisement:* Any comparative advertisement that explicitly names/shows two or more competing brands.

(c) *Implicit Comparative Advertisements:* Any comparative advertisement that is not judged to be strictly comparative i.e. that does not name or show the competing brands, but compares a product to any ordinary brand 'X' or implies the comparison without giving 'X' brand.

The content analysis has been used previously in consumer and advertising research. Kassarjian (1977) has recommended these types of studies in consumer and advertising research to investigate the communication methods being used by advertisers and marketers. It is appropriate both for longitudinal and cross sectional studies such as this one. By examining the advertisements on the basis of content analysis, relevant database was generated. Though, much care has been taken to maximize the reliability of the database, yet, there is a possibility of observer bias. To increase the reliability and to test the clarity of the definitions as well as the observer's ability to follow the instructions, an independent observer also assessed the advertisements. Finally, only those advertisements were considered and included in the database for the present study on which there was unanimity between the researcher and the independent observer.

ANALYSIS AND FINDINGS

After collecting the information regarding each of the 400 advertisements, a detailed content analysis was undertaken. The data were transferred on a master sheet. Then it has been tabulated and cross tabulated and a detailed percentage analysis was performed. No advance inferential statistical technique was used as the purpose for the present study was exploratory. The analysis for the present study was performed in the following manner:

Comparative and Non-Comparative Advertisements

Table 8.1 reports on the number of comparative and non-comparative advertisements with respect to the total TV advertisements studied and indicates their respective percentages. As evident from Table 8.1, vast majority of messages were non-comparative i.e. almost 92.5%. Only about 7.5% of total advertisements telecast during the study period, were comparative in nature. This includes both the strictly comparative as well as implied ones. When more restrictive definition of comparative advertising was employed it was found that there was no advertisement using the explicit comparison i.e. naming or showing the competing brands against the advertised brand. Thus, all the 30 comparative advertisements studied were of implied nature either with brand 'X' or without brand 'X'.

Table 8.1
Comparative Versus Non-Comparative Television Advertising

Nature of Advertisements	*No. of Advertisements*	*% of Total Advertisements*
Explicitly Comparative	0	0
Implicitly Comparative	30	7.5
Non-Comparative	370	92.5
Total	400	100

Table 8.2 clearly indicates that the use of comparative advertising was more popular in the case of Fast Moving Consumer Goods (FMCGs) and durables, whereas, in the other two categories i.e. industrial goods and services, comparative advertising was conspicuous by its absence. One of the possible reasons for the popularity of comparative advertising in the consumer goods category *vis-a-vis* the other goods may be due to the high level of competition and brand proliferation.

Exhibit 1—Content Analysis Proforma

(1) Name of the Product advertised

(2) Type product :

(a) Non-durable ( ) *(b)* Durable ( )

(c) Industrial Product ( ) *(d)* Services ( )

(3) Duration of the advertisement:

(a) < 10 seconds ( ) *(b)* 10-20 seconds ( )

(c) > 20 seconds ( )

(4) Nature of Advertisement :

(a) Comparative ( ) *(b)* Non-comparative ( )

(5) Nature of comparison:

(a) Comparison name/shown ( )

(b) Comparison implied by 'X' brand given ( )

(c) Comparison implied without given 'X' brand ( )

(6) Comparative Advantage stressed :

(a) Price ( ) *(b)* quality ( )

(c) features ( ) *(d)* any other specify ( )

(7) Number of brands compared

(a) One ( ) *(b)* two ( )

(c) three or more ( ) *(d)* implied all ( )

(8) Method of comparative advertising presentation used :

(a) opening statement ( ) *(b)* demonstration ( )

(c) body ( ) *(d)* concluding statement ( )

Table 8.2

Comparative Advertising and Product Type

Type of Product	*Nature of Advertisements*				*Total*
	Comparative		*Non-Comparative*		
	No.	*%*	*No.*	*%*	
FMCG Goods	24(6)	8.14	271(67.75)	91.86	295
Consumer Durable	6(1.5)	6.98	80(20)	93.02	86
Industrial	0	0	8(2)	100	8
Services	0	0	11(2.75)	100	11

Note: Figures in the parenthesis are percentages to grand total.

In Table 8.3, the analysis is restricted to comparative advertisements only. This table indicates very clearly that the comparative advertisements are of implicit nature only, either the comparison was made with the brand 'X' or without brand 'X'. The majority of TV commercials which were analysed here belonged to implied comparison category with brand 'X' i.e. 66% and the remaining advertisements i.e. 33% were compared without any brand 'X'. It seems that advertisers are generally hesitant to show or name the competitor. This may be because of two reasons. Either they may not be able to substantiate their claims *vis-à-vis* the main competitor's brand or they may be avoiding an advertising battle of claims and counter claims.

Table 8.3
Nature of Comparative Advertisements

Nature of Comparison	*Number of Advertisement*	*%*
Strict or Explicit comparison	0	0
Implied Comparison	30	100.00
(a) With Brand 'X'	20	66.60
(b) Without Brand 'X'	10	33.33

Comparative Advertisements and Comparative Advantage Stressed

In Table 8.4, the information about the comparative advertisements was classified in terms of the type of comparative advantage being stressed. This table clearly shows that quality is the primary basis for comparison followed by features and price. Even when this was further analyzed in terms of product categories, the same trend continued. In case of FMCGs, quality was found to be the modal reason of comparison while in case of durables features were highlighted. This is quite logical in the sense that the feature can be easily ascertained by the consumers on the one hand and they can easily be sustained by the marketers. Quality being intangible in nature and having many dimensions can not be ascertained easily in the short run. Therefore, quality, it seems does not find favour in making comparisons by the advertiser and marketers alike. In case of durables price is not of much use as the basis of comparison because consumers generally relate price with quality. In consumers' perception quality and price are directly proportional to each other as far as durables are concerned. However, in case of FMCGs price is more determining factor, particularly, in case of price sensitive consumers.

Table 8.4
Comparative Advantage and Type of Product

Type of Product	*Comparative Advantage*								*Total*
	Price		*Quality*		*Features*		*Both Price & Quality*		
	No	*%*	*No.*	*%*	*No.*	*%*	*No.*	*%*	
FMCGs	1	4.2	15	63	6	25	2	8.3	24
Consumer Durables	0	0	1	16.6	4	66.7	1	16.7	6
Total	1	3.33	16	53	10	33.3	3	10	30

Type of Product and Number of Brands Compared

Another dimension of the study examined the number of products compared in the comparative advertisements. The results compiled in Table 8. 5 clearly show that the modal type of comparison in the various comparative advertisements was with one brand only. This was followed by 'implied all' i.e. 33.3%. Making comparisons with two or three brands simultaneously did not find favour with the advertisers. The advertisements in which two and three brands were compared simultaneously comprised 26% and 16% of the total advertisements respectively.

Table 8.5
Number of Brands Compared and Type of Product

Type of Product	*Number of Competing Brands*								*Total*
	One		*Two*		*Three or More*		*Implied All*		
	No.	*%*	*No.*	*%*	*No.*	*%*	*No.*	*%*	
FMCGs	11	45.8	1	4.2	3	12.5	9	37.5	24
Durables	2	33.3	1	17	2	33.3	1	16.6	6
Total	12	43.3	2	27	5	16.7	16.67	33.3	30

The final aspect of comparative advertising which was analysed related to mode of presentation and the comparative advantage stressed for the purpose of comparison. The findings are arranged in Table 8.6. It is quite evident from this table that in more than half of the advertisements (53.4%), comparison was through the body of the message i.e. through songs and dialogues. Advertisers of both FMCGs and durables, extensively used this method for comparison through demonstration technique (30%). Rarely the comparisons were made in the opening or concluding statements.

Table 8.6
Type of product and Method of Comparative Advertising Presentation

Type of Product	*Number of Competing Brands*								*Total*
	Opening Statement		*Demonstration*		*Body*		*Concluding Statement*		
	No.	*%*	*No.*	*%*	*No.*	*%*	*No.*	*%*	
FMCGs	3	12.5	7	29	13	54.2	1	4.16	24
Durables	0	0	2	33	3	50	1	16.7	6
Total	3	10	9	30	16	53.3	2	6.7	30

CONCLUSIONS

The various conclusions that can be drawn from the study are as follows:

1. In India, comparative advertising strategy is not very popular among the advertisers. However, in case of television commercials, lately, there has been a sharp rise in the use of comparative commercials.
2. The study demonstrated that the advertisers prefer to use implied comparison rather than boldly naming/showing the specific competing brands in the television commercials. Also, the implied comparisons with brand "X" are more popular than without brand "X" comparison.
3. Product-wise analysis showed that comparative advertising is not popular in case of industrial goods and services, whereas, it is used frequently by the marketers of FMCGs such as detergents, soaps, bars, tea, tooth paste, oils etc., and consumer durables such as refrigerators, automobiles, and televisions.
4. Quality of products is widely used for comparison is case of FMCGs, while features form the primary basis for comparison in case of durables. Price in comparison to

quality and features did not find favour with the advertisers as the basis of comparison.

5. Most of the comparisons were made against one brand in case of FMCGs. The comparison with all the competing brands was the second most popular technique.
6. Most of the comparative advertisements use *body copy* for comparison. This was equally popular among FMCGs and in durables. For showing the comparative advantages in terms of price and features, advertisers were found to employ demonstration techniques.

SUGGESTIONS

The following suggestions may help in the effective use of comparative advertising:

1. If an advertiser feels that his brand is substantially superior to other similar brands in the market, with respect to price, quality, features, or any other factor and if this advantage can be verified by the consumer, then it is better to explicitly compare his brand with the competitor's brand.
2. It seems, in India advertisers are hesitant to use direct comparisons as they fear this may lead to unnecessary advertising wars. But boldness helps in comparative advertising as it may enable the consumers, if they believe in the advertisement, in choosing the specific brand.
3. Advertisers must refrain from attacking the competition without any substantial competitive advantage. They must try to incorporate authentic and adequate information about the brand.
4. Advertisers must compare related or similar attributes of the brands, whenever possible, by side-by-side demonstration. The attribute being compared should be significant in terms of value or usefulness to the consumers.
5. While using comparative messages, marketers should avoid exaggeration or puffery, and the comparison should be based on undeniable facts that are measurable and significant.

REFERENCES

Bitta Albert J. Della, Monroe Kent B., and McGinnis John M. (1981), "Consumer Perceptions of Comparative Price Advertisements", *Journal of Marketing Research*, Vol. 18, pp. 416-427

Bodewyn, J.J. and Marton Katherin (1978), *Comparison Advertising: A Worldwide Study*, NY: Hasting House.

Brown Stephen W. and Jackson Donald W., Jr. (1977), "Comparative Television Advertising: Examining Its Nature and Frequency", *Journal of Advertising*, Vol. 6, No. 4, pp. 15-18.

Golden, Linda L. (1979), "Consumer Reactions to Comparative Advertising", In B. B. Anderson (Ed.) *Advances in Consumer Research*, Vol 3, Atlanta: Association for Consumer Research.

Goodwin Stephen and Etgar Michael (1980), "An Experimental Investigation of Comparative Advertising: Impact of Message Appeal, Information Load, and Utility of Product Class", *Journal of Marketing Research*, Vol. 17, pp. 187-203.

Jackson D. W., Brown Stephen W. and Harmon R. Robert (1979), "Comparative Magazine Advertisements", *Journal of Advertising Research*, Vol. 19, No. 6, pp. 21-26.

Jain, Subhash C. and Hackleman Edwin C. (1978), "How Effective is Comparative Advertising for Stimulating Brand Recall?" *Journal of Advertising*, Vol. 7, No.3, pp. 20-25.

Levine Philip (1976), "Commercials That Name Competing Brands", *Journal of Advertising Research*, Vol. 16, No.6, pp. 7-14.

McDougall Gordon H. G. (1977), "Comparative Advertising: Consumer Issues and Attitudes", In Barnett A. Greenberg and Danny N. Bellenger (Eds.) *Contemporary Marketing Thought: 1977 Educators' Proceedings*, Chicago: American Marketing Association.

Muehling Darrel D., Jeffrey J. Stoltman, and Sanford Grossbart (1990), "The Impact of Comparative Advertising on Levels of Message Involvement," *Journal of Advertising*, 19 (December), 41-50.

Rose Randall L., Miniard Paul W., Barone Michael J., Manning Kenneth C. and Till Brian D. (1993), "When Persuasion Goes Undetected: The Case of Comparative Advertising," *Journal of Marketing Research*, 30 (August), 315-330.

Rose, Randall L., Miniard Paul W., Barone Michael J., Manning Kenneth C. and Till Brian D. (1993), "When Persuasion Goes Undetected: The Case of Comparative Advertising," *Journal of Marketing Research*, 30 (August), 315-330.

Shimp A. T. and Dyer D. C. (1978), "The Effects of Comparative Advertising Mediated by Market Position of Sponsoring Brand", *Journal of Advertising*, Vol 3, pp. 13-19.

Wilkie L. William and Farris P. (1975), "Comparative Advertising: Problems and Potential", *Journal of Marketing,* 39, pp. 7-15.

Wilson R. D. (1976), "An Empirical Evaluation of Comparative Advertising Messages: Subjects' Responses on Perceptual Dimensions", In B. B. Anderson (Ed.), *Advances in Consumer Research,* Vol. 3, Atlanta: Association for Consumer Research.

9

The Role of Financial Advertising in Influencing Investment Decisions

STATUS OF FINANCIAL ADVERTISING

Financial advertising is a specialised type of advertising whose main objective is to attract the potential and existing investors and it is carried out for the purpose of promoting different financial instruments. These instruments include new issues of equity shares, preference shares, debentures, convertible debentures, saving schemes, units etc. Financial advertising is also known as public issue advertising. However, public issue advertising is relatively narrower in scope as compared to financial advertising. Usually, companies resort to corporate or institutional advertising before releasing a financial advertisement but this is not a norm. It is distinct from corporate advertising. Financial advertising deals with the promotion of a specific financial instrument whereas the institutional/corporate advertising's main aim is to build corporate image (Ogilvy, 1983).

Financial advertising is more or less akin to the product/service advertising but with one difference. Here the company promotes a specific financial instrument for raising funds and tries to use its image as one of the factors of influence. In case of brand advertising the target market comprises some customer groups whereas in financial advertising the target market comprises both potential and present investors. Another factor, which makes financial advertising somewhat different from other forms of advertising, is the time factor. Financial instruments have to be marketed within a specified period, usually a fortnight, unlike consumer goods or industrial products, which can be sold over an indefinite period.

With the increased attention and vigor in the marketing of new issues, financial advertising is today considered to be the fastest growing segment in the advertising business. Though, the share of financial advertising is relatively small as compared to the total advertising expenditure, yet, it is expected to grow substantially in future. In 1990, the share of financial advertising to the press advertising was 8.9 percent (Rao, 1991). The value of capital issues approved is increasing with a fast pace. In 1985 it was Rs. 2,579 Crores, rising substantially to Rs. 6,168 Crores in 1986 and was around Rs. 12,000 Crores in 1988. In 1993-94 the release of 1,149 issues led to the raising of funds to the tune of Rs. 22,000 Crores, nearly a 300 percent as compared to 1991-92 (Annuncio, 1994). During 1988 over Rs. 45 Crores were spent on financial advertising out of which Rs. 25 Crores were reported to have been shared between two agencies Pressman and Shobhagya. In 1989, financial advertising touched the figure of Rs. 120 Crores and major part of it was spent on new issue advertisements (Pervez, 1991). In the new millinium the financial advertising has crossed the figure of Rs. 500 Crores. A new dimension, which has been added in the recent years to the marketing of public issues, is that foreign institutional investors, mutual funds and corporate bodies have been permitted to invest in the Indian market causing a huge influx of funds. This development is bound to have far reaching implications.

Financial advertising in India dates back to 1960's. Pressman Advertising and Marketing Pvt. Ltd., a pioneer in this business, was established in 1964. A mini boom in the stock market was experienced in the late 1960's by Indian firms, when owing to FERA, a number of foreign companies had to dilute their equity base. This was particularly true with the pharmaceutical companies. So the ground for the active market was laid then. The real boom in the stock market came in 1985-86 which changed the entire industrial scene dramatically, with the economic liberalisation and broadbanding of industries, large number of companies went public. This resulted in launching of mega issues running into hundreds of crores of rupees. To cater to this growing market a number of advertising agencies entered this field. Initially, there were only two or three agencies who captured a sizable market share. However, with the increase in the financial advertising several larger advertising agencies also made considerable investments in setting up separate financial or corporate advertising cells. The top five agencies in financial advertising are Shobhagya Advertising Services, Pressman Advertising and Marketing Private Ltd., Clea Advertising, Imaads and Concept Communication Private Ltd. Between Shobhagya and Pressman there is an undeclared war of supremacy. In 1988 Shobhagya was on top followed by Pressman and Clea. In 1990 Pressman snatched the number one spot in financial advertising from Shobhagya and still retains its position as the largest financial advertising agency. The financial advertising agencies in the early 90s were the hottest acts in the town, however, due to recession there growth has been considerably slowed down (Jyothi, 1997).

The success of public issues, particularly from the new and lesser known companies is very important and depends largely on how these issues are promoted to the potential investors. This is largely a specialised function. Those agencies that specialised early got the stronghold in this field and those who entered the field later had to face lot of difficulties. Even bigger and established agencies, which entered later, failed to attain a respectable share of this business. Some agencies had to close down their financial advertising cells. The basic reason for their failure was lack of specialisation and expertise. A financial advertising agency is expected to render the following specialised services:

- Organising the printing of prospectus and application forms in a stipulated time schedule at a reasonable price.
- To organise the distribution of prospectus and application forms to at least eight important share markets located in the four regions of the country.
- Planning the media schedule advertising mix and submitting estimates for pre-launch, launch and post-launch advertising supported by creative visuals highlighting the strengths of the issue and also a corporate image building campaign if needed.
- To hold press conference at all important business centres and ensure proper press coverage.
- To organise broker conference at all important stock exchange centres and to prepare suitable publicity material concerning the issue.

- To organise advertising in overseas media in order to attract NRI investors.

In order to carry out these activities, the agency's task involves a significant creative element. And that makes the job rather tough since financial advertisements have to carry voluminous mandatory copy mentioning issue highlights, risk factors, names of promoters, registrars, plus the statutory warnings and conditions. These occupy a lot of space. Therefore, the financial advertising needs the creativity of the highest order, strategic planning, the right media options, and brand building activity similar to product advertising.

Among the various media available for financial advertising, the print media is considered to be most effective which accounts for almost 65 per cent of most advertising budgets. Till late 80s, print media was the only major medium available to the private sector companies for promoting their public issues. It was in April 1989 that television was thrown open to private sector companies for launching of public issues. Previously, only public sector companies were allowed to use television for marketing of new issues, bonds and debentures. This was announced in a Doordarshan circular which stated that it will accept advertisements relating to new public issues of shares/bonds/debentures by private companies. According to a government guideline, the cost of public issue advertising has to be kept within 5 percent of the issue amount. This figure of five percent includes not only the cost of advertising and publicity but also fees to merchant bankers, underwriters and brokers. After paying these fees, one to one and a half percent is left for advertising.

There was a mixed reaction to this in the industry circles and particularly among agencies. Some criticised the requirement of 5 percent of the issue amount as unrealistic. They were of the opinion that only companies making large capital issues would be able to afford to advertising on television. Only issues of Rs. 100 Crore and above with advertising budget exceeding Rs. 1.5 Crore will find adequate residual budgets to advertise on television. Companies with smaller public issues will have to restrict themselves to print and other media, while companies with larger issues will have the additional option of using television commercials as a powerful tool to raise money in the capital markets (Taneja, 1989). The use of television is bound to bring major changes in the advertising expenditures. Through this medium one can reach great many potential investors who have not yet been tapped–particularly in smaller towns and semi-urban areas.

A major problem that is faced by the agencies is related to "cluttering". In the recent years this has become a major problem as far as TV media planning is concerned. Cluttering refers to the screening of large number of advertisements in a short duration. High level of cluttering is considered to be detrimental for attention and recall (Bhasker, 1990). There are two major effects of cluttering on advertising. Firstly, cluttering decreases the noticeability and recall substantially and, secondly, it also decreases the advertising effectiveness (Pillai, 1990). cluttering in case of financial advertising takes two forms. First type occurs whenever there is a boom in the capital market and large number of companies come out with public issues. This may lead to overcrowding in the capital market, which can not be really avoided because every company wants a share in the cake when the going is good. The second type of cluttering occurs when a mega issue is launched and all the smaller issues have to be postponed for the time being. But, when the mega issue is closed, they all come in the market, at the same time, in a bunch. There is no proper spacing among the different issues and consequently, this may lead to under subscription. The stringent regulations set by the SEBI pose another problem for the advertising agencies dealing with financial advertising. Agencies cannot go for fancy copy, or use adjectives, or visual element which may attract the wrath of SEBI and distract potential investors. They have to concentrate more on presentation of facts.

With the boom in stock market in the early 90s, financial advertising was considered a burgeoning area with a promising future. Another change that one could easily notice was the changing investor profile. Issue culture had come to the middle class. Today's middle class investor is more frequently exposed to the happenings in foreign markets through satellite TV channels (Annuncio, 1994). A new breed of investors comprising middle and low income groups, salaried class, young professionals and even students are increasingly going in for investing in the public issues. New media, including the Internet, are expected to be increasingly used. Many financial institutions such as ICICI have launched their web sites to entice the modern day investor. The future holds new opportunities and challenges for financial advertising. Therefore, it is imperative for the agencies to become more creative and competitive in order to effectively promote and market the public issues to the prospective investors. However, one advertising professional criticised the financial advertising in the following words "Unfortunately, most financial advertising in the country has so far been unspectacular. Memorable campaigns are still few and far between" (Pervez, 1991). The need of the hour is in creating better and memorable advertisements that will distinguish them from those of their competitors. This is particularly difficult when the financial instruments on offer are very similar.

One of the most important characteristics regarding these advertisements is that the investor should get all facts. It is imperative to give potential investors all possible information that might be useful to them. And convey it in language that the target can easily understand. This means financial advertisement must be concrete, specific and down to earth. One error, which many agencies commit, is the belief that long copy does not get read. All the evidence points to the contrary. A person who wants to invest money will read every word of the copy. It is an obvious fact that one has to develop an atmosphere of trust to persuade the people to part with their savings. People will never invest their hard earned money in a company, which they do not trust. Financial advertising must build on a company's image.

THE OBJECTIVES OF THE STUDY

Since financial advertising requires special skills to render services specific to the client's requirements, there is a strong need to explore and investigate its impact on the potential investors. The success of a public issue, apart from other things, largely depends how effectively a financial advertisement influences the investing public. More specifically, this study pursues the following objectives:

- To identify the sources of information utilised by investors for obtaining information about different companies which enter the capital market with their equity issues.
- To find out in which type of companies investors are more likely to purchase shares.
- To measure the relative weightage or importance given to different information sources by investors in share subscription.
- To find out the relative importance attached by investors to the different aspects or characteristics of the company

given in the advertisement.

RESEARCH DESIGN

To accomplish the above mentioned objectives this study was designed to gather information from those who invest their money in different companies' equity shares. A structured questionnaire was designed keeping in mind the research objectives.

Respondents were selected from Delhi. Sampling was carried out at two stages. In the first stage, from the Delhi Stock Exchange, a list of authorised brokers was obtained and five brokers were selected randomly – one from each parliamentary constituency. In the second stage these brokers were contacted and from them names and addresses of regular investors were obtained. From the list obtained from the stock exchange brokers, the names of 60 investors from each constituency were selected on a random basis and they were first contacted through telephone. Those who agreed to participate and cooperate with the study were later contacted personally. The questionnaire was administered personally. In this way, data were obtained from two hundred and forty respondents. The profile of the respondents in terms of experience and income is given in Table 9.1. The decision to categorise the investors on the basis of years of experience was taken on the assumption that experienced investors exhibit different investment behavior than those who have less experience in stock investment.

Table 9.1
Profile of Respondents

		No.	%
Experience	Less than 5 years	112	46.66
	More than 5 years	128	53.34
Income per month	Less than Rs. 4500	70	29.16
	Rs. 4501 to Rs. 6000	120	50.00
	Rs. 6001 and above	50	28.84
Total		240	100

ANALYSIS AND INTERPRETATION

Sources of Information

Respondents were asked to indicate the sources from which they get information about various companies. For this purpose a close-ended question was framed and they were provided four sources of information namely, friends and relatives, financial advertisements, brokers and company sources. The respondents were then asked to tick the source/s from which they usually come to know about a new equity issue.

The responses were cross-tabulated and are presented in Table 9.2. This table shows the investing experience and sources of information as independent and dependent variables respectively. It is clearly evident from this Table that out of the four information sources, financial advertisements were the most frequent used source by both categories of investors. More than three fourth (75.5 per cent) investors upto five years category use financial advertisements to get information about the new equity issues. The percentage of experienced investors is slightly less (62.7 per cent) as far as using financial advertisements is concerned. This variation may be due to chance factor or it may be that experienced investors get information from other sources. In case of less experienced or new investors financial advertisements assume greater importance.

Second important source for both the categories of investors is stockbroker. Brokers usually send literature and information regarding different issues to the regular subscribers on a periodic basis whenever a company enters capital market. Therefore, it seems that investors having considerable experience in investment utilise this source more often (23.9 per cent) than those who have less than 5 years experience in investments (11.3 per cent).

It is surprising to note that new investors seek advice and guidance from friends and relatives for purchase of shares. This is understandable because being relatively inexperienced they may feel a bit insecure before they purchase shares and, therefore, they try to reduce their pre-purchase dissonance by taking advice from friends who might be having more experience in share dealings. This is not the case with experienced investors (having more than 5 years experience) as far as purchase of shares is concerned. Not a single investor in this category had mentioned friends and relatives as a source of information. Another finding, which can be deduced from the Table, is that no investor in the less than five years category uses company sources, such as company executives, employees or top management, as a source of information. However, experienced investors seem to have more access to the company sources and 13.4 per cent of them mentioned that they get information about the forthcoming capital issues from this source. This may happen because, they may develop personal relations and contacts with the company people on account of their prior experience.

Table 9.2

Investing Experience and Information Sources

Sources	*Experience*				*Total*
	< 5 Years		*> 5 Years*		
	No.	*%*	*No.*	*%*	
Friends & Relatives	16	62	10	38	26
Financial Ads.	82	49	84	51	166
Brokers	14	32	30	68	44
Company Sources	0	0	14	100	14
Total	112	47	128	53	240

Respondents were also asked to indicate the type of company in which they would prefer to invest in equity share. Three types of companies were mentioned to them, namely, companies with proven track records, multi-product companies and companies launching new products. Both categories of investors preferred to invest in those companies with proven track record i.e. 78 per cent. Multi-products companies came second with 14 per cent of investors and only 8 per cent investors wanted to invest in those companies who are launching new products in the market.

Relative Weightage to Information Sources

The second important research objective of this study was to find out the relative weightage given to five information sources by investors before they make a decision to purchase shares. For this purpose investors were asked to rate five information sources, in order of importance. These five sources were friends and relatives, financial advertisement stock brokers and agents, company sources and press reporting and review. Respondents were requested to assign numbers for each of the five sources according to their importance. '1' stood for 'most important', '2' for somewhat important', '3' for 'neither important nor unimportant'. The raw scores of respondents were converted into composite mean scores by adding the scores of all respondents and then dividing by number of respondents in each category. Again the category of investors was considered to be independent variable and the relative importance to each source as dependent variable. The data were cross tabulated according to the type of investors and importance mean of each information source are given in Table 9.3. Examining Table 9.3 one can easily discern that of all the five sources of information, press reportings and reviews were given top ranking by both types of investors. This clearly demonstrates that press reportings and reviews (publicity) command highest credibility in the eyes of investors as far as subscribing the shares of a particular company is concerned. This is understandable because press reviews and coverage comes under publicity and publicity is considered to carry maximum credibility among the four elements of marketing mix. This is because press reviews published by independent media are considered relatively unbiased and less subjective. However, the utility of press reviews is somewhat limited because press does not give much coverage to the equity issues of small, or medium sized and newly established companies.

Next most important source after press reviews is financial advertisements published on behalf of the issuing companies in newspapers and magazines. No significant difference was found when the mean score of both type of investors was tested using 't' distribution. The difference between the scores of press reviews and financial advertising was also not found significant. This shows that financial advertisements are as important as press reviews for both types of investors. Company sources occupy the third place after press reviews and financial advertising. When 't' test was applied to find out any significant difference between two types of investor it was found to be significant. Though, friends and relatives occupy the bottom position for both the investors, yet, less experienced investors give more importance to this source and this was found to be significant at 5 per cent level.

Table 9.3
Relative Importance Weightages of Information Sources

	Less than 5 years		*More than 5 years*	
Sources	*Mean*	*Rank*	*Mean*	*Rank*
Friends & Relatives	3.31	V	4.35*	V
Financial Advertisements	2.04	II	2.1	II
Brokers	2.45	III	2.18*	III
Company Sources	3.22	IV	2.65*	IV
Press Reviews	1.95	I	1.92	I

Note : 1. Rating was done on a five point scale, "1" for "most important", and "5" for "least important".
2. * = Significant at p = 0.05 of "t" values.

Company Highlights

Almost every financial advertisement displays different aspects related to the issuing company's performance with a sub-heading "Highlights". After content analysis of a number of financial advertisements eight aspects were delineated. These are as follows:

1. Continuous dividend paying company.
2. High dividend paying company.
3. Excellent track record.
4. Tax benefits.
5. Foreign collaboration.
6. Export oriented company.
7. Easy liquidity.
8. Company managed by professionals.

Respondents were first asked whether they go through the highlights of the company given in the advertisement or not. Only 4 per cent said that they do not go through it, whereas, an overwhelming 96 per cent gave their answers in affirmative. Next, they were asked to rate the above eight aspects given in the highlights according to their importance on a five-point scale ranging from "highly important" to "least important". They had to assign '1' for 'highly important' and '5' for 'least important'. Mean score for each aspect was calculated. The mean scores and ranking of eight aspects are shown in Table 9.4. Higher rank is associated with lower mean and vice versa.

Table 9.4

Relative Weightage to Different Aspects of Highlights

	Less than 5 years		*More than 5 years*	
Sources	*Mean*	*Rank*	*Mean*	*Rank*
Continuous Dividend Paying Company	2.10	IV	2.45	V
High Dividend Paying Company	1.95	III	2.41	IV
Excellent Track Record	1.63	I	1.33*	I
Tax Benefits	3.00	VIII	2.98	VII
Foreign Collaborations	2.77	VII	3.08	VIII
Export Oriented Company	2.68	VI	2.48	VI
Easy Liquidity	1.68	II	1.34*	II
Company Managed by Professionals	2.40	V	2.08*	III

Note : 1. Rating was done on a five point scale, "1" for "most important", and "5" for 'least important"
2. * = Significant at p = 0.05 of "t" values

Perusing Table 9.4 one can find that the importance given to different aspects of the company are more or less the same for both types of investors. A company's track record is considered the barometer of performance whenever a firm is evaluated. This is also true as far as the investors are concerned. Track record stood as the first rank aspect of company from the point of view of the both types of investors. However, it can be safely surmised that experienced investors give more weightage to the company's track record and this was found statistically significant too. Close to track record was easy liquidity. This was followed by company managed by professionals in case of experienced investors and high dividend paying company by less experienced investors. Medium importance was given to continuous dividend paying companies. Export oriented company, foreign collaboration and tax benefits were considered least important by both types of investors.

CONCLUSIONS

Summary of Results

The results indicated that out of the four sources of information maximum number of investors (70%) use financial advertisements for equity issues. The other three sources i.e. company sources, friends and relatives and stock brokers were used by just over one fourth of the investors.

As far as relative weightage given to different sources is concerned, press reviews and financial advertisements were given maximum importance. Because press reviews are not completely under the control of the company their utility is quite restricted. This is not the case with financial advertisements. These can be pretested, before they are launched, to maximise their impact. Financial advertisements must build on a company's image. These advertisements should be memorable and convincing if they are to have any impact on prospective investors. Other sources are less important on the one hand and less exploitable by the company on the other.

Highlights of the issuing company are the most important ingredient of an advertisement. Whenever a company has proven track record, it should be given maximum prominence in the financial advertisement. Nothing is important for the subscriber than the company's track record. The actual sale of a financial instrument depends to a great extent on the trust. Trust of the investors can be established only when a financial advertisement can bring all the relevant facts before them. High liquidity is also highly important aspect. Companies should increase the liquidity of shares and other financial instruments and mention this fact in their financial advertisements.

Future Directions

The present study represents an initial exploration of investing behavior and impact of financial advertisements on prospective equity subscribers. The results suggest that the investors give significant importance to financial advertisements before making an investment decision. However, it should be noted that the procedures employed in the present study represent one of the possible approaches in investigating investment behavior and impact of financial advertisements. The same can also be assessed by using an experiment where different copy approaches are manipulated to see the effect on investors. Instead of ex-post-facto research, as the present one, an experimental research can also be used. This will enable the agencies in improving their advertisements considerably before they are placed in a specific media vehicle.

It should also be noted that the present results are the outcome of an exploratory research work. If the reliability is to be increased the present research design can be improved further. Sampling procedures can be improved to increase the reliability and then the generalisations can be made with more confidence.

Finally, this type of research can be undertaken by the business organisations who frequently resort to public issue of their equity shares or by independent research agencies which may provide useful information obtained by this type of exercise to the interested business organisations on payment basis. Advertising agencies, which specialise in financial advertising, should commission these type of studies on a regular basis. Apart from being advantagious from the client's point of view, this would also immensly benificial to the creative team in the prepation ofdeveloping advertising campaigns.

REFERENCES

Anriuncio Charubala, (1994), "Marketing Public Issues", *Advertising and Marketing,* (June), pp. 27-31.

Balsara Pervez, (1991), "The Fundamentals of Financial. Ads", *The Economics Times*, June, 11, p. 5.

Bhasker S. Iyer (1990), "Clutter: Seen But not Heard", *'Advertising And Marketing,* pp. 54-56.

Jyothi, P. T. (1997), "Financila Advertising Agencies Down But Not Out", *The Financial Express, June 16.*

Kotler, Philip (2000), *Marketing Management: Analysis, Planning, Implementation , and Control*, 10th ed. New Delhi, Prentice-Hall India Ltd.

Ogilvy, David (1983), *Ogilvy on Advertising*, London: Multimedia Publications.

Pillai Shanker (1990). "Impact of Clutter on Advertising Viewership and Recall", *Solus*, October, pp. 12-13.

Rao, N.Bhaskara, (1991). "The Media 1990: Ups and Downs", *Advertising and Marketing*, April, pp. 46-51.

Taneja Shiv, (1989). "TV Commercials: Detergents to Debentures", *Business India*, May, p. 25.

10

Selling Appeals, Demonstration Techniques and Basic Approaches Used in Audio Visuals

INTRODUCTION

Audiovisuals commonly refer to all those advertisements which combine sight, motion and sounds. Audiovisuals are used in three advertising media, namely, cinema, television and video, and have assumed great importance because of their increased use in Indian advertising. Prior to the emergence of television as one of the major media, audiovisuals were mainly used in cinema. But with phenomenal growth of television audiovisuals are now being produced mainly for television and are popularly called advertisement films. However, these are also being used in cinema and video advertising because of common production process.

Making of an Audiovisual

Making an audiovisual is a challenge, because, in brief 30 seconds one has to put everything in it i.e. try to mould people's behaviour, attempt to change their habits and alter life styles in order to sell the advertised brand. In doing so one has to keep in mind two important points. Firstly, the script should be written according to the characteristics of target audience, and secondly, the type of response sought from them. Making a good television commercial requires four things. Suresh Mulick, creative director of the then OBM, said, "you have to have a good client, a good product, a good script (agency) and a good producer" (Vatsayana, 1987).

An element of prime importance in the making of an audiovisual is the client–a company which wants to sell its product. It now depends entirely on the advertising agency to devise a campaign and the script for the television commercial. Earlier, the job of writing the script was handed over to the producer, but now this important task is handled by the agency itself. This is important because it is the agency which researches, devises, and launches a campaign in all the major media. Therefore, it is appropriate that creative people in the agency should write the script because the message should be in harmony with the objective of the campaign.

After the script is written, the advertising agency contacts a producer. In the selection of a producer a great deal of significance is attached to his reputation in industry and his standing with agency. Schedule is the most important aspect of making an advertisement film. Indeed, the first thing that a producer is asked to do is to give a schedule for making of a film. Normally, an advertisement film is made in about 4 to 6 weeks. Before the shooting begins, the producer is called for pre-production meetings by the agency. In these meetings different issues related with production and script are discussed and an understanding is developed. The producer is apprised of the research that the agency has carried out and its findings. The script is discussed and all the differences about its interpretations are ironed out at this stage.

Next, the models are chosen by the agency and the producer together, keeping in mind the requirements of the story. The life style and milieu of the target audience is kept in mind. Sometimes, a client is also present in these meetings and his approval is sought on these and allied matters. After selecting the models/actors, the cameraman is also selected at this stage. As with the producers, the cameraman is also selected on the basis of his reputation and standing in the industry and rapport with the agency.

After the pre-production discussions are over and after the script is explained, the model(s) is/are chosen. Now it is the responsibility of the producer who has to meticulously plan the details beforehand to avoid anything going wrong on the day of the shooting, which is done either in studios or on outdoor locations and the size of the budget depends to a large extent on these factors. During the shooting, representatives of the agency and the client are also present.

Assuming that everything proceeds smoothly, the actual shooting of a commercial is generally completed in two shifts.

After the shooting is over, the exposed film is sent to the laboratory for processing and then for editing. What makes editing even more crucial in a commercial is the extremely short length of the shots. A 30 second commercial works out to 45 feet of film length. Sometimes, after shooting an editor has more than 2,000 feet on his desk. It is his job to reduce it to the required length. Then comes the post production work which includes work on music, the jingle, animation, special effects etc. which can further stretch upto four weeks.

Once the film is complete and ready, it is first screened before the agency representatives. Either the film is accepted as it is or some changes are suggested. After the required changes have been incorporated and the agency has approved the film, the client is invited for a screening. Sometimes a producer is present when the film is screened but many agencies feel safer in dealing with the client, alone, particularly if the producer happens to be a newcomer.

Audiovisuals have finally come of age in India. The introduction of colour television and the advent of new video technology have given tremendous boost to audiovisual making. Since the early eighties there has been an increase of 300 to 400% in business.

The contribution of a copy writer in making a television commercial is crucial because he has to think in terms of advertising, the medium, marketing and communication objectives, selling appeals to be conveyed, different demonstration techniques to be utilised, and principal approaches. The following section discusses these aspects of audiovisuals and heavily draws on the models developed by Huntley Baldwin (1970) and writings of advertising legend David Ogilvy (1983). Later, this study analyses television commercials on the basis of these aspects.

Selling Appeals/Themes

A selling appeal is the benefit that can be derived from the characteristics of a product itself which contributes to the satisfaction of need or desire of the consumer (Right, Winter and Zeigler, 1989). This benefit becomes the central theme generally called the selling idea or unique selling proposition (USP). There is usually one main selling appeal which is given prominence in the message and, others, if they are used, are secondary to the theme. Various types of selling ideas are used in the audiovisuals. Some of the major ones are explained below:

1. Newness

This appeal highlights the new product, product size, new features, new models, new package etc., and used quite often in advertisements. Campaigns using introduction of fast food items, larger size soaps, automatic defrosting systems in refrigerators, and flat TV screens are some of the recent examples.

2. Ingredients and manufacturing process

Many a time commercials emphasise the ingredients and constituents used in the specific brand or the way, a specific brand or product is made.

3. Company Image

Under this selling appeal the company tries to take advantage of its good reputation in the market for some of its brands and products.

4. Major uses, versatility and convenience

Here the emphasis is laid on the product's major uses, its versatility and convenience in use.

5. Quality

This is one of the most powerful and widely used campaign themes and is used for products as diverse as coconut oil, paints, TV, tyres and suitings.

6. Economy

This is another very powerful appeal commonly used in audiovisuals. Here virtues of product and economy in using are emphasised.

7. Results of using and not using

This appeal is often based on creating fear among the audience by showing that if the brand is not used what would be the consequence and if the brand is used what could be the benefits. Forhans commercial is a classic example of where this type of appeal was used effectively.

8. User life styles

This type of appeal or theme tells prospective consumers about the type of people using the advertised product. Through this appeal the brand is tried to be positioned to a specific market segment which exhibit this life style or wants to emulate this type of lifestyle. Most often in textiles and cosmetics this type of selling idea is used.

9. Number of users

Companies with established brands use this appeal. Through this type of appeal the advertiser tries to make the audience think that "there must be something in this brand which has made it popular among different types of people". Usually, this type of selling appeal is more appropriate for those brands which have mass appeal and the basic aim of the advertiser is either to maintain the existing market share or to increase it further. "Hamara Bajaj" campaign is a classic example.

Demonstration Techniques

These are the ways or methods through which the central theme or appeal is demonstrated. Various demonstration techniques are used all over the world in commercials to persuade the target audience and to change attitude and ultimately to purchase the brand. Some of the common demonstration techniques are discussed below:

1. Product alone or with spokesman

This is the simplest way to show what a product can do i.e. by making it do it. The demonstration is accompanied by a spokesperson explaining what is happening on the screen. He/she may be a celebrity, a satisfied customer or even a corporate symbol. This demonstration techniques is extensively used in fans, tyres, soaps, detergents etc.

2. Before and after

Under this technique it is shown how the consumers can get their want fulfilled after using the product. A comparison is made in the condition of the consumer before using and the change after using it.

3. Torture test

For some products when the durability and the toughness have to be demonstrated in the commercial, the products are subjected to extremely tough and stressful situations. Examples of this technique in the Indian advertisements can be found in case of Kitply, VIP suitcases and Eveready torches.

4. Side by Side

In the commercials two or more brands are compared and the superiority of the advertised brand is established. The comparison is sometimes with no specific brand but other brand is depicted as brand X or an ordinary brand. Sometimes the comparison is done explicitly with a specific brand whose identity is revealed. This type of advertising technique is also known as comparative advertising. Some of the famous advertisements in this category are Surf washing powder (where Surf is compared to ordinary brand X), Captain Cook Salt and Thomson colour televisions.

5. Slice of life and vignettes

These techniques try to dramatise the situations in which the advertised brand saves the people from their real life problems. This may involve a long look at one person's problem or situation (slice of life) or may try a series of short and amusing looks at a lot of different people's problems (vignettes). Well known examples of this technique are Colgate toothpaste and Amrutanjan pain reliever balm.

6. Testimonials

This technique is variation of the spokesperson technique where the spokesperson either interviews a satisfied customer or the spokesperson himself/herself is shown as the user of the brand. Testimonials can use non-celebrities as actual users or celebrities are depicted as satisfied consumers. Godrej and Hindustan Lever have been successfully using the same for shaving creams and detergents.

7. Symbolism

If the selling idea or appeal is abstract or difficult to substantiate, the demonstration may be symbolic in nature. Kawasaki Bajaj advertisement where it is compared in power and speed with the qualities of a *Cheetah* come under this category.

8. Fantasy

Here the selling appeal is demonstrated through certain situations which may be classified as fantasy or exaggerations. This technique tries to create a world where most of the prospective consumers will like to be. Often, the situation is beyond the reach of the common man yet he aspires to achieve it.

BASIC APPROACHES USED IN AUDIOVISUALS

There are three kinds of basic approaches which one finds in the advertisements. These approaches are used for the entire commercial or they are the basic tone which run through the advertisement. They are explained below:

1. Straight forward

Here the advertisement has a matter of fact approach, the selling appeal and the other aspects of the brand are presented in a straight forward and serious manner.

2. Humorous

A little bit of humour is considered to bring a refreshing change in the advertisements. Here the selling appeal and the demonstration techniques are used in a funny and a humorous way.

3. Exaggerated

The approach of the commercial is slightly exaggerated one. The effect of a specific brand, the features or qualities are shown in an exaggerated manner. In advertising puffery i.e. slight exaggeration is considered by many experts as desirable because it grabs the attention of the audience and gains favourable response. However, there is a thin dividing line between puffery and exaggeration and many a time exaggeration may be taken as misleading and false. If this happens, a particular advertisement may come under the category of unfair practices and is liable for corrective steps if regulating agencies such as MRTP take exception to this type of advertising.

PURPOSE AND SCOPE OF THE PRESENT STUDY

With the tremendous increase in the reach of television in India, large number of business organisations are now promoting their products through audiovisuals. Thus, audiovisuals have become a big business and their making a highly professional affair in India. Audiovisuals are made using sophisticated techniques to ensure their desired impact on the target audience. The purpose of the present study is to analyse audiovisuals i.e. TV commercials in the context of their various facets. This involves studying, which products are advertised, using what kind of selling appeals or themes, demonstration techniques and basic approaches. An attempt has also been made to see whether any sub-category of one technique is used to a larger extent with any specific sub-category of other. For instance, whether to see whether any sub-category of one technique is used to a larger extent with any specific sub-category of other. For instance, whether advertisements using slice-of-life demonstration technique based more on user lifestyle appeal or theme.

OBJECTIVES OF THE STUDY

The effectiveness of an advertising message depends to a great extent not only on what has been conveyed to the target audience. It means a message's effectiveness depends on its structure as well as on content (Kotler, 2000). Therefore, the basic objective of the present study was to find out the relationship between the types of products and the selection of selling ideas, demonstration techniques and the basic approaches in TV commercials. More specifically the following objectives were delineated in analysing TV commercials:

- To find out the relationship between type of products and the type of selling ideas used.
- To find out the relationship between type of products and the type of demonstration technique.
- To find out the relationship between type of products and basic tones or approaches used.
- To find out the relationship, if any, between selling ideas and demonstration techniques.
- To find out the relationship between selling ideas and basic tones or approaches.

METHODOLOGY

In order to fulfill the above stated objectives of the study it was thought appropriate to undertake the content analysis of audiovisuals.

All commercials screened on various TV channels on alternate days at prime time were recorded for one month period. Both spot as well as sponsored commercials were included in the study. This led to the recording of a large number of commercials. For the purpose of analysis, repetition was avoided and if a specific commercial appeared more than once in that period, then that commercial was analysed only once. In this way a list of 266 commercials was made and subsequently they were analysed for the present study.

Firstly, a content analysis proforma was prepared taking into consideration all variables of the study. On the proforma, name of the brand, product category, selling appeals, demonstration techniques and the basic approaches were categorised. This proforma is shown in Exhibit-1. Secondly, each audiovisual was analysed for the specific selling appeal, demonstration technique and basic approach. After all the 266 audiovisuals had been analysed using the said proforma, the contents were transferred to a master sheet. The data from the master sheet were then converted into different tables according to the objectives and hypotheses of the study. Finally, the data were subjected to statistical techniques, wherever applicable, to test the hypotheses.

A number of problems were faced during the analysis phase. Firstly, repetition of commercials had to be taken care of which took a lot of time and effort. Secondly, the total number of categories—two for the products and twenty-three for the other variables i.e. twenty-five in all, were very difficult to analyze and therefore each audiovisual had to be played back several times. Since there was a possibility of subjectivity, as there is a thin dividing line between the sub-categories of each variable, discretion had to be used to put a particular variable in a specific sub-category. However, as far as possible, care has been taken to analyse audiovisuals according to the specifications of each sub-category.

ANALYSIS AND RESULTS

Type of Product and Selling Ideas

The data arranged in terms of product category and selling ideas are shown in Table 10.1. Our first null hypothesis in this connection was "there is no relationship between the type of products advertised and the various selling themes used to convey the message". To prove or disprove null hypothesis one has to examine Table 10.1 which depicts the use of selling appeals/themes arranged according to the product categories of durable and non-durable nature. Out of the total 266 commercials analysed for the present study, 116 were durable products i.e. 43.6% and 150 were non-durable products i.e. 56.4%. This indicates that television as a medium is more popular amongst the advertisers for non-durable products than for durables. The classification of durable and non-durable products was done on the basis of the normal life or consumption time of the product. All those products which are consumed in two years or less than two years time were put in non-durable category and all those products which are consumed in more than two years were categorized as durables. It is not claimed that this procedure is perfect but under the given circumstances this classification scheme was considered suitable. This classification of products into two distinct categories has been used throughout the study and an attempt has been made to establish relationship with selling ideas, demonstration techniques and basic tones.

Table 10.1

Relationship Between Product Categories and Types of Selling Ideas

Selling Ideas		*Product Category* *Durables*	*Non-Durables*	*Total*
Newness	F	16	14	30
	%	13.8	9.3	11.28
Ingredients and Mnfg. process	F	5	16	21
	%	4.3	10.7	7.89
Company Image	F	8	6	14
	%	6.9	4	5.26
Major Uses	F	22	20	44
	%	19	13.3	16.54
Quality	F	20	32	52
	%	17.2	21.3	19.55
Economy	F	5	12	17
	%	4.3	8	6.39
Result of Using/Not Using	F	6	22	28
	%	5.2	14.7	10.53
User Lifestyles	F	23	22	45
	%	19.8	14.7	16.92
No. of Users	F	11	6	17
	%	9.5	4	6.39

Note: Calculated χ^2 = 20.79
Critical values of χ^2 for 8 df at 5% level of significance = 17.53 $P<.05$.

Table 10.1 was analysed to find out the relationship between product categories and selling ideas. Perusing this table one may find certain distinct trends. It seems that there is some correlation between the nature of products and specific selling appeals. In case of durable products three selling themes were found to be very popular. These in order of their prevalence were user lifestyle (19.8%), major uses (19%) and quality (17.2%). Emphasising newness came next to the first three appeals i.e. 13.8%. Number of users (9.5%) company image (6.9%), results of using and not using (5.2%), economy (4.3%) and ingredients (4.3%) were the other selling appeals which were used in decreasing order. When the selling appeals of non-durable products were examined there emerged a somewhat different trend. The top three appeals in case of non-durables were quality (21.3%), results of using and not using and user lifestyle (14.7%). Next important appeals in non-durable categories in terms of their prevalence were major users (13.3%). ingredients (10.7%), newness (9.3%), economy (8.0%), number of users (4.0%) and company image (4.0%). To test the null hypothesis, chi-square analysis was performed and it was proved that there exists some amount of correlation between the product categories and type of selling appeal used ($\chi^2 = 20.79$, $p < 0.05$). Therefore, one may reject the null hypothesis that there is no relationship between type of product and type of selling appeals used in television commercials.

Type of Products and Demonstration Techniques

The commercials were content analysed to find out the relationship between type of products and demonstration techniques used in commercials. It was found that in audiovisuals that were analysed, eight different demonstration techniques were being used in varying degrees. The frequency and percentage of these eight demonstration techniques in different television commercials were arranged in relation to product categories and are given in Table 10.2.

From Table 10.2 it is clear that some of the demonstration techniques were quite popular among both categories of products i.e. durable and non-durable. Whereas, some of the techniques were found to be more popular for one category of products and some for other category of products. The techniques which are more or less equally popular in both types of products are slice-of-life (30.7% in non-durables and 25.0% in durables), and testimonials (21.3% in non-durables and 12.1% in durables). When the demonstration techniques for separate product categories are analysed product alone/with spokesman is more popular in durable product category than non-durables. This is understandable because consumer durables are being purchased infrequently. Further, consumers purchase these products after giving considerable thought and they are interested more in how the product actually performs. Another interesting finding in case of durables is the use of torture test to demonstrate the toughness, sturdiness and quality of products being advertised. The use of torture test is associated more with durables (10.4%) as compared to non-durables. The use of symbolism was also found to be more popular in non-durables as compared to durables. Before and after, side-by-side and fantasy demonstration techniques were sparsely used in both categories of products. Chi-square analysis has shown a significant statistical difference between the product categories and use of specific demonstration techniques χ^2 =23.32, $p < 0.01$).

Type of Products and Basic Tone/Approach

The third research objective was related to the use of basic approach in presentation of message along with the selling ideas and demonstration techniques.

Table10.3

Relationship Between Product Category and Basic Tones

Basic Tones	*Straight Forward*		*Humorous*		*Exaggerated*		*Total*	
Product category	*F*	*%*	*F*	*%*	*F*	*%*	*F*	*%*
Durables	39	33.6	29	25	48	41.4	116	43.6
Non-durables	30	20	53	35.3	67	44.7	150	56.4
Total	69	25.9	82	30.8	115	43.2	266	100

Calculated χ^2 = 7.82
Critical Value χ^2 = 7.38

In message presentation, whatever demonstration is used, the advertiser, copywriter and the producer have to think what approach should be employed so that it may create a positive impact on the audience. It was thought that using of a particular tone or approach is product specific. Therefore, our third null hypothesis was "there is no relationship between type of product and basic tone used in commercials". To test this hypothesis we analysed the audiovisuals on this aspect and arranged the analysis with respect to the type of products. The same is presented in Table 10.3. Three types of basic tones were considered. They were straight forward, humorous and exaggerated approaches. Examining Table 10.3, one can find that the frequency of using these approaches seems to be related to the type of products. As far as the exaggerated approach is concerned, it seems that advertisers of both types of products feel that the message can be made effective if it is presented in an exaggerated way. Table 10.3 indicates that 41.4% of commercials in durable category and 44.7% in non-durables category used advertising message in an exaggerated way. As far as the other two approaches i.e. straight forward and humorous are concerned, the former was found to more popular for durable products (33.6%) and latter i.e. humorous approach was found more popular for non-durable products (35.3%). In durables category humorous approach was less commonly used (25%) while the was true with respect to straight forward approach in case of non-durables (20.7%). The chi-square analysis also confirmed that use of the two approaches i.e. straight forward and humorous are related with the type of product ($\chi^2 = 7.83$, $p<.05$).

Selling Ideas and Demonstration Techniques

After analysing the first research question i.e. the relationship between the type of product with selling ideas, demonstration techniques and basic tones the next research question was to find out the relationship between selling ideas and demonstration techniques irrespective of the type of product. An aspect which requires further investigation is "does a specific selling idea/theme go well with a specific demonstration technique or all the demonstration techniques are equally popular"?

To answer this research question, our null hypothesis was "there is no relationship between selling ideas and demonstration techniques". For this purpose the data were arranged on these two variables and presented in Table 10.4. In arranging the data only those selling ideas were taken which were used in advertisements repeatedly. In this way six selling ideas were analysed with respect to the use of different demonstration techniques. Table 10.4 shows that the frequency distribution of different demonstration techniques is not uniform with a specific selling idea/theme.

Table 10.2
Relationship Between Product Category and Demonstration Techniques

Demonstration Techniques		*Product Category* *Durables*	*Non-Durables*	*Total*
Product alone with spokesperson	F	28	18	46
	%	24.1	12	17.3
Before and after	F	5	14	19
	%	4.3	9.3	7.1
Torture test	F	12	2	14
	%	10.3	1.3	5.3
Side-by-side	F	6	8	14
	%	5.2	5.4	5.3
Slice of life-vignettes	F	29	46	75
	%	25	30.7	28.2
Testimonials	F	14	32	46
	%	12.1	21.3	17.3
Symbolism	F	11	20	31
	%	9.5	13.3	11.6
Fantasy	F	11	10	21
	%	9.5	6.7	7.9
Total	F	116	150	266
	%	43.6	56.4	100

Note: Calculated $\chi^2 = 23.32$.
Critical values of χ^2 for 7 df at 5% level of significance = 16.01 $P<.05$.

The first theme to be considered was "newness". Out of the 30 commercials which used "newness" as the basic theme, 30% employed testimonial more often than the other techniques. Slice-of-life was used next(26.7%), then torture test (16.7%), product along/with spokesperson (13.3%), and side-by-side in descending order. As far as selling idea "ingredients and manufacturing process" is concerned it used four demonstration techniques. Here product alone/with spokesperson came on top (33.3%), followed by slice-of-life (22.4%) and testimonials (22.2%).

Exhibit —1: Content Analysis Proforma for Selling Ideas, Demonstration Techniques and Basic Tones

1. Serial No. ( )
2. Brand Name ____________
3. Product Category
   (1) Consumer Durables ( )
   (2) Consumer Non-durables ( )
4. Selling Ideas:
   (1) Newness ( ) (2) Ingredients ( )
   (3) Quality ( ) (4) Major Uses ( )
   (5) Company Image ( )
   (6) Results of using/not using ( )
   (7) User life-style ( ) (8) Economy ( )
   (9) Number of users ( )
5 Demonstration Techniques:
   (1) Product alone/with spokesperson ( )
   (2) Before and after ( )
   (3) Torture test ( )
   (4) Side-by-side ( )
   (5) Testimonials ( )
   (6) Slice-of -life and vignettes ( )
   (7) Symbolism ( )
   (8) Fantasy ( )
6. Basic Tones:
   (1) Straight forwar ( )
   (2) Humorous ( )
   (3) Exaggerated ( )

In the case of "major uses", almost all the major demonstration techniques were employed with varying frequency. The two most commonly employed techniques under this theme were side-by-side (38.1%) and product along/with spokesperson (28.6%). Others such as testimonials, before-after, torture tests, symbolism and fantasy were employed sparingly. Out of 266 commercials analysed in the study, 52 used quality as main selling idea and here the advertisers employed five demonstration techniques to convey this idea. Product alone/ with spokesperson (26.0%) and fantasy (26.0%) were employed most frequently. It is also interesting to note that torture test was used more often than in any other selling appeal for demonstrating the quality of advertised brand. Other techniques such as slice-of-life and testimonials were also used but with less frequency. An interesting finding is that all those commercials which used user lifestyle as basic selling idea, more than half (54.5%) employed slice-of-life technique. Finally, under using-not-using selling idea four different techniques were being used. Because using-not-using theme tries to convey the difference, so slice-of-slice (35.3%), testimonials (29.4%) and before-after (23.5%) demonstration techniques were predominantly employed.

The above discussion clearly indicates that advertisers were of the opinion that a particular demonstration technique will be more useful than others in conveying the theme. For example, torture test, before-after and side-by-side demonstration techniques were used only with respect to newness, major uses and quality selling ideas, and they were not at all employed with ingredients or user lifestyle themes. Before-after-technique was more suitable with using not-using theme, whereas torture test was more associated with quality. Testimonial alone as demonstration technique was being used with all the basic selling ideas/appeals. This shows the popularity of this technique on the one hand and versatility of its use on the other. Though no statistical test is applied here to test the null hypothesis, yet, the findings are so obvious and clear that one can reject the null hypothesis with confidence.

Selling Ideas and Basic Tones

Final research objective was to find out the relationship, if any, between selling ideas and basic tones/approaches. The basic issue here was to investigate whether a specific selling idea is conveyed to the target audience through a specific approach or not. To answer this question the data was anlaysed in terms of selling ideas and basic tones used in audiovisuals and are presented in Table 10.5.

Here six different selling themes were examined in terms of basic tones. Straightforward (46.7%) and exaggerated (40.0%) were the two basic tones used for conveying "newness" selling idea. Here humorous tone was used sparingly. As a matter of fact, exaggerated tone was the modal way for using-not-using (76.5%), major uses (52.4%), user-life-style (40.9%) and quality (34.6%) selling ideas. Humorous tone found favour with ingredients (55.6%), and major uses (33.3%). Straightforward tone was found to be less popular with majority of selling ideas except for newness where it is a modal

Table 10.4
Relationship Between Product Categories and Demonstration Techniques

Demonstration Techniques	*Selling Ideas*							
	Newness	*Ingredients*	*Major Uses*	*Major*	*Quality*	*User life style*	*Using not using*	*Total*
Product alone with spokesperson	F	4	6	12	13	0	0	35
	%	13.3	33.3	28.6	26	0	0	
Torture test	F	5	0	2	10	0	0	0
	%	16.7	0	4.8	20	0	0	
Before and after	F	0	0	4	0	0	8	0
	%	0	0	9.6	0	0	23.5	
Side-by-side	F	4	0	16	0	0	0	0
	%	13.3	0	38.1	0	0	0	
Slice of life vignettes	F	8	4	0	8	24	12	0
	%	26.7	22.4	0	16	54.5	35.3	
Testimonials	F	9	4	4	8	8	10	0
	%	30	22.2	9.4	16	18.2	29.4	
Symbolism	F	0	2	2	0	4	4	0
	%	0	11.1	4.7	0	9.1	11.8	
Fantasy	F	0	2	2	13	8	0	0
	%	0	11.1	4.8	26	18.2	0	
Total	F	30	18	42	52	44	34	0

approach. The analysis has shown that there seems to be a definite relationship between selling ideas and approaches used. This was further verified by chi-square statistics (χ^2 = 36.63, $p < .01$).

Table 10.5
Relationship Between Selling Ideas and Basic Tones

Basic Tones	*Straight Forward*		*Humorous*		*Exaggerated*		*Total*
Selling Ideas	*F*	*%*	*F*	*%*	*F*	*%*	
Newness	14	46.7	4	13.3	12	40	30
Ingredients	2	11.1	10	55.6	8	33.3	18
Major Uses	6	14.3	14	33.3	22	52.4	42
Quality	18	34.6	16	30.8	18	34.6	52
User Life-Style	12	27.3	14	31.8	18	40.9	44
Using-Not-Using	2	5.9	6	17.6	26	76.5	34
Total	54		64		112		

INTERPRETATIONS AND CONCLUSIONS

The analysis in the preceeding section has shown that quality, followed by user-life-style, was the most frequently used appeal irrespective of the type of product. This reveals a general tendency among advertisers to persuade the target audience by employing superior quality theme and thereby increasing their positive predisposition and at the same time removing doubts about the quality. It was also observed that user lifestyle appeals were being used to show a lifestyle slightly out of reach of the target audience and it becoming accessible to those who purchased the advertised brand. This is a powerful appeal, and if used judiciously can pull the target audience effectively. The most commonly used selling appeals for durables were user lifestyle, major uses, versatility and convenience. These appeals try to show the brand performance and the advantages of owning it. These appeals are generally considered to be effective because durables are purchased after considerable deliberations and evaluation on account of being big ticket items. For non-durables, quality appeal occupies the top position, followed by results of using and not using the brand.

As far as the demonstration techniques were concerned slice-of-life stood at the top and side-by-side at the bottom. The popularity of slice-of-life lies in its melodramatic impact. There is a possibility that advertisers feel it is more in tune with the Indian milieu. Side-by-side requires comparing two brands and many advertisers do not want to create a controversy by explicit comparison (Khan and Aijaz, 1988). One technique which found favour in commercials for durables was product alone/with spokesperson. Being a simple technique it is more suitable for durables, because the distractions are very few.

As regards to basic approaches irrespective of type of product, advertisers seem to favour slightly exaggerated approach.

Exaggeration is quite subjective in nature – to one person a message may seem to be highly exaggerated while for the other it may not be so. There is a possibility of bias occuring on this count as the researchers may have interpreted the approach as exaggerated one though in reality it may not be so. However, care was taken to minimize the bias and to evaluate the same as objectively as possible. It would be appropriate to point out that people feel that advertisements generally try to show more than what the brand can actually accomplish. If this is the case, it is obvious that exaggerated claims may create higher expectations and if these expectations are not fulfilled by the performance of the brand it may lead to dissatisfaction (Swan and Combs, 1976). When there is a gap between expectation and perceived performance, some consumers themselves magnify the gap and as a result they experience high levels of dissatisfaction. Sometimes other consumers minimise the gap and experience less dissatisfaction (Anderson, 1973). Whatever be the case, it would be prudent on the part of the advertisers to avoid exaggeration, if possible. However, one can not rule out the use of puffery which is considered to enhance the effectiveness of message (Pestion, 1977). Torture test, where the toughness and sturdity of the brand has to demonstrated, are used more with consumer durables and it was not at all being used for non-durables.

Of all the demonstration techniques, slice-of-life and testimonials were being frequently used with all the major types of selling appeals. This shows two things; firstly, their popularity among the advertisement film makers and secondly, their versatility to go with every appeal. The use of side-by-side and before-after techniques were confined to major uses, newness and results of using and not using appeals. Because these techniques employ some sort of comparison, their utility is limited. Product alone/with spokesperson is one of the oldest techniques but its popularity is on the decline. It can not be used or is less effective in user lifestyle and results of using or not using the products.

Finally, we can say that audiovisuals have arrived in India with a bang and have come of age. In this connection the producers of audiovisuals are using different appeals, different demonstration techniques and different approaches for promoting various types of products and services. In order to be in tune with the trends in this field, periodic longitudinal studies are needed.

REFERENCES

Anderson E. Ralph (1973), "Consumer dissatisfaction: The Effect of Disconfirmed Expectancy on Perceived Product Performance", *Journal of Marketing Research*, February, pp. 38-44.

Balwin Hunley (1970), *How Television Commercials are Made* (Department of Advertising, Northwestern University: Evanston III).

Khan, Kaleem Mohd and Mohd. Ajaz (1988), "Comparative Advertising: Content Analysis of Magazine Advertisements, *Indian Management*, vol. 27, No. 12, pp. 4-10.

Kotler Philips (2000), *Marketing Management. Analysis, Planning, Implementation and Control*, 10th Ed. (Prince-Hall India Ltd., New Delhi).

Ogilvy David (1983), *Ogilvy on Advertising* (Crown Publishers, Inc, New York).

Pestion L. Ivan (1977), "The FTC's Handling of Puffery and Other Selling Claims", *Journal of Business Research*, June, pp. 155-181.

Swan E. John and Linda Jones Combs (1976), "Product Performance and Consumer Satisfaction: A New Concept", *Journal of Marketing Research*, April, pp. 25-33.

Vatsayana, Mukesh (1987), "Ad Films: Making of a 30 Second Wonder", *Business India*, March 21, pp. 82-86.

Wright S. John, Willis L. Winter and, Sherilyn K. Zeigler (1989), *Advertising* (Tata-McGraw-Hill Publishing Company, Limited, New Delhi).

11

Sex Role Portrayal of Women in Advertising: Effect on Company Image and Purchase Intentions

INTRODUCTION

For centuries, women have been treated as inferior to men in India. Indian women have been taken to be submissive, a decoration piece and blamed for every misdeed or calamity that befell on the family.

With the breaking up of joint family system and a gradual change in the attitude of the male dominated Indian society towards the education of women, especially, during the last three decades, the role of women has changed dramatically in India. These changes are more pronounced in metropolitan cities of India, where women have entered the work force in substantial number. Increasing number of educated and professionally qualified women have now entered the formal settings of organisations, which include private, government and even multinationals operating in sectors such as communications, media, travel, education, banking, life insurance, etc.

The 1991 census reveals that women have now come into the open. Professions like accountancy, administration, engineering, air transport, air craft maintenance, architecture and town planning are being followed by women and that too in a sizable number. Apart from these, there are other professions into which Indian women have entered like as journalists, lawyers, marriage counsellors, managers, pharmacists, photographers, pilots, police officers and detectives and even as railway drivers. Interestingly, during the last three decades or so, women have entered the management field also. They have made important contributions in the entire spectrum of economic activities in the organised sector. In modern India, though women are quite visible in the traditional fields like education, medicine, law and clerical jobs, they are also making significant contributions in less conventional fields such as engineering scientific research and professional business management (Sinha, 1985).

The increased participation of women in different professions and the role that they are playing in the modern society as co-decision makers in almost every human endeavor has brought a profound change in the thinking of marketers to re-examine this important market segment. However, a cursory glance of present day advertising proves that many marketers and advertisers are still insensitive to this change. Women are often shown in tradition bound roles like housewife in the kitchen, mother taking care of her children, or in a slightly advanced role as a secretary making an appointment for her boss. In many instances, she is not even needed in the advertisement, nor does she have any relation with the product, but still she is used as a decorative piece or just to attract attention of the viewers and readers of advertising.

In recent years, wide spread attention has been focused on the certain stereotypic role portrayals of women in advertising. Both journalistic and academic research has taken this issue of stereotypic portrayal of women in advertising. Even in the Western countries where women are more prominent and have more equality than their counterparts in the developing countries, this question has been raised in many studies. One area of marketing is likely to be strongly influenced by women's changing role in advertising. Weiss (1972) observed that if advertising to the new women is to persuade it must teat women as intelligent adults who will respond to a reasonable and believable presentation of the product's case. Many writers have been critical about the treatment of women in advertisements, particularly their limited role portrayal (Mazis and Beuttenmuller, 1992; Courtney and Lockeretz, 1971; Wagner and Banos, 1973). In one study of women in magazine advertisements over the thirty years period from 1955-1985 indicated movement towards more egalitarian role definitions but revealed that women continue to be shown in unrealistic and steriotypical roles (Mays and Braddy, 1991). Many of these studies have concluded that advertisements have depicted the following major sexual stereotypes for women (Lundstrom and Sciglimpaglia, 1977).

- That women's place is in the home.
- That women do not make important decision.
- That women are dependent on men.
- That men regard women primarily as sex objects
- That women are physically beautiful and therefore, should be used as attention grabbers.

Recent research on contemporary women's perceptions of their role portrayals in advertising indicated that serious disenchantment still exists (LaTour and Lundstrom, 1991).

These studies have also found that the number of occupational roles showing women outside the home was much less than that for men and those shown were fairly traditional sex roles (e.g., secretaries, teachers, nurses).

OBJECTIVES OF THE STUDY

Not much empirical research has been reported which examines the questions of how the Indian consumer in general and women in particular view sex role portrayal in advertising. There are diverse views amongst advertisers and marketers regarding the sex role portrayal of women. The present study attempts to address the question of current status of consumer's attitude towards sex role portrayal of women on company image and purchase intentions towards those companies who still portray women in traditional bound roles. Specifically, the following research questions were considered:

- What are the attitude of men and women consumers towards sex role portrayal in advertising.
- Does the sex play any role in forming the attitude towards sex role portrayals in advertising.
- Does role portrayal affect the attitude of men and women consumers towards company image.
- Does role portrayal affect the attitude of men and women consumers towards purchase intention.

RESEARCH INSTRUMENT

A questionnaire was developed to determine the attitudes of males and female consumers towards role portrayal of women in advertising. The questionnaire was developed keeping in mind three major areas i.e. advertising role portrayal, effect on company image, and effect

Table 11.1
Demographics of Respondents

Variable	*Sex* *Females(n=200)* *Percentage*	 *Males(n=200)* *Percentage*
Age		
Less than 20 years	31	17
20-25 years	47	43
More than 25 years	22	40
Education		
Under Graduates	28	14
Graduates	44	55
Post Graduates	28	31
Marital Status (Women Only)		
Married working women	8	
Housewives	20	
Non-working Unmarried women	54	
Working Unmarried women	18	

on purchase intention. Help has been taken in the selection of the items from an earlier study on the same issue done by Lundstrom and Sciglimpaglia (1977). After pretesting, some statements were rephrased to eliminate ambiguity or difficulty in comprehension, from the Indian point of view. Thus, the questionnaire in the final form contained a series of 15 attitudinal statements dealing with advertising role portrayals of women and men, the company image of firms using sexual role portrayal practices, and intentions to buy from the aforementioned companies and also certain classification information. Each statement had five-point Likert type scale responses with *strongly disagree* and *strongly agree* as the scale anchors. A *strongly disagree* response was given a weight of 1 and *strongly agree* a weight of 5; thus a possible 1 to 5 range with 3 as the *neutral point.*

The sample consisted of 400 respondents, with equal number of men and women. Care has been taken to select the respondents from all age groups and from diverse background. In choosing the respondents systematic random sampling was used. The respondents were personally contacted and the researcher explained whenever the respondent sought any clarification regarding any statement of the questionnaire. The demographic profile of the respondents is given in Table 11.1.

RESULTS AND DISCUSSION

Results showed a marked difference in male and female attitude towards role portrayal in advertising, its effect on company image and finally on purchase intentions. This happened in four out of the ten statements in case of role portrayal, two in case of the effect on company image and one in case of purchase intentions. The results are thus grouped in three categories, namely, attitude towards role portrayal, attitude towards company image and the attitude towards purchase intentions.

Attitudes Towards Advertising Role Portrayal

As stated earlier, this dimension was investigated by providing ten statements to the respondents and asking them to give response in *agree-disagree* form. Both for men and women respondents the responses were given weightage and for each statement the mean response has been calculated. These mean responses have been compared and t-test applied to find whether any significant differences exist between male and female attitudes. The results are shown in Tables 11.2 and 11.3. The Table 11.2 indicates that out of the ten statements pertaining to role portrayal, in case of four statements, attitudes of men and women found to be significantly different. An analysis of attitudes towards sex role portrayal shows that in certain statements women held more critical attitudes and in some less critical attitudes than men. Table 11.3 gives the percentage of responses of men and women who agree/disagree to ten statements of this section. The first statement concerned the attitude toward advertisements which portray women as they really are. Both male and female respondents held negative attitude towards this statement. However, female respondents were more critical than their male counterparts. This difference was found statistically significant. Table 11.3 indicates that large number of women agreed with this statement. Whereas, only a small number (25%) of male respondents agreed. An interesting aspect was that even though the extent of agreement with the statement had significant difference, there was not much difference as far as disagreement towards this statement was concerned (47% and 41% respectively).

The next statement was "advertisements suggest that women are fundamentally dependent on men". From Tables 11.2 and 11.3 it is clear that there were marked differences between male and female responses on this statement. Majority of males and females disagreed with this statement. However, the percentage of female swho strongly disagreed with this statement was substantially higher (39%) than males (14%). This suggests that women have more favourable attitude towards this facet. There has been a change in the status of women in the Indian society. They are now equally sharing the responsibilities with men. Advertising has recognised this fact and females are now being shown as being less dependent on males. Looking from a different angle, only 17 per cent females and 23 per cent males agreed with thei statement. The mean responses of males and females also showed perceptible difference and were found significant at 5 per cent level of significance.

The third statement was almost the same as the first except that here the attitude of respondents was measured regarding the portrayal of men in advertisements. Both the categories of respondents held positive attitude regarding this statement. It means that both males and females think that advertisements portray men as they really are. No statistical significance was found on this statement.

The fourth statement dealt with the role of women in family decision making. A very interesting pattern emerged. Males reacted negatively to this statement as compared to females. More than one third (32%) female respondents strongly agreed and overall degree of agreement was 59 per cent. When this is compared with men, only 13 percent agreed with the statement. This indicates that unconsciously men still feel that in the real world they are the decision makers and they have not yet reconciled to the idea that females can also be good in decision making. Inadvertently, they have shown, if allowed to use hackneyed phrase, their "male chauvinism". Females reacted favourably to this statement. Whatever may be the reasons, mean scores of both men and women were found statistically significant. The reaction of women to this statement may not depict reality.

Table 11.2
Attitude Towards Role Portrayal

S.No.	*Statements*	*Mean Response* *Men* *n=200*	*Women* *n=200*	*t-value*
1.	Advertisements which I see show women as they really are.	2.58	2.97	2.02*
2.	Advertisements suggest that women are fundamentally dependent on men	3.21	2.73	2.34*
3.	Advertisements which I see show men as they really are	3.41	3.24	0.79
4.	Advertisements suggest that women make important decisions	2.88	3.37	2.56*
5.	Advertisements treat women mainly as sex objects	3.39	3.85	2.30*
6.	Advertisements suggest that women don't do important things	2.97	2.79	0.94
7.	Advertisements suggest that a women's place is in the home.	2.57	2.69	0.64
8.	I am more sensitive to the portrayal of women in the advertising than I used to be.	3.19	3.27	0.43
9.	I find the portrayal of women in the advertising to be offensive.	2.97	2.98	0.05
10.	Overall, I believe that the portrayal of women in advertising is changing	3.31	3.41	0.59

In the profile 5 = Strongly Agree and 1 = Strongly Disagree.
* = 95% significance level of difference between means based on t distribution.

Strangely enough, there was not much difference in the attitude of men and women with regard to this statement. The mean scores of men and women are slightly different but this difference can be attributed to sampling variations. Though, the percentage of men agreeing with this statement is higher (58%) than females (43%), this difference has not been found statistically significant (see Table 11.2).

The fifth statement "advertisements treat women mainly as sex objects" was negatively worded and disagreement with this statement may indicate a new kind of thinking. The level of agreement among females was almost 70 per cent and among the males it was 59 per cent. This indicates that majority of males also think that women are primarily used as sex objects in the advertisements. Though, both of them are critical as far as use of women in advertising is concerned females are highly critical. This is evident in their mean scores and t-value (see Table 11.2).

The next statement is contradictory to the fourth statement which concerned decision making. This is a negatively worded statement and disagreement indicates a positive attitude. Table 11.3 shows that 44 per cent males and 37 per cent females agreed with this statement. Though, the females are less in agreement as compared to males. This has not been found significant. Both males and females were found to be moderately critical on this count.

The seventh statement addressed the issue of women's place in the society. Criticism has been leveled that advertising projects stereotypic roles of women, such as, mother, housewife and traditional occupations. This is an important issue for career women. There was no marked difference in the attitude of men and women. Both men and women have almost similar views about the place of women in the society. Those who subscribe to the view that advertisements suggest that women's place is in the home, are younger, and more educated on demographic traits.

In the next statement, an attempt was made to find out, in the changed circumstances, whether the respondents were sensitive to the portrayal of women in advertising. Surprisingly, both men and women agreed. However, in the break-up of responses, quite a substantial number of men (41%) were indifferent towards this issue, whereas, only 23 per cent women fell in this category. The degree of indifference was found to be substantially lower (21%). Though, the attitude of men and women regarding sensitivity was not found to be significant yet men seemed to be more indifferent than women.

The penultimate statement in this section dealt with the offensive portrayal of women in advertisement. There was a mixed opinion in this regard and attitudes varied considerably. Strangely enough, there was a considerable polarisation of opinion regarding offensive portrayal which resulted in mixed feelings. Women who found their portrayal in advertising most offensive tended to be highly educated, came from higher income households, and to a lesser extent, were younger.

The last statement concerned the perception of men and women towards the changing portrayal of women. A substantial number of males and females agreed that the portrayal of women is changing for the better. This is a good omen for the advertisers and marketers. Previously, many women were critical of advertising practices in general and their role portrayal in particular. But with the change in their perception , future maketers can take advantage and attract this segment which may eventually lead to increased liking for their products and services. Further, advertisers should note that they need to portray women in a more realistic manner and not depict them in stereotypic roles.

Table 11.3
Degree of Agreement Towards Role Portrayal

S.No. Statements	*Men*		*Women*	
	Agree %	*Disagree* %	*Agree* %	*Disagree* %
1. Women show as they really are.	25	47	49	41
2. Women are fundamentally dependent	44	32	39	44
3. Man show as they really are.	58	28	43	36
4. Women make important decisions.	35	40	59	22
5. Women treated as sex objects	59	17	70	18
6. Women don't do important things.	44	40	37	46
7. Woman's place is in the home.	29	50	37	47
8. More sensitive to the portrayal of women.	37	22	49	28
9. Portrayal of women offensive.	40	36	39	37
10. Portrayal of women changing for better.	48	22	44	24

Role Portrayal and Effect on Company Image

In this section we present responses pertaining to the effect on company image as a consequence of offensive role portrayal of women in advertising. There are two statements in this section and the results are shown in Tables 11.4 and 11.5.

Table 11.4
Attitude Towards Effect on Company Image

S.No.	*Statement*	*Mean Response*		*t-values*
		Men	*Women*	
1.	Companies that portray women offensively in their advertising are more likely to discriminate against women in the job promotion and advancement compared to other companies in the same business or industry.	2.63	3.21	2.35*
2.	I believe that how women are portrayed in advertisements merely reflects the general attitude of that company towards women's place in the society.	3.98	3.63	2.04*

In the profile 5 = *Strongly Agree* and 1 = *Strongly Disagree.*
* = 95% significant level of difference between means based on t distribution.

The purpose of the first statement in this section was to find out the image of those companies who use women in their advertisements offensively. It was stated that those companies which use women offensively in their advertising generally discriminate against women in job promotions and career advancement. Agreement with this statement indicates a negative attitude towards company image. Analysis has shown conclusively that women hold more critical opinion towards this type of companies than do men. The difference between the mean scores of men and women was found significant.

Second aspect which was investigated in this section was the attitude of those companies towards women's place in society who portray women offensively in their advertisement. The results show certain interesting findings.

Three fourth (75%) of males and two third (64%) females agreed with this statement indicating positive attitude towards the statement.

This shows that men are more critical than women and think that women are not highly viewed by these companies. This difference was found to be statistically significant.

Table 11.5
Degree of Agreement/Disagreement Towards Company Image.

S.No.	Statements	Men Agree %	Men Disagree %	Women Agree %	Women Disagree %
1.	Companies more likely to discriminate.	26	44	49	29
2.	Advertisements reflect company's view of women.	75	13	64	19

Table 11.6
Attitude Towards Purchase Intentions

S.No.	Statement	Mean Response		
		Men(n=200)	Women(n=200)	t-value
1.	If a new product is introduced with advertisements, that I find offensive, I might still buy it if it offers me benefits which I find attractive.	3.46	3.31	0.64
2.	If a new product or service which I use adopt an ad. campaign which I find offensive I will discontinue using it.	3.16	3.34	0.96
3.	Even though I may see an ad. which is offensive for one product, I would continue to purchase other products that I have been using from the same company.	4.25	3.96	1.72*

* = 95% significant level of difference between means based on t-distribution.

Role Portrayal and Effect on Purchase Intention

Apart from investigating the attitude of men and women towards role portrayal, and its effect on company image the objective was also to find out the attitude towards purchase intentions. This was necessary because prior to purchase, favourable disposition towards the company, and its brands, generally lead to purchase intention. To find out the attitude towards offending companies and their produces/services three statements were used. The results are tabulated in Tables 11.6 and 11.7 below.

Table 11.6 indicates that for the first two statements no significant differences were found between male and female attitudes. However, in case of third statement the difference in attitude was slightly signiificant (P=.10). From the overall attitude point of view, the females were slightly more critical than males.

Table 11.7

Degree of Agreement/Disagreement Towards Purchase Intentions

S. No.	*Statements*	*Men*		*Women*	
		Agree %	*Disagree* %	*Agree* %	*Disagree* %
1.	Might still buy new product.	52	43	48	32
2.	Would discontinue using product.	43	27	48	26
3.	Would continue buying new products.	77	6	73	11

CONCLUSIONS

The results discussed in the preceding section have led the researchers to conclude that the role portrayal of women is a real problem. Not only a sizable proportion of women appeared to be critical but a substantial number of enlightened males were also equally apprehensive about the existing role portrayal of women in advertising. Indeed many of those who were most critical were women who were younger, better educated, working, and belonged to upper strata of society. These women rejected their depiction in stereotypical roles in society. In coming years, as the number of young and better educated, career conscious women enter the work place, the degree of criticism will likely increase unless certain remedial steps are taken by advertisers and marketers alike.

To the extent that generalisations can be made from the analysis of reported purchase intentions, the effect of dissatisfying role portrayals may be both large and small. A sizable proportion of women surveyed indicated that they would alter their purchasing behavior due to advertising which they considered offensive. Even if they do not alter their future purchase behavior they may create dissentions in the minds of more gullible people. Even if this is does not happen, they may become vociferous critics of advertising and marketing practices.

Taking into consideration the empirical evidence and recognising the fact that increasing number of women are joining non-traditional professions and their being a perceptible shift in the locus of family authority, a number of implications/suggestions for marketers can be delineated:

- It is no longer appropriate to think of women in general or even women of the same age group as members of one monolithic target market. With different values, lifestyles and role related aspirations being found in women, an appropriate marketing and communication strategy has to be devised keeping in mind the relevant market segment.
- If a product happens to be purchased by a large number of women belonging to varying socio- economic backgrounds and with different demographic profiles, then it will be advisable that advertising may use a variety of life style scenarios instead of one which is stereotypically traditional.
- As the number of working women increases and as the actual role of women in the society changes, advertising, instead of portraying traditional image of women should reflect reality.
- Hitherto, products which were traditionally purchased by men alone, are now being increasingly purchased by women too. In addition, as the role orientation of women changes, she is likely to exert increased influence at every stage of family purchase decision process. More and more families, even in the Indian context, are becoming syncratic, where both husband and wife play equal role in family decision

making and purchasing decisions alike. Therefore, it is imperative that advertisers should be very careful in the role portrayal of women in future.

REFERENCES

Courtney A. E. and Lockeretz S. W. (1971), "A Women's Place: An Analysis of Role Portrayed by Women in Magazine Advertisements", *Journal of Marketing Research*, Vol. 8, p. 95.

LaTour M. S. and Lundstrom J. William (1991), "Contemporary WOmen's Evaluation of Female Role Portrayal in Advertisement", *Journal of Consumer Marketing,* Vol. 8, pp. 19-21.

Lundstrom J. William and Sciglimpaglia Donald (1977), "Sex Role Portrayals in Advertising", *Journal of Marketing*, July, pp. 72-79.

Mazis M.B. and Beuttenmuller M. (1972), "Attitudes Toward Women's Liberation and Perception of Advertisements, in M. Venkateshan (Ed.) *Proceedings of Third Annual Conference,* Association for Consumer Research, Chicago pp. 428.

Sinha Debjani (1985), "Women MBA's: A Status Report", *Business World*, October 14-17, pp. 38-39.

Wagner L. C. and Banos J. B. (1973), "A Women's Place: A Follow-up Analysis of the Roles Portrayed by Women in Magazine Advertisements", *Journal of Marketing Research*, Vol. 10, p. 213-214.

Weiss E.B. (1972), "New Life Styles of 1975-1980 Will Throw Switch on. Admen, *Advertising Age*, p.62.

12

A Woman's Place: An Analysis of Portrayal of Women in TV Commercials

INTRODUCTION

Of all the marketing activities, advertising is the most visible one. And perhaps because of its visibility it has attracted a lot of criticism from people belonging to diverse fields. In the present day world, advertising has become an important institution, all pervasive in nature, affecting large number of people. Consequently, it has a formidable influence on the people's minds without them even being aware of it. Given its all pervasiveness and persuasive character, advertising has been criticised because of its social and economic side effects.

In recent years the role of women has changed drastically. In the past, women were considered to be inferior or sub-servient to men. In terms of role differences women have historically been cast as home makers with the responsibility of child care and men as providers or bread winners. While such roles are no longer strongly associated with members of specific sex, nevertheless they are still largely prevalent. Many advertisers still appeal to such sex-linked stereotypical roles (Schiffman and Kanuk, 2000). The present study is directed towards this facet of advertising i.e. portrayal of women in advertising.

More specifically, off late, advertising has been accused of stereotypical representation of women. It has generally been argued that women are usually portrayed as housewives and mothers and only rarely in working roles and practically never in professional roles. In a number of studies employing content analysis the role portrayal of women in advertising has been explored extensively. These studies have generally indicated that women have been depicted inaccurately in terms of the range of their current roles. For instance, general audience magazine advertisements tended to stereotype women into four restrictive feminine roles:

(1) women's place is in the home;
(2) Women do not make important decisions or do important things;
(3) Women are dependent and need man's protection;
(4) Men regard women primarily as sexual objects.

Courtney and Lockeretz (1971), in the US context, made an attempt to determine how women were portrayed in advertisements. They examined 729 advertisements appearing in seven general interest magazines published in April 1970. None of the advertisement showed women in professional capacity, whereas 35 of them so portrayed were men. Only 9% of the women shown were in working roles, and they were clerks, stewardesses and the like. They also reported that the advertisement reflected the stereotype that women do not perform important things, are dependent on men, or regarded by men primarily as sex objects and should be in the home. In a follow-up study Wagner and Banos (1973) also came up with the same results. In an another study of over 6000 television commercials in 1976 it has been found that 18.3% women were portrayed as working outside the home and 21% as home makers. However, this finding is substantially different from the one found by Courtney and Lockeretz (1971).

During the last few decades, a large number of studies have been carried out in USA to investigate the role portrayal of women in advertising. Most of the studies have relied on content analysis technique. Dominick and Rauch (1972); Sliverstein, (1974); McArthur and Resko (1975) analysed the TV commercials. Prather and Tidall (1975) content analysed advertising in specialised fields from the point of view of psychological and behavioural influences on stereotypical role portrayal of women. Wortzel and Frisbie (1974) investigated female reaction to different female roles associated with various product advertising situations. Using an imaginative methodology they had subject, "Construct" advertisements from portfolios containing pictures of different products and women occupying different roles. In addition, subjects completed an attitudinal scale designed to categorize them as favourably or negatively predisposed to women's liberation movement. No consistent preferences were found for specific female roles that would enhance desirability across all product categories. More importantly, individuals classified as either supporters or non-supporters of the women's liberation movement indicated no significant differences in preferred roles for men. The role preferences of those with positive attitude (towards the women's liberation movement) were remarkably similar to the pattern for those with negative attitudes. The researchers concluded that the major determinant of the appropriate role type appeared to depend on the nature of the product being advertised.

Using a somewhat different methodology Duker & Tucker (1977) studied the preferences for women's roles in advertisements. In their study they categorised the women as independent (those who expressed pro-feminist attitude) and not independent. The study had indicated that women who were independent and expressed pro-feminist attitude did not react significantly to the women's roles in advertisements from women who were not independent and did not express pro-feminist attitude.

Apart from the behavioural studies on women's portrayal, a number of content analyses have been performed on the portrayal of women in magazines. Most often these investigations have been 'image-studies' drawing conclusions based upon counting the number of women shown in advertisement and the quality of those images. Content analysis has been found to be one of the favourable research techniques by the researchers in this area. In one study Sextant and Haberman (1974) content analysed the magazine advertisements by coding latent contents. Using a more extensive research method they concluded that the 'Overall Results would appear to corroborate the feminist charges that the images of women reflected in advertisements are quite narrow'. They suggest that although working women roles featured in advertising were more prevalent, the tasks depicted tend to be traditional. The authors, however, did find a decrease in the number of advertisements depicting females as home makers or mothers. A subsequent study of Venkatesan and Losco (1971) suggested that only the proportion of sex-object role portrayals have decreased significantly. Other stereotypes had not. The latest changes occurred in women magazines rather than general audience or men's magazines. However, from the late 1970s through the 80s, there appears to have been some real improvement in the proportion of magazine advertisement that portray women in working environment, or in some other non-traditional yet realistic settings (Schiffman and Kanuk (2000).

India, being a developing country, lags behind the more advanced countries of the West in terms of various social and economic dimensions. However, with the availability of modern means of communication, increased competition in the market and more thrust towards professionalisation in management techniques, advertising has also improved tremendously in the recent years. One can say that advertising has come of age in India, as far as techniques, approaches and persuasive abilities are concerned. On the other front the role and status of women is also changing rapidly. One of the major changes in the Indian family is the breaking up of joint family system. This has lead to emergence of three important developments:

(1) women have started getting more and more education;
(2) their status in the family has been elevated;
(3) they are now entering into the job in sizeable numbers.

One study suggested that increasing number of educated and professionally trained women were entering different jobs in diverse fields (Parikh and Kumar, 1987). Another important qualitative change in the status of women is the perceptible change in attitudes towards women in the corporate sector. This change in attitude has come because of the increasing number of female students passing out from the management institutes. Women are not only joining traditional jobs but they are opting for many non-traditional professions (Ramachandran, 1990). For example, women have excelled in the advertising profession.

One question that comes to the mind is whether advertising in India is reflecting has taken this change in its advertising campaigns by depicting women realistically or not. Unfortunately no serious research has been done to find out the role portrayal of women in advertisement in the Indian context. Present study is an attempt to analyse the TV commercials in terms of role portrayal of women.

RESEARCH METHOD

In their review of literature on sex stereotyping in advertising, Courtney & Whipple (1984) suggest the following:

1. There is mounting evidence that sex stereotyping in advertising does play a role in reflecting societal ills and helping to sustain them. There is also mounting evidences, however, that more responsible advertising could play a positive and beneficial role in helping to change them.
2. This shows the importance of advertising content on the society and places a heavy burden of responsibility upon the advertising industry.

Therefore, to examine this impact of advertising content, TV commercials over a period of time were taken for analysis. Because role portrayals have been found to vary across the product category (Sexton and Haberman, 1974), we also explicitly examine the functional relationship between role portrayals and product classification.

The Instruments

The instruments employed in the present study are mainly drawn from scales developed by Sexton and Haberman (1974) and Pingree, *et al.* (1976). The Sexton and Haberman rating system included traditional measures of manifest content such as number and gender of adults, advertisement composition, environment, role and manifest relation of woman to others in the advertisement (interpersonal context). These included: relation of woman to the product, appearance, and traditional versus non-traditional depiction (see Figure 12.1 for detailed classification).

The Scale of *Sexism* ("level of consciousness scale") employed by Pingree *et al.* (1976), is outlined in Figure 12.1. It has classified media portrayals of woman into five conceptually driven categories which are believed to possess an ordinal relationship to each other. As such, it allows the "meaning" of an image to reside in the interpretation of that image rather than in some objective measure of content elements. Another instrument used in analysing the advertisement content was to examine the relationship between general product category and classification of women in terms of the manifest interpersonal "sex roles". housewife/mother, social companion/date, employee/ consumer, and model/other. In this method, the individual advertisement was taken and from the advertising content the portrayal of women as housewife/mother, social companion/date, employee/consumer and model/other was ascertained. The female was classified as housewife/mother in the advertisement showing her as a typical Indian female doing household chores or looking after family or children.

Figure 12.1 Latent Content Variables in Advertisement (Sexton and Haberman's 1979)

Relation of Women to Product

Participating in the Product's use (functional)

Decorative (no functional relation to the product)

Appearance

Obviously alluring

(following pilot tests, defined as "the model's body or face is being used to entice or tempt the viewer of the advertisement into liking or using the product")

Non-alluring

Traditional/Non-Traditional

The situation in which the woman appears would be considered by society as traditional/non-traditional for a woman.

Usually the product advertised was any household product or appliance such as the Maggie Noodles advertisement or washing machine advertisement.

Social Companion/date

In this role women is shown as an appendage attached to male so as to glamorise the product or to add social value to the product. She is shown as a companion of men which could be necessary (in case of gender specific products) or unnecessary (advertisements showing females promoting products which are exclusively used by men).

Employee/Consumer

In this case the female is rightfully depicted as the user of the product.

Model/Other

In this category the female is there just to advertise the product.

She is used as glamorous sex-object and not be user of the product.

This pattern suggests that the sponsors of advertisements appearing in TV tend to portray women in a sex role that is consistent with (or relevant to) the product type. This sex role/ product congruency is a pattern that some researchers (Wortzel and Trisbie, 1974) have found women to prefer.

Figure 12.2 Pingree et al.'s (1976) "Scale of *Sexism*" Dimensions Coded in the Study

Level-1. Put her down and belittle her.

Dumb blonde, Sex object, Victim.

Level-2. Keep her in her place

Woman shown in romantic situation

Traditional role of wife, mother, secretary, nurse; unwomanly traits, a woman shown as doctor, engineer, etc.; seems to be doing something beyond her capabilities.

Level-3. Woman in two places

May be a lawyer, but must still have dinner on the table.

Career is something extra, after housework.

Level-4. She is fully equal

Woman treated as a professional.

Not necessary to mention home or mothering.

Men can do housework as well as the woman.

Level -5. Non-stereotypic

Woman shown as superior to men in some cases; inferior in others.

People not judged by sex.

Women may be have in a traditionally masculine way, men may behave in traditionally feminine way.

A related manifest content dimension examines the content of interpersonal relationship depicted in the advertisements. This "relationship to other" variable was coded into the following typology: family context, social context, business context, in personal context, nobody else. This type of classification tells about the set-up of the advertisement.

Another dimension in this study is the "latent advertising content" for the different product classes (Sexton and Haberman, 1974). The content dimension "latent" requires not only observation but also interpretation of the woman's role. That is, latent content categories require assessment of the connotative meaning of the role portrayal. The three latent content dimensions drawn from the Sexton and Haberman (1974) study within which each of the two broadly defined categories are:

1. a "decorative" rather than functional role of the women in relation to the product;
2. a "traditional approach of the woman" interpreted as enticing the consumer into liking or using the product.

Instrument Reliability

Two female coders were trained to completely understand operational definitions of the manifest and latent content variables. In a recent study of commercial content, Wilkes and Valencia (1984) noted that the ethnicity or race of coders may be significant factor biasing their observations. These findings, seen in the light of Bruner's (1954) earlier work, suggest that when feasible, coders should be members of the medium's natural audience.

In this study the two female coders had to fill up the proforma (Figure 12.3) for the content analysis of TV commercials. The advertisements for which there was a consensus in responses of the two female coders were taken into account.

Procedure

A total of around 700 advertisements were recorded on video cassettes. These advertisements included commercials that were televised during the period from October 1996 to January 1997. The commercials recorded were the ones telecast at prime time on various channels. To avoid duplication and repetition of commercials, a commercial (for the same brand) was considered only once. In total, 495 individual advertisements were considered for analysis. Out of these only 422 advertisements, featuring women, were considered for the ultimate analysis. Of these, 73 commercials did not have any female and showed children, males or animals. A structured proforma was filled up by the two coders to know the manifest content variables i.e. product category, manifest sex roles, latent advertisement content, level of *sexism* and relationship with others.

In order to examine whether or not observed frequencies of the various manifest and latest content categories and level of *Sexism* in the TV commercials are related to product class or not, chi-square analysis was performed. Further, frequency distributions of product and content variables were also analysed on individual basis. The chi-square figures and subsequent degrees of freedom are shown at the end of each table and they have been discussed in the section on analysis.

ANALYSIS

Categorisation of Products

At the outset, TV commercials appearing on prime time and prime 'A' time were analysed. On the basis of the question number 3 of the content analysis proforma, the products were broadly categorised in the following manner:

1. Toiletries (Soap, Detergents, Toothpastes)–68 (13.6%)
2. Drinks and Eatables (Tea, Coffee, Softdrinks and others)–34 (6.8%)
3. Medicine and Health products–64 (12.8%)
4. Personal Appearance (Cosmetics, Clothing, Footwear)–115 (23.2%)
5. Home products and Home appliances – 106 (21.2%)
6. Services–6 (1.2%)
7. Paints and home furnishings–30 (6%)
8. Automobiles and Vehicles–14 (2.8%)
9. Chocolates and Biscuits–34 (6.8%)
10. Miscellaneous items (Watches, mosquito repellent and related gadgets office equipment) – 32(6.4%)

(*In front of the product category, the frequency of the advertisements with the percentage is given. Here, the total number of advertisements taken into account is 495*).

These ten product categories were further combined into five categories for the purpose of analysis. These are as follows:

1. Drinks and confectionary products

This category included all types of drinks, whether hot or cold, beverages like tea and coffee, and confectionary items like biscuits, chocolates etc. The number of advertisements under this category

Figure 12.3 Content Analysis Proforma for Role Portrayal of Women in TV Commercials

1. Advertisement number.
2. Brand name
3. Product category
4. Manifest Sex Role of Women
   - *(a)* Housewife/Happy mother
   - *(b)* Social Companion of men
   - *(c)* Employee/consumer
   - *(d)* Model/other
5. Relationship with other
   - *(a)* Family set-up
   - *(b)* Social set-up
   - *(c)* Business
   - *(d)* Impersonal
   - *(e)* Nobody else
6. Latent Advertising Content in TV Commercials
   - *(a)* *(i)* Functional (Using/User of the Product)
     - *(ii)* Decorative
   - *(b)* *(i)* Traditional
     - *(ii)* Non-traditional
   - *(c)* Appearance
     - *(i)* Alluring
     - *(ii)* Non-alluring
7. *Sexism* Scale
   - *(a)* Level 1 (Put her down and belittle her)
   - *(b)* Level 2 (Keep her in her place)
   - *(c)* Level 3 (Women in two places)
   - *(d)* Level 4 (She is fully equal)
   - *(e)* Level 5 (Non-stereotypic)

were 68 out of 495 i.e. 13.6%.

2. Personal appearance products

Under this included cosmetic items, feminine hygiene products, clothing and footwear. All the items included in this category were the ones that were for personal use. The number of advertisements in this product category were 116 which accounted for 23.2% of the total commercials.

3. Home products, appliances and furnishings

Items included in this category were edible oils, glues, spices, sewing machines, automobiles, pressure cookers, suitcases, bulbs, paints, etc. Number of advertisements falling in this category were 30% i.e. 150 advertisements. Maximum number of advertisements were related to this category.

4. Medicine and Toiletteries

Items under this category were OTC drugs like painkillers, balms, ointments, health drinks, toothpastes, detergents and soaps. All such items were put in one category because of their chemical nature. These advertisements constituted around 24.8% (124) of the total.

5. Miscellaneous

Under this category rest of the items were placed. They include services, tobacco products, and office equipments like filing cabinets etc. There were 42 advertisements in this category constituting 8.4% of the total.

Latent Content of Role Portrayal of Women

As mentioned earlier, the TV commercials were analysed on the content dimension that may be considered latent. These contents were considered to be latent because not only they require observation but also interpretation of the women's role in advertisement. There was a possibility of misinterpretation of the latent content by the coders. However, the latent content was analysed strictly in accordance with the Sexton and Haberman's (1974) coding procedure.

As given in figure 12.1, the latent content of role portrayal of women was divided into three variables:

1. Relation of women to product,
2. Apearance of women, and
3. The role depicted in the advertisement.

These variables analysed in terms of different product categories and the results are given in Tables 12.1, 12.2 and 12.3. Examining Table 12.1, one finds that the role of women in relation to the product categories is more or less similar, of course with a few exceptions. Predominantly, in almost all product categories one observes the functional role of women in the advertisements and higher percentage as compared to the per entage of women portrayed in decorative roles. The same is clearly evident from Table 12.1. However, when chi-square analysis was applied, these differences were found to be insignificant, indicating more or less equal portrayal of women in both functional and decorative roles (chi-square = 3.02, df = 2, P<.9).

Table 12.1
Latent Advertising Content in T.V. Commercials for different Product Categories

Product Categories	*Relation to the Product*		*Product Category*
	Functional	*Decorative*	*Totals*
Personal appearance	32 (59.25%)	22 (40.75%)	54 (25.6%)
Drinks & Confectionary items	15 (57.69%)	11 (42.31%)	26 (12.32%)
Home product and appliances	31 (50.81%)	30 (49.19%)	61 (28.9%)
Medicine & Toiletries	28 (54.90%)	23 (42.1%)	51 (24.17%)
Misc.	13 (68.42%)	6 (31.58%)	19 (09.00%)

Chi-square χ^2 =3.02, 4 df, P<.9.
(Based on 211 advertisements containing women).

Table 12.2 categorises the role portrayal of women in terms of their appearance as alluring or non alluring. In the alluring role, the women are suposed to entice the consumers into liking or using the product. Surprisingly, in only 37% of the advertisements featuring personal appearance products, alluring women were used. In case of drinks and confectionary products, least number of women were used in alluring role (23.07%). Alluring appearance of women was most frequently observed in miscellaneous products category (68.42%) and home products and appliances (65.57%). Chi-square analysis showed significant differences as far as the alluring appearance of women was concerned (χ^2 = 19.86, df = 2, P < .001).

Table 12.3 summarises the third latent content variable i.e. traditional versus non-traditional role in which the women appear. Interestingly, the traditional role was most frequently observed in advertisements for personal appearance products (79.62%) and drinks and confectionary products (80.76%). The least frequent traditional

Table 12.2
Latent Advertising Content in T.V. Commercials for different Product Categories

S.No.	*Product Categories*	*Appearance*		
		Alluring	*Non-alluring*	*Totals*
1.	Personal appearance	20 (37.03)	34 (62.79)	54 (25.60%)
2.	Drinks & Confectionary items	06 (23.07)	20 (76.93)	26 (12.32%)
3.	Home product and appliances	40 (65.57)	21 (34.43)	61 (28.9%)
4.	Medicine & Toiletries	27 (52.34)	24 (47.06)	51 (24.17%)
5.	Misc.	13 (68.42)	06 (31.58)	19 (09.00%)

Chi-square χ^2 =19.866, 4 df, P<.9.
(Based on 211 advertisements containing women)

role occurred in miscellaneous products (31.58%) followed by home products (42.62%) and medicine and toiletteries (43.13%). This trend corroborates the findings of Fergusen, Kreshel and Tinkham (1990). This indicates the under representation of women and persistence of traditional "happy housewife" and "keep her in her place" role stereotypes in personal apearance and drinks and confectionary products. However, the non-traditional aspects are highlighted in the remaining three product categories. The chi-square analysis was found to be significant across product categories (chi-square = 29.14, df = 2, P < 0.001).

Level of Sexism and Product Categories

Three additional latent content dimensions derived from the ordinal Scale of *Sexism* used by Pingree *et al.* (1976) were analysed with respect to the five product categories. The original five levels were converted into low, moderate and high categories of *Sexism*. Level 1 (portrayal as a sex object) and level 2 (keep her in her place) were considered to high and moderate levels of *Sexism*, resepctively. The final latent content dimension reported here (considered lowest in sexist role portrayal) combines level 3, 4 and 5 of the Scale of *Sexism*. This last dimension thus includes portrayals featuring women in multiple roles at once; as fully equal professionals; or in completely non-stereotypical roles. The regrouping of Scale of *Sexism* measures was done in accordance with the Fergusen *et.al.* (1990). study. This regrouping of Scale of *Sexism* measures and the different product categories is given in Table 12.4. It is interesting to note that high level of *Sexism* i.e. women as sex objects was more pronounced in personal appearance (56.7%), drinks and confectionary products (65.4%). This pattern was consistent with the traditional and alluring dimensions described earlier.

In aggregate terms for all the product categories, the prevalence of low level of *Sexism* was found to be low, indicating the persistence of advertisers and advertising professionals on portraying the women either as sex objects in romantic situations, or traditional roles of wife, mother, secretary and nurse. In Table 12.4, the moderate level of *sexism* is evident in case of home products and appliances (70.5%), miscellaneous products (52.6%) and medicines and toiletteries (47.1%). It is clear from this table that in spite of emancipation of Indian women and the changing role of women in the society, advertisers still continue to portray women in their traditional roles. A chi-square anaylsis of data contained in Table 12.4 indicates that these patterns are statistically significant (chi-square=36.14, df=4, P<0.001).

Manifest Sex Roles in TV Commercials

The manifest contents in an advertisement are traditional measures and have been examined by many researchers. These include such variables as number and gender of adults, presence or absence of children, advertisement composition, environment, role and manifest relation of women to others in the advertisements. For the present study only the manifest relation of women to others has been taken.

Table 12.5 examines the relationship between five general product categories and classification of women in terms of the manifest interpersonal sex roles: housewife/mother, social companion/date, employee/consumer and model/others. The portrayal of these roles varies significantly across product class (chi-square = 52.55, df = 12, P < .001). For personal appearance products, one can note that the modal sex role depicted is model/others (40.74%); while for drinks and confectionary products, women are

Table 12.3
Latent Advertising Content in TV Commercials for different Product Categories (Sexton and Haberman)

S.No.	*Product Categories*	*Appearance*		*Product Category*
		Traditional	*Non-traditional*	*Totals*
1.	Personal appearance	43 (79.62)	11 (20.35)	54 (25.6%)
2.	Drinks & Confectionary items	21 (80.76)	5 (19.23)	26(12.32%)
3.	Home product and appliances	26 (42.62)	35 (57.38)	61 (28.9%)
4.	Medicine & Toiletries	22 (43.14)	29 (56.86)	51(24.17%)
5.	Misc.	6 (31.58)	13 (68.42)	19 (9%)

Chi-square χ^2 =29.142, 4 df, P<0.9
(Based on 211 advertisements containing women)

most frequently portrayed in the social companion/date role (38.5%). In the home product appliance category, housewife/mother role (75.4%) was the most frequently portrayed one. Again, in medicine and toiletteries housewife/mother was the modal sex role (49%). In miscellaneous products also, housewife/mother sex role was frequently used. This pattern indicates that the advertisers and copywriters tend to portray women in a sex role i.e. consistent with the product type. As home products and appliances, medicine and toiletteries are consumed in the household, the housewife/mother role is emphasised in the advertisements. The congruency between the sex role and product category has been found to be the dominant pattern by some researchers (Wortzel and Frisbie, 1974). Both personal appearance products and drinks and confectionary products are consumed/used on an individual basis, therefore, the model/other and social companion/date sex roles are being used more frequently than others.

The relationship to *others* with different product categories is given in Table 12.6. This table indicates that the modal category for personal appearance products is impersonal (59.2%) followed by social setup (26%). In case of drinks and confectionary items, social content relationship (53.8%) was the most frequently depicted relationship. In the remaining three product categories i.e. home

Table 12.4
Latent Advertising Content in TV Commercials for Different Product Categories

S.No.	Product Categories	Level of Sexism			Product Category
		Low	Moderate	High	Totals
1.	Personal appearance	3 (05.6)	15 (27.70)	36 (66.70)	54 (25.60%)
2.	Drinks & Confectionary items	3 (11.5)	6 (23.10)	17 (65.40)	26 (12.32%)
3.	Home product and appliances	5 (08.2)	43 (70.50)	13 (21.30)	61 (28.90%)
4.	Medicine & Toiletries	4 (07.8)	24 (47.10)	23 (45.10)	51 (24.17%)
5.	Misc.	4 (21.1)	10 (52.60)	05 (26.30)	19 (09.00%)
	Sexism and Totals	19 (9.0)	98 (46.44)	94 (44.56)	211 (100%)

Chi-square = χ^2 =36.1463, 4 df, P<.001;

Low = Level 3, 4, 5; Moderate = level 2; High = level 1 on "Scale of Sexism"

Table 12.5
Contingency Table Analysis of Manifest of Sex Roles in Commercials by Product Category

S.No.	Product Categories	Level of Sexism				Total
		Housewife/ Mother	Social Consumer	Employee/ Consumer	Model/ Others	
1.	Personal appearance	8 (14.8)	9 (16.6)	17 (31.5)	22 (40.74)	54 (25.60%)
2.	Drinks & Confectionary items	5 (19.2)	10 (38.5)	4 (15.38)	7 (26.9)	26 (12.32%)
3.	Home product and appliances	46 (75.4)	5 (8.2)	3 (4.9)	7 (11.47)	61 (28.90%)
4.	Medicine & Toiletries	25 (49)	6 (11.76)	10 (19.6)	10 (19.6)	51 (24.17%)
5.	Misc.	9 (47.3)	2 (10.5)	3 (15.8)	3 (15.8)	19 (9.00%)

Chi-square χ^2 =52.55, 12 df, P<.001.

Table 12.6
Contingency Table Analysis of Women's Relationship to other People in TV Commercials by Product Category

S.No.	*Product Categories*	*Level of Sexism* *Family Setup*	*Social Setup*	*Business*	*Impersonal*	*Total*
1.	Personal appearance	6 (11.1)	14 (26)	2 (3.7)	32 (59.2)	54 (25.6%)
2.	Drinks & Confectionary items	4 (15.3)	14 (53.8)	2 (7.7)	6 (23)	26 (12.32%)
3.	Home product and appliances	41 (67.2)	11 (18)	2 (3.27)	7 (11.47)	61 (28.9%)
4.	Medicine & Toiletries	22 (43.1)	11 (21.56)	0 (0)	18 (35.2)	51 (24.17%)
5.	Misc.	10 (52.6)	4 (21)	2 (10.5)	3 (15.8)	19 (9.00%)

Chi-square χ^2 =69.3691, 12 df, P<.001

products and appliances, medicines and toiletteries and miscellaneous items, modal category was the family setup. However, in home products, appliances category, the family setup relationship was disproportionately large (67.2%) and was proportionately small for medicines and toiletteries (43.1%). Business context relationship is disproportionately small across all the product categories. Again, this significant pattern suggests a consistency between product categories and the interpersonal content featured in the advertisements.

CONCLUSIONS

Summary of Results

Using the latent content method of Sexton and Haberman one can conclude that both the functional and decorative role of women are equally used in TV commercials. Chi-square analysis revealed that there was no significant difference between functional and decorative roles. From this we can say that female portrayal is congruent with the product category. In case of alluring appearance and relation to the product, surprisingly, only 37% of the advertisements featured women in personal appearance products. As far the drinks and confectionary items are concerned, women were found to be sparingly used in alluring appearance. In case of miscellaneous products and home products and appliances category, alluring appearance of women was most frequently observed in the advertisements. From this one conclude that in the above said categories, alluring women were used so that the female buyers could associate themselves with the glamorous image of the female models shown in the advertisements. This attaches social value to the product too. Thus, we may conclude that, off late, the image of Indian female is changing, no longer the female working in kitchen is drab and unglamorous in appearance. Moreover alluring appearance of women is used in home products to show that the glamorous women can also be seen in home settings.

From the third latent content variable study of traditional versus non-traditional role in which women appeared, traditional role was most frequently observed in advertisement for personal apearance products and drinks and confectionary products indicating that the woman is still stereotyped in the traditional "happy house-wife" role. Even today Indian female is "looked down upon" and treated as a dumb passive sex object.

By the "Level of *Sexism*" we can see that the use of women as sex objects is more pronounced in personal appearance and drinks and confectionary products which is consistent with the traditional and alluring dimensions described earlier. Even from the chi-square analysis we can see that these pattern are statistically significant. Thus, even in the changing times there is a long way to go to free the Indian female from the chains of traditional Indian society which considers women as inferior and subservient to their male counterparts.

While examining manifest sex roles in TV commercials, it was noted that the modal sex role in the personal apearance product categories is model/others. In drinks and confectionary products women are most frequently portrayed in the social companion/ date role. In home product and appliances the housewife/mother role portrayal is dominant. Again, we can see that product category is related to role portrayal of women. Products consumed on individual basis have advertisements depicting model/other whereas in other product categories female is depicted according to the setup i.e. in home products, housewife/mother is used.

In "relationship to other" manifest content dimension, modal category for personal appearance product is nobody else/impersonal followed by social context. Business context relationship with regard to women was being depicted in small proportion across all the product categories in the advertisements. This clearly shows that Indian woman, despite their substantial presence in the business world, are not shown realistically in the advertisements. Small representation of women in medicines and toiletteries implies that female are still not considered to have significant role in the purchase of such articles. Her domain is still restricted to home products and appliances.

DISCUSSION

Modal level of *Sexism* differed across product categories. This lack of uniformity was evident in measures of both manifest and latent content. In general, in advertisements for personal apearance and drinks and confectionary products, highest level of *Sexism* was observed. Women are still depicted in romantic situations portraying traditional role stereotypes. Moderate level of *sexism* is depicted in home products and appliances. This phenomenon may, in part, be explained by the management concept of "sex-role/product congruency". That is to say, for certain products which are "sexually relevant" (e.g. cosmetics, clothing) the association of the product with sexually oriented role portrayals may be seen to be appropriate and effective.

From a management perspective, striving for such congruency appears intuitively sound. However, it may in fact diminish an advertisement's effectiveness in communicating with the target audience (and in extreme cases may even among the audience) in so far as the specific role portrayals are perceived to be negative or inappropriate. Alternatively, role portrayals that were once perceived to be inappropriate may become acceptable over time. This suggests, the need for constant management re-evaluation of message content.

The results of the study do raise several questions regarding the ability of the measures to truly capture all the nuances of the dynamic *Sexism* construct. Certainly, it is clear that simply counting manifest content elements in an advertisement fails to tap the subtlety and complexity of *sexism*. This argues strongly for the inclusion of interpretive measures of latent content such as those employed here.

Since stereotypes derive meaning from culture, advertisers who rely upon stereotypic role portrayals, and researchers who attempt to evaluate those portrayals must be particularly cognizant of cultural changes as it might impact the interpretation of meaning. Further, in the light of increased interest in fitness and health, greater acceptance of intimacy in persuasive appeals, and greater tolerance of nudity, one can no longer assume that negative stereotypes characterize advertisements which simply "focus on the body". In fact, such advertisements may now seen to be quite positive.

The use of latent as well as manifest content measures in this study provided insights into the complexity of the concept of *Sexism*, insights that would not have been apparent from an examination of manifest content alone. In light of these insights, researchers in this area would do justice if they consider the adoption of other methodologies (perhaps drawn from disciplines such as interpretive sociology, cultural anthropology and rhetorical criticism) in their efforts to further understand the nature of "sexist" role portrayals. Such methods should consider the relationship of stereotypes to the legitimisation of social power and should address both the descriptive and evaluative aspects of those stereotypes as well as their grounding in social structure.

It should be noted that even using both manifest and latent content measures, any content analysis is inherently descriptive and can provide only limited insight into why significant relationship or trends are observed (Kassarijan, 1977). In this particular study, possible explanations have been discussed for findings in the context of changing social milieu. Another possible avenue of inquiry might be to explore the effect of economic influences on the sex role portrayal of women.

REFERENCES

Bruner, Jerome, S., 1957, "On Perceptual Readiness", *Psychological Review*, 64(March), pp. 123-152.

Courtney, Alice and Thomas Whipple, 1984, "*Sex Stereotyping in Advertising*", Lexington, MA: D.C. Health and Company.

Courtney, E.A. and W.S. Lockeretz, 1971, "A Woman's Place: An Analysis of the Role Portrayed by Women in Magazine Advertisements", *Journal of Marketing Research*, 8, pp. 92-95.

Dominick, J. and G. Rauch, 1972, "The Image of Women in Network Commercials", *Journal of Broadcasting*, 3, pp. 259- 269.

Duker, K.M. and L.R. Tucker, 1977, "Women's Libbers Versus Independent

Women: Study of Preferences for Women's Roles in Advertisements", *Journal of Marketing Research*, 14, pp. 469- 475.

Fergusen, Hick J., Peggy. J. Kreshel and F. Spencer, 1990, "In the pages of MS: Sex Role Portrayal of Women in Advertising", *Journal of Advertising*, 1, pp. 40-51.

Kassarjian, Herold, H, 1977. "Content Analysis in Consumer Research", *Journal of Consumer Research*, 4 (1), pp. 8-18.

McArthur, L.Z. and B.G. Resko, 1975, "The Portrayal of Men and Women in American Television Commercials", *Journal of Social Psychology*, 97, pp. 209-220.

Parikh, I. and Rakesh Kumar, 1987, "Research on Women on Management: A Developmental Prospective", *W.P. No. 663* (Indian Institute of Management, Ahmedabad).

Pingree, S., R. Hawkins, M. Butler and M. Paisley, 1976, "A Scale for Sexism", *Journal of Communication*, 24(4), pp. 193-200.

Prather, J. and L.S. Tidall, 1975, "Sex Differences in Content and Styles of Medical Advertisement", *Social Sciences and Medicine*, 9, pp. 23-26.

Ramachandaran, A., 1990, "Women Managers: Will they make it to the top?" *Business India*, p. 181.

Scheive, C., 1979, "Sex Role in TV Commercials", *Journal of Advertising Research*, 90, pp. 23-27.

Schiffman, G.L. and L.L. Kanuk 2000, *Consumer Behaviour*, 6th ed. (New Delhi, Prentice Hall of India Pvt. Ltd).

Sexton, D. and Haberman, 1974, "Women in Magazine Advertisements", *Journal of Advertising Research*, 14, pp. 41-46.

Sliverstein, A. and R. Sliverstein, 1974, "The Portrayal of Women in TV Advertising", *Federal of Communication Bar Journal*, 1, pp. 71-98.

Venkatasan, M. and J. Losco, 1975, "Women in Magazine Ads: 1959-1971", *Journal of Advertising Research*, 15, pp. 49-54.

Wagner, C.L. and B.J. Banos, 1973, "A Woman's Place: A Follow-up Analysis of the Role Portrayal by Women in Magazine Advertisements", *Journal of Marketing Research*, 10, pp. 213-214.

Wilkes, Robert E. and Humberto Valencia, 1989, "Hispanics and Blacks in Television Commercials", *Journal of Advertising*, 18 (1), pp. 19-25.

Wortzel, L. and J. Frisbie, 1974, "Women's Role Portrayal Preferences in Advertisement: An Empirical Study", *Journal of Marketing*, 28, pp. 41-46.

13

A Cross Cultural Study of Role Portrayals of Men and Women in the Advertisements of India and USA

INTRODUCTION

Advertising profoundly influences our daily life not only in choosing various products and services, but also shapes our attitudes, values and aspirations. Because of its omnipresence, if not omnipotence, advertising has been criticised by many social thinkers on various issues of importance. One such issue is the portrayal of men and women, especially women, in advertising. This issue has further gained importance because of the changing role of women in the society.

Researchers in general and feminist advocates in particular have expressed their concern about the role portrayal of women in advertising. They are of the opinion that depicting women in narrowly defined roles gives the impression to a layman that this is proper and natural (Hawkins and Coney, 1976). In other words, this type of portrayal of women in advertising is injurious to society because it creates, or perpetuates, misconceptions about women (Silverstein and Silverstsein, 1974) and encourages stereotyping. These stereotypes serve as poor role models and inhibit sympathetic understanding of individual differences (Polay, 1986) and such stereotypes encourage the people to think and speak of women primarily in terms of their narrowly defined roles in the society (Courtney and Whipple, 1983).

Defenders of advertising's portrayal of women argue that advertising simply reflects what is already prevalent in the society. Though, this is debatable, yet, there is no doubt that advertising is reflective of cultural sex-role norms to some extent (Pollay, 1986; Holbrooks, 1987). There are differences in cultural norms including role portrayal of women across the countries. In order to find out the differences, if any, of role portrayal of men and women in advertising, the present study was undertaken. This study, through content analysis technique, attempts to compare the role portrayal of men and women in advertements of two countries i.e. India and United States. Only TV commercials have been considered and compared for two reasons. Firstly, the data of United States was available (Gilly, 1988) and secondly, inclusion of other media would have made the comparison difficult.

Literature Review

In the 1970's several researchers examined sex-roles in US advertising, both in print and electronic media, and concluded that women were portrayed differentially than men in advertising (Courtney and Lockeretz, 1971; McArthur and Resko, 1975; Belkaoni and Belkaoni, 1976). Further, women were portrayed as younger and more likely to be married than males. In addition women were depicted as unemployed or employed in traditional female occupations (Schneider and Schneider, 1979). As spokespersons, women were also used less frequently and often were shown as recipient of help and advice from men (Silverstein and Silverstein, 1974). Lysonski (1983) compared the sex roles in magazine advertisements during 1974-1980 and found that women were depicted less frequently dependent on men and more frequently as career oriented. TV commercials, however, had not kept pace with changing sex roles in the American society during that period (Courtney and Whipple, 1983).

As far as India is concerned, very little amount of literature is available on women's role, and if at all it is available, it is in the form of journalistic articles. One thing which makes the Indian culture different from US is the traditional role of women in Indian society. Since times immemorial, women have been relegated to secondary position in the traditional Indian society. Despite various constitutional provisions granting equal privileges to both men and women, yet, women either do not seek employment, or predominantly choose those professions which are considered *suitable* for women. The situation has changed considerably during the last few decades. But, a cursory glance at the present day advertising reveals that marketers and advertisers are still quite insensitive to these changes.

OBJECTIVES AND PURPOSE

The basic aim of this study was to compare the role portrayal of men and women in TV advertisements of India and US Keeping in mind this aim, the following specific objectives were delineated:

- To get acquainted with the TV commercials screened in India.
- To analyse the differences in role portrayals in Indian TV commercials through content analysis.
- To analyse and compare the role portrayals of sexes as depicted in advertisements of India and US

The need for this type of study arose because the sex role differences are prevalent almost in every country of the world and a systematic study is the need of the hour. In advanced countries of the world, these type of exercises are being undertaken at regular intervals. However, in the developing countries, because of late realisation and lack of systematic thinking on the part of researchers, very few or no attempt have been made to analyse the sex role portrayal of men and women in advertising. This study is a modest attempt in this direction. To find out the difference due to culture and technology the TV advertisements of India – a developing country and US – a developed country, were compared on the role portrayal of men and women.

DESIGN OF THE STUDY AND METHODOLOGY

Present study is exploratory as well as comparative in nature and hence it was carried out in two phases. The first phase analyses the sex role portrayal in Indian TV commercials and in the second phase a comparison was made between Indian and US advertisements.

Further, the scope of this study was limited to television commercials aired during prime-time. All non-commercial programmes, programme announcements and social advertisements were excluded from this study. The study of sex-role portrayal in Indian TV advertisements is based on the methodology employed by Gilly (1988). This has been done deliberately to make the comparison with US TV commercials more meaningful.

The following steps were followed for both phases:

1. Prime-time advertisements telecast on major TV channels were videotaped for a one week period. Duplication of commercials was avoided. This resulted in a total of 402 TV commercials.
2. After editing, a content analysis proforma was prepared taking the same variables as used in Gilly's (1988) study. It had the following variables:

   (a) Variables of each commercial

   Under this category four variables were coded:

   (i) Product: Product category being advertised.

   (ii) Product user: Voice of the off-camera announcer.

   (iii) Setting: Locational setting of advertisement.

   (b) Variables of each character in the commercial

   Under this category different variables of each character appearing at least 3 seconds in the commercial were coded with the following categories:

   (i) Demographic variables:

   Age-approximate age of the character.

   Marital status-Married/unmarried/not identified.

   Sex-male/female.

   Employment-Work situation/non-work situation but appears to be employed/no indication.

   Occupation: If employed then type of job.

   (ii) Advertisement Approach variables:

   Advertisement approach variables depict how each character in the advertisement is used. It includes the following:

   Spokesperson: On camera spokesperson.

   Credibility: Characters credibility in terms of a product user or an authority.

   Help: Is the character a recipient of help or

provider of help or neither.
Advice: Is the character a receiver of advice or giver of advice or neither.
Role: In what role is the character primarily portrayed i.e. spouse/boy/friend/girlfriend/ parent, home maker, worker real life celebrity, interviewer etc.

(3) All 402 commercials were analysed on the separate content analysis proforma. Thus, four variables were analysed for each commercial and 10 variables were analysed for each character as defined in the preceeding steps. For coding each variable, two graduate students were explained the procedure and in case of any disagreement the researchers used their discretion after discussing the same with the two raters.

(4) For comparison of Indian TV commercials with the US commercials, the data reproduced by Gilly (1988) was taken in the same form.

RESULTS

Table 13.1 compares the distribution of commercials across product categories. This table reveals various differences in commercials of India when compared with those of the US. In order to facilitate the comparison between Indian and US commercials, the products were divided into the same number of categories as given in Gilly's (1988) study. The comparison has shown the following differences.

In both the countries, the food, snacks and cold drinks category comprises the largest percentage. However, the percentage is more in case of US (30.97) than in case of India (21.25). Another important difference is that household appliances and furnishings category has the same percentage as that of food snacks and cold drinks in India whereas in case of US household appliances are rarely advertised and they cover only 2.2% out of the total commercials. Personal and health care products represent 20.75% of Indian advertisements, whereas, their percentage is only 10.9 in US advertisements. Retail and Restaurant advertisements represent nearly 9% in US advertisements and none in Indian commercials.

Table 13.1
Distribution of Commercials Across Product Categories

Product Category	*India*		*United States*	
	No.	*%*	*No.*	*%*
1. Food, Snacks & Cold Drinks	87	21.75	85	30.9
2. Personal & Beauty Care	83	20.75	30	10.9
3. Automobiles & Accessories	20	5	7	2.5
4. Restraunts & Retail Outlets	0	0	24	8.7
5. Drugs & Medicines	47	11.75	36	13.1
6. Household Appliances	85	21.25	6	2.2
7. Institutional/Public Services	5	1.25	4	1.5
8. Alcoholic Beverages	0	0	0	0
9. Pet & Related Foods	0	0	7	2.5
10. Household Cleaning Agents	25	6.25	30	10.9
11. Clothings	30	7.5	11	4
12. Finance & Real Estates	8	2	3	1.1
13. Others	10	2.5	32	11.7
Total	400	100	275	100

Another important finding was that in both the countries, there was no representation of industrial product advertisements. The comparison of commercials across the product categories of the two countries has been made to examine the sex role portrayals in these countries. However, the purpose of research was to examine sex role stereotypes regardless of the product advertised.

As regards the *sex*, the character primarily portrayed in US commercials were women (54.7%). In Indian commercials, the percentage of male portrayals (48.4%) exceeded that of females. However, we did not found any significant differences in the primary character portrayal in the commercials of both the countries.

Table 13.2 compares certain characteristics of commercials in which men and women appear. First, the sex of the user of the product being advertised was identified and the percentage of male and female characters appearing in each kind of commercial was calculated. Significant differences were observed

Table 13.2
Comparison of Men & Women in the Indian & US Commercials

Advertisement Characteristics	*India* (%)		*United States* (%)	
	Women	*Men*	*Women*	*Men*
Product User				
Female	31.76	1.1	13	2.3
Male	2.36	15.47	0.6	3
Either	65.88	85.43	86.4	94.7
	$\chi^2 = 27.77$*		$\chi^2 = 13.52$**	
Setting				
Home	61.11	33.7	33.5	22.7
Store	5.2	9.3	9	6.8
Occupational	4.7	11.6	3.6	15.2
Outdoors	28.8	48.3	11.4	7.6
Other	0	2.3	42.5	47.7
	$\chi^2 = 24.83$*		$\chi^2 = 16.30$**	
Voice-over				
Female	18		12.5	
Male	78.5		67.2	
Chorus	6.25		9.5	
None	3.25		10.5	

*$p \leq 0.001$
**$p \leq 0.01$

between the two countries. In US, women were featured in those product advertisements which were exclusively used by women or by both the sexes, but rarely appeared in commercials for men's products. Men appeared primarily in commercials for products used by either sex. However, Indian commercials reflected sex stereotyping to a greater extent as compared to US commercials. In India, female characters appeared more in advertisements for products used by women (32%) than in the US (13%).

As far as *setting* variable was concerned, male and female characters were portrayed significantly in different settings in both US and Indian commercials. Women were more likely to be portrayed in homes and outdoors, in US advertisements, whereas, men were more likely to appear in work situations and outdoors. This was more pronounced in the case of Indian commercials. Indian women were portrayed mostly in home setting (61%) as compared to those in US (33%). Another interesting finding is that along with men, women appeared outdoors more in Indian ads (28.8%) than in US ads (11.4%).

In terms of *voice-over* used in commercials, the male voice was dominant in both countries. However, it was more pronounced in case of Indian commercials (see Table 13.2).

Table 13.3 shows how male and female characters in commercials differed on the demographic variables of age, marital status, employment status and occupation. In both the countries, women were significantly more likely than men to be portrayed as young (under 35 years of age). The discrepancy between men's and women's ages is more in the American advertisements with 40% of the female characters appearing to be younger than 35 in contrast to only 19% of the male characters. In Indian advertisements the percentage of younger women was higher (67%) than US (40.2%), and surprisingly, the percentage of younger males was also quite high (50%) *vis-a-vis* US commercials (19.7%).

In case of *marital status*, significant differences were found so far as Indian ads are concerned. Nearly 50% women were shown as married whereas only 23% men were shown as married. However, in case of American ads no significant differences were found in the marital status of men and women. For most characters, both male and female, no indication of marital status was given. In US, some characters were rarely portrayed as being obviously single.

As far as the *employment status* was concerned, significant differences were observed in both the countries *vis-a-vis* male and female characters. Women were consistently less likely to be portrayed as employed (whether at work or not) than men in both US and India. In case of India almost three fourth of male characters were depicted in the employment (at work as well not at work) and female characters were shown employed only in one fifth of the cases.

Finally, in terms of *occupation*, female characters, in either US or Indian commercials, were not portrayed in occupations that would be classified as professional/top level business executive. In case of Indian commercials the modal occupation of women was entertainers which constituted nearly seventy per cent. In case of US advertisements, the modal category was middle level managers followed by blue collar workers and entertainers. In Indian commercials the distribution of various occupations for male characters was broad as compared to the female characters. In terms of differences of character portrayals between the two countries, no significant differences were found as far as the occupations of men and women were concerned. But in India, this was found to be highly significant. This clearly indicates the narrow depiction of women in certain predetermined occupations in India, whereas, in US women were shown in as many occupations as men were shown.

In the last phase of the study, an attempt was made to analyse various ad approach variables–how male and female characters are used in commercials. The results are shown in Table 13.4. This table shows the comparison of male and female characters in the way they were used in the commercials. Here five ad approach variables were analysed. They are spokesperson, credibility of character shown, help recipient/provider, advice taker/giver and type of role portrayed.

As far as the use of *spokesperson* in the commercials for both the countries was concerned, the table 13.4 shows both women and men were being used as spokesperson in more or less same proportions. This was also corroborated by the chi-square analysis which showed no significant differences. However, the basis for credibility as spokesperson did vary between men and women in both the countries. Both in Indian and US commercials, women were used as spokespersons because they were depicted as product users more often than men but they were presented as authorities less often than men.

Results did not differ between the two countries on sex of characters portrayed as recipient or provider of *help* which is defined in physical terms. In both the countries, both the males and the females were shown receiving as well as providing help in the advertisements in more or less same proportions. However, in US commercials women were portrayed more often as recipients of *advice* and men were the providers of advice. In case of Indian commercials the situation is slightly different. Here women were portrayed less often as providers of advice as compared to men.

Table 13.3
Comparison of Indian & US Commercials on Demographic Variables

	India (%)		United States (%)	
Advertisement Characteristics	*Women*	*Men*	*Women*	*Men*
Product User				
Demographic Variables				
Age				
< 35	67.64	50.82	40.2	19.7
35 to 50	31.17	44.75	50.9	62.1
> 50	1.19	4.43	8.9	18.2
	$\chi^2 = 11.52$**		$\chi^2 = 16.64$**	
Marital Status				
Married	48.23	23.21	21	20.5
Not Married	5.29	11.04	0.5	0
Not identified	46.48	65.75	78.4	79.5
	$\chi^2 = 25.08$*		n.s.	
Employment Status				
Employed-at work	7.05	22.65	16	32.6
Employed-not at work	13.52	50.82	8.9	18.9
Not Employed	79.43	26.53	75.1	48.5
	$\chi^2 = 28.09$*		$\chi^2 = 22.73$*	
Occupation				
Top Executives	0	27.81	0	8.7
Entertainers	67.64	15.03	26.2	20.3
Mid-Managers	20.56	46.61	35.7	29
White Collar	14.7	1.5	4.8	7.2
Blue Collar	0	9.05	14.9	24.6
Others	0	0	19	10.9
	$\chi^2 = 34.42$*		n.s.	

*p ≤ 0.001
**p ≤ 0.01

The role variable was divided into three categories as was done by McArthur and Resko (1975):

(1) roles that defined the character in terms of his or her relationship to the other i.e. spouse, parent, housewife, son etc.

Table 13.4
Comparison of Indian & US Commercials on Ad-Approach Variables

Advertisement Characteristics	*India* (%) *Women*	*Men*	*United States* (%) *Women*	*Men*
Spokesperson				
Yes	48.23	42.54	60.4	56.1
No	51.77	57.54	39.6	43.9
	n.s.		n.s.	
Credibility				
User	95.29	82.87	85.3	67.6
Authority	4.71	17.13	14.7	32.4
	χ^2 = 13.69**		χ^2=6.82***	
Help				
Recipient	10	14.36	7.7	9.8
Provider	10.58	11.6	13	12.1
Neither	79.42	74.04	79.3	78
	n.s.		n.s.	
Advice				
Recipient	18.23	19.33	11.8	9.1
Provider	27.05	23.75	7.1	15.9
Neither	54.72	56.92	81.1	75
	χ^2=6.12***		n.s.	
Role				
Relative to others	71.76	35.35	37.3	21.2
Independent	17.64	41.43	30.2	58.3
Neither	10.06	23.22	32.5	20.5
	χ^2=46.65*		χ^2=24.12**	

*$p \leq 0.001$
**$p \leq 0.01$
***$p \leq 0.05$

(2) roles that defined the character independently of others such as worker, celebrity, executive, scientists, etc. and
(3) other.

In both the countries significant differences were found as far as *role* characters were concerned. In India, most of the female characters were portrayed in roles that defined them relative to others, whereas, majority of male characters were portrayed in US in a manner that defined them independently of others. It is interesting to note that in case of Indian commercials male characters were portrayed in substantial number both independent to others and related to others. This may be due to the fact that the family ties are still very strong in India as compared to US.

CONCLUSIONS

The content analysis findings regarding the sex role portrayals in Indian and US commercials provides valuable insights into the cultural influences on advertising.

The television commercials from these countries generally reflect stereotypes of male-female roles. In both the countries male voices are more likely to be used than female voices in voice-overs. As far as the product use was concerned, in both the countries, main product users belonged to either sex. However, the percentage of *either* is very high in US commercials where both men or women appear. Female product users are very high in Indian commercials than in the US. In Indian commercials women were more often portrayed as being young than men, and men more likely to be portrayed in independent roles, whereas, women were portrayed in roles related to others. Also, in case of Indian commercials, women were more likely to be portrayed in the home settings as compared to their US counterparts. This difference was quite pronounced when *setting* was compared with the other categories. US commercials were more likely to portray women in *other* settings than women in Indian commercials.

On most of the variables studied, the Indian commercials exhibited more differences between men and women than US commercials. One interesting finding with respect to Indian commercials was the age of male models. More than half (50.82%) of the male characters shown were less than 35 years old, whereas, in case of US, the modal age ranged from 35 to 40 years. In both the countries, older age models i.e. above 50 years, were used sparingly.

Another interesting difference between Indian and US commercials was with regard to the explicit/implicit depiction of marital status.

In nearly half of the Indian commercials, women were shown as married–either in the roles of a mother, wife or daughter-in-law. Explicit/implicit depiction of married women was less likely in case of US commercials. This indicates that in India the portrayal of women in typical traditional roles is much more prevalent as compared to the US advertisements. Women are also more likely to be portrayed as being less independent in Indian commercials than in the US. As far as the depiction of employment status in the commercials was concerned, in both the countries, significant differences did not exist. In both the countries' advertisements more men were shown as being employed than women. Interestingly, a high percentage of women (67.64%) in Indian commercials were shown as entertainers, whereas, this figure was quite low (26.2%) in case of US commercials. In both the countries' commercials, not a single woman was shown occupying high managerial/organisational position. This is understandable in case of India as the process of women emancipation started during late 1970s. However, the absence of women's portrayal as top executives in US commercials is surprising. In this context it is interesting to note that the concept of egalitarian society has long been recognised in US and women are actively involved in nation building activities.

As far as the comparison of women's portrayal for *ad approach* variables is concerned, we did not find any significant difference. In both countries' commercials, little differences existed as far as spokesperson was concerned. On other ad approach variables too, the commercials of the two countries did not exhib much difference. However, in case of Indian commercials the depiction of women in stereotypical roles was more prevalent than US. Only in case of women's role *relative to others* Indian commercials showed women as being more dependent on others rather than in independent roles as showed in the US commercials.

The Indian commercials reflected more traditional sex roles than the US advertisements, but the differences, given the traditional sex role played by women in the Indian society, were not as pronounced as expected. But with the advent of globalisation and liberalisation of Indian economy and the exposure to international mass media, particularly satellite television, women are expected to be portrayed in a more realistic and egalitarian way in future.

The findings of the present study suggest that there is a possible relationship between the culture of the country and the appeals used– at least to the extent of *sex roles* in advertising. For a country like India, perceived to be developing one, and much more tradition bound than US, sex role stereotyping was not much different than in US. It is possible that while depicting stereotype sex roles, the advertisers may not even be aware of the fact that they are responsible for perpetuating this trend.

Finally, while concluding, we suggest that these type of content analysis studies should be undertaken on a periodic basis, but in addition, qualitative evalution of advertising is needed. This will be of great help in ascertaining the message contained in the commercials *vis-a-vis* sex roles (Courtney and Whipple, 1983). Further, as suggested by Pollay (1986), there is a need to ascertain the unintended consequences of sex role portrayal in advertising on society at large.

REFERENCES

Belkaoui, Ahmed and Janis M. Belkaoui (1976), "A Comparative Analysis of the Role Portrayed by Women in Print Advertisements : 1958, 1970, 1972", *Journal of Marketing Research,* 13, pp. 168-72.

Courtney, Alice E. and Sarah Wernick Lockeretz (1971), "A Woman's Place : An Analysis of the Role Portrayed by Women in Magazine Advertisements", *Journal of Marketing Research*, 8, pp. 92-95.

Courtney, Alice E. and Thomas W. Whipple (1983), *Sex Stereotyping in Advertising*, MA : Lexington Books.

Gilly, Mary C. (1988), "Sex Roles in Advertising : A Comparison of Television Advertisements in Australia, Mexico, and the United States", *Journal of Marketing*, Vol. 52, pp. 75-85.

Hawkins, Del I. and Kenneth A. Corey (1976), "Advertising and Differentiated Sex Roles in Contemporary American Society", *Journal of the Academy of Marketing Science,* 4, pp. 418-428.

Holbrook, Morris B. (1987), "Mirror, Mirror on the Wall, What's Unfair in the Reflections on Advertising"? , *Journal of Marketing*, 51, pp. 95-103.

Lysonski, Steven (1985), "Role Portrayals in British Magazine Advertisements," *European Journal of Marketing* , 19(7), pp. 37-55.

McArthur, Leslie, Zebrowitz and Beth Gabrielle Resko (1975), "The Portrayal of Men and Women in American Television Commercials", *Journal of Social Psychology*, 97, pp. 209-220.

Pollay, Richard W. (1986), "The Distorted Mirror : Reflections on the Unintended Consequences of Advertising", *Journal of Marketing*, 50, pp. 18-36.

Schneider, Kenneth C. and Sharon Barich Schneider (1979), "Trends in Sex Roles in Television Commercials", *Journal of Marketing*, 43, pp. 79-84.

Silverstein, Arthur Jay and Rebecca Silverstein (1974), "The Portrayal of Women in Television Commercials", *Journal of Communications*, 27, pp. 71-93.

14

Moderating Effect of Family Type on Husband and Wife Involvement in Purchase Decisions

INTRODUCTION

Marketers have acknowledged the role of family in general and involvement of husband-wife dyad in the purchase decision-making process in particular (Grashef and Dickshaw, 1980). The information about who influences the purchase decision within a family setup serves as the basic input in designing the marketing communication and subsequently in media selection. Researchers have categorised household decision-making as husband dominated, wife dominated, syncratic (joint decision) and autonomic (individualised decisions) (Davis and Rigaux, 1974 and Lavin, 1986).

This study attempts to investigate the relative influence of husband-wife in purchase decisions *vis-a-vis* four product categories. Type of family has been taken as moderating variable and level of involvement of husband-wife as dependent and nature of product as independent variable.

Previous Research

Research in this area has indicated that husband/wife influence in purchase decision process depends to a great extent on three factors. Firstly, this influence is product specific (Ferber and Lee, 1974); Woodside and Motes, (1979). Secondly within a specific product category the husband-wife influence is also the function of stages in purchase decision process (Davis and Rigaux, 1974: and Park and Lutz, 1982). Thirdly, it also depends on the specific purchase factors (Bonfield, 1978).

Since 1970, after the pioneering work of Davis (1970, 1971, 1974, 1976), the interest of consumer researchers has increased in examining the extent and nature of husband-wife influence in purchase decisions. Davis's studies have served as an impetus to the other researchers who investigated the relative influence of husband-wife in a number of purchase decisions. They focused their attention on various types of products. Husband dominated decisions were more prevalent in the purchase of such products as automobiles (Cunningham and Green, 1974). Wife was found to exert considerable influence on furniture purchase (Burns, 1981), food products (Haley and Overholser, 1975), and small appliances (Burns and Divere, 1981). In a number of purchase decisions syncratic pattern was found such as in buying homes (Munsinger, Weber and Hansen, 1975) and vacation (Filiatrault and Ritchie, 1980). Cunningham and Green (1974) found that with the passage of time, relative roles of husband and wife in purchase decisions change. Several moderating variables, such as, spousal involvement and empathy have been found to be positively associated with syncratic decisions (Burns 1976; Burns and Granbios, 1977). Families with modern sex role norms showed less wife influence and more joint and husband influence in those areas which were considered traditionally under the domain of wife and conversely there was lessening influence of husband and greater joint and wife influence in those areas which were traditionally handled by the husband (Schaninger, Buss and Grover, 1982). Qualls (1987) identified three factors that strongly effect a member's influence in the family: the financial resources of the family member, the importance of the decision to the family member and the sex role orientation of the family member. Another study by Foxman and Burns (1987) found that role overload in the family also effects the relative involvement of husband-wife in various purchase decisions. Rosen and Granbios (1983) indicated that family role structure is a function of sex-role attitudes and educational level. Working women tend to make more autonomic decisions on various aspects of their family's finances. It has also been found that relative influence of husband and wife changed during the decision making process (Davis and Rigaux, 1974). Replicating the same basic research design, Bonfield (1978) explored changes in husband and wife decision making for twenty products using multi-stage decision making model: problem recognition, search for information and final purchase decision. Results showed that for the majority of products the initial decision making pattern established in problem recognition stage continued during the subsequent two stages. However, for a few products the decision making pattern was found to shift among these three stages. Woodside and Motes (1979) have concluded that in case of automobiles, husband played dominant role in the initial stage of decision process but in the second stage it was more of a joint decision. The final purchase decision, however, generally was husband dominated.

Some studies focused on cultural factors. Imperial, O'Guinn and Mac Adam (1985) in a cross cultural study found that Mexican-American families tend to be more husband-dominant than Anglo-Sexon families and that Angle-Sexon families engage in more syncratic purchase decisions. Husbands in less developed nations were found to make more unilateral decisions than their counterparts in the developed nations and that significantly more syncratic decisions take place in developed nations as compared to less developed nations (Green, *et. al.*, 1983).

This study's objectives were to ascertain the relative influence of husband and wife in the purchase of certain products in the Indian context. India being a developing country, the socio-economic conditions prevailing here are vastly different from those of the developed countries. Women, in general, were less active in the various walks of life including household affairs as compared to their male counterparts. However, during the last three decades because of education, women are increasingly joining the work force. Today, the number of families with working couples has increased considerably, particularly in the metros. The employment of women might have created some social problems in the family, nevertheless, it has increased their influence in the family affairs including the purchase decisions. In the present study the family has been categorised into two types i.e. families where only the husband works (single earning family) and families where both work (Dual earning family). An attempt has been made here to measure the moderating effect of family on the husband-wife involvement in purchase decision. One of the reasons for taking up present work was the paucity of serious research work in this area in India. The authors have found two recent studies of serious nature in the Indian context (Nathan, 1997; Khan, 2000).

RESEARCH METHODOLOGY

As indicated in the preceding section, the present study attempts mainly to find out the moderating effect of the type of family and the husband and wife involvement in purchase decisions. For this purpose four products were selected i.e. refrigerator, television, two-wheelers, and toothpaste. Keeping in mind the socio-economic conditions prevailing in India these products are used by majority of Indians. The rationale behind their selection was that these products represent buying situations ranging from complex buying decisions to routinised ones. The basic objectives of this study were three fold. Firstly, to investigate the relative involvement of husband-wife dyad in the purchase of specific product i.e. product specific influences. Secondly, to measure the relative role of husband-wife dyad during the decisions making process with respect to three stages i.e. idea initiation, information search and final decision (stage specific influences). Finally, the objective was to investigate the product specific and stage specific husband-wife involvement moderated by the type of family, because type of family may exert some moderating effect in the purchasing decisions within the family. On the basis of the above objectives the following hypotheses were proposed:

- H_1: The relative involvement of husband-wife is product specific and stage specific.
- H_2: Both product specific and stage specific involvement of husband and wife moderated by the type of the family.

Method and Instrument

One problem constantly faced by the researchers in this area relates to the reliability and validity of the data collected. Substantial disagreement has been found between spouses as to their relative influence in purchase decisions (Spiro 1983, and Woodside and Motes 1979). Burn (1977) reported that in certain cases husband was found to inflate his influence/involvement and/or authority in household purchase decisions and in certain cases wife was found to do the same or underestimate her influence. Burn and Hopper (1986) and Moore-shay and Wilkie (1988) have found that significant disagreement existed in the reported relative influence of the spouses and this disagreement ranged between 10 to 50 percent of couples. Though a number of researchers (Seymour and Lessne 1984; Gupta Hagerty and Myers 1982; and Buss and Schaninger, 1982) have proposed several ways to increase the reliability and validity, still this question is not completely resolved. Keeping this consideration in mind the present study tried to reduce this discrepancy in reporting of influence by the couples, and undertook the following steps. Firstly, a more neutral term involvement has been used, instead of influence. Secondly, the information has been obtained about the relative involvement from both the partners. Thirdly, husband and wife were asked to fill up the questionnaire in the absence of the other. And finally, the respondents were asked to provide the information as regard to their involvement in case only when the product has been purchased during the last two years. This has been done to minimise the forgetting effect and social impact. These steps hopefully may reduce the respondents' bias, if any, to a great extent. The data were gathered from husband and wife dyads. For this purpose help was taken from the derived five-point relative scale developed by Szybillo, Sosainie and Tenenbein (1979). The original scale was been reduced to derived three-point scale. The measurement procedure is explained later in this section. In order to get a representative heterogeneous sample of respondents it was decided to collect the data from two cities. The telephone directories served as sampling frames. With a sampling interval of 50 a list of possible respondents was prepared from the directories which resulted in 225 addresses. After preparing this list, they were contacted on telephone to:

1. verify the address
2. identify the husband and wife couple and
3. sought permission for information.

Of the 225 addresses, 49 did not answer or had disconnected numbers, 9 moved to some other places and 47 refused to participate. Hence the information was collected through a personal interview from one hundred and twenty couples.

The procedure adopted to measure the relative involvement of husband-wife was as follows:

- Respondents (couples) were requested to state their level

of involvement for four products for three stages of purchase, i.e. idea initiation, information search, and final decision for each product class by assigning 1 if "not involved", 2, if "moderately involved" and 3, if "very much involved". These responses were then converted into a 5 point relative influence scale.

- A wife score of 2 or 3 and a husband score of 1 were considered as "wife decides".
- A wife score of 3 and a husband score of 2 were considered as "wife more than husband".
- Husband-wife combination score of either 1-1, 2-2, or 3-3 were considered as "husband-wife equal influence".
- A husband score of 3 and a wife score of 2 were considered as "husband more than wife".
- A husband score of 2 or 3 and wife score of 1 were considered as "husband decides".
- Further, the above five categories were collapsed into three types of influences.
- This finally resulted into three types of influences:
  (i) Wife's influence greater than husband (W>H)
  (ii) Husband-wife equal influence (H=W)
  (iii) Husband's influence greater than wife (H>W)

RESULTS AND DISCUSSION

Results are arranged product-wise and the effect of type of family on the involvement of husband-wife discussed for each product in terms of three stages viz. idea initiation, information collection, final decision and three level of involvement, wife's influence greater than husband (W>H); husband-wife equal influence (H=W); and husband's influence greater than wife (H>W)

Refrigerator Purchase

Table 14.1 presents the results of level of husband-wife involvement in refrigerator purchase. As stated earlier, refrigerator is basically a family product and every member of the family uses it with varying frequency. However, the lady of the house, irrespective of whether she works or not, is the prime user. It is clear from the table that the wife is increasingly more involved in the purchase of refrigerators in all the three stages of purchase decisions in those families where she works along with her husband

On comparing the two types of families (i.e. single earning and dual earning), the modal level of involvement in the single earning family for three stages i.e. idea initiation, information collection and final decision, was husband's influence greater than wife (H>W). In case of dual earning families this was considerably less and wife's involvement was found to have increased significantly. Combining W>H and W=H or H=W, the of wife's influence for idea initiation was found to be quite high (87.80%) in dual earning families. For information collection this was 66.02% and for final decision it was 82.92%. For all the three stages of purchasing decisions these differences were found significant.

Television Purchase

Though, TV has been around in India for more than three decades, the real impetus to TV viewing came in the late 1980s after the introduction of colour transmission. Today TV has become a common household product and a sizeable number of Indian homes today have either colour or B/W TV sets. The relative involvement of husband wife in the purchase of TV is shown in table 14.2. Perusing this table we also find that the role of wife has increased tremendously in the dual income family. This trend continued in all the three stages of purchase decisions, and was found to be significant too.

Two-Wheeler Purchase

In India, of all the personal modes of mechanised transport, two-wheelers – scooters, motorcycles and mopeds – are most commonly used. It would not be wrong to say that two wheelers occupy the same position in India as car occupies in advanced economies of the world.

Interestingly, in India, even those who possess cars, keep two-wheelers owing to convenience and easy maneuverabilty on the crowded, narrow and pot-holed Indian roads. Historically, two-wheelers were predominantly used by males and female's role was that of pillion rider. But during the last decade, women, esspecially girls, have started riding two-wheelers, particularly scooters and mopeds, in substantial numbers. Table 14.3 shows predominant involvement of husband (in more than three fourth cases) in all the three stages of two-wheeler purchase in case of single earning families. While the involvement of wife increased substantially in dual earning families for all the three stages. Though, the results for two-wheeler are not as significant as they are for earlier two products, yet, we find considerable increase of wife's influence in two-wheeler purchase. A significant trend that emerges from the table 14.3 is that the syncratic pattern i.e. equal involvement of husband and wife was found to be quite high in idea initiation and information collection stages for dual earning families. However, in making the final decision for purchase, husband's role was quite high even in dual earning families.

Toothpaste Purchase

Toothpaste being frequently purchased, low priced convenience good, people are not much involved in its purchase. Nevertheless, it is a product which is used by people belonging to all socio-economic strata, not only in the cities but also in the rural areas. As per current estimates (for the year 2000) 47% of the Indian population uses uses toothpaste (http://www.indiainfoline.com). Table 14.4 shows the results in terms of relative involvement of husband and wife in toothpaste purchases. Here results are vastly different from those for other products under study. Predominantly, it was found to be a wife dominated decision and type of family did not have any bearing on the relative involvement of husband and wife in purchase decisions. Chi-square analysis also showed insignificant results.

DISCUSSION AND CONCLUSIONS

Type of family does appear to influence the purchase decision process, particularly, for the refrigerator, television, and two-wheelers, but this was not observed in case of toothpastes. The impact of type of family on the purchase decision for all the three stages appeared to be equal. It seems that working wives are more involved in major household purchases as compared to non-working (house) wives. In India, dual earning families are moving either towards syncratic decisions or towards wife dominated ones, both in case of refrigerator and television. This is understandable because of two reasons. Firstly, she is the prime user of both the products and secondly being an earning member she is equally contributing towards the family income.

As far as two-wheeler purchase is concerned, the influence of

Table 14.1
Involvement of Husband-Wife in Refrigerator Purchase

(N=105, n_1=63, n_2 = 42)

Stages in Purchase	*Type of Family*	*Level of Involvement %*			χ^2
		W>H	*H = W*	*H > W*	
Idea Initiation	Single Earning Family (n_1)	29.82	29.82	40.36	9.79*
	Dual Earning Family (n_2)	36.58	61.22	12.2	
Information Collection	Single Earning Family (n_1)	8.77	24.56	38.67	30.84*
	Dual Earning Family (n_2)	41.46	24.56	38.67	
Final Decision	Single Earning Family (n_1)	17.54	22.81	59.65	18*
	Dual Earning Family (n_2)	41.46	41.46	17.08	

* = Significant at 1% level.

wife no doubt increased in the dual earning families but this shift was not towards wife domination. For two wheelers, where the husband is the prime or main user, still it is husband-dominated purchase decision but male dominance has decreased considerably and given way to syncratic pattern. Toothpaste purchase being a minor purchase decision, it is predominantly wife's forte and her domination was rather pronounced in dual earning families.

Finally, from the managerial perspective, it may be concluded that the findings of this study may prove to be useful in selection of media mix, message formulation and advertisement execution. Appropriate female oriented appeals need to be employed for these products. In the selection of media mix, those advertising vehicles should be given more weightage which are women specific.

Limitations

Though, precautions have been taken to increase the reliability of the present study, yet, the researchers feel there are certain limitations which may be given due consideration in interpreting the results. These are enumerated as follows:

(i) The sampling frame used i.e. telephone directories of two cities provided the addresses of only those persons who

Table 14.2
Involvement of Husband-Wife in Television Purchase

($N=113$, $n_1=70$, $n_2=43$)

Stages in Purchase	*Type of Family*	*Level of Involvement %* W>H	H = W	H > W	χ^2
Idea Initiation	Single Earning Family (n_1)	11.94	40.29	46.88	15.93*
	Dual Earning Family (n_2)	34.88	51.16	13.95	
Information Collection	Single Earning Family (n_1)	10.44	25.38	64.18	23.48*
	Dual Earning Family (n_2)	44.19	34.88	20.93	
Final Decision	Single Earning Family (n_1)	7.46	26.87	65.67	18*
	Dual Earning Family (n_2)	46.51	34.88	18.6	

* = Significant at 1% level.

possess telephones. This might have given some upmarket bias because normally in India people with high to medium income and high qualifications possess telephone. This may preclude the inclusion of sample elements who are having low income and low education.

(ii) The sample size of 120 couples may not be reflective of of the population characteristics.

(iii) India being a multilingual, multi-religious and multi-regional country, the sample drawn from two cities may not be representative of the population and therefore, generalisation has to be done with caution.

Table 14.3
Involvement of Husband-Wife in Two-Wheeler Purchase

(N=102, n_1=60, n_2 = 42)

Stages in Purchase	*Type of Family*	*Level of Involvement %*			
		W>H	*H = W*	*H > W*	χ^2
Idea Initiation	Single Earning Family (n_1)	5.2	8.7	86.1	20*
	Dual Earning Family (n_2)	10.81	45.94	43.25	
Information Collection	Single Earning Family (n_1)	8.77	17.59	75.44	7.95†
	Dual Earning Family (n_2)	10.81	40.54	48.65	
Final Decision	Single Earning Family (n_1)	10.04	8.7	77.26	7.91†
	Dual Earning Family (n_2)	24.32	24.32	51.36	

* = Significant at 1% level; † = Significant at 5% level.

issue, the respondents may have given the answers which may be desirable from their and social point of view.

(v) The relative influence of other family members especially parents and children were not considered. For example, a husband-wife score of "1-1" has been taken as husband-wife equal influence (H=W). Whereas, in reality other family members might have played a considerable role in influencing the purchase of that particular product. Researchers have found that children, particularly grown-up children, do influence family purchase decisions (Szybillo and Sosanie, 1977; Nelson, 1979; Szybillo, Sosainie and

Table 14.4
Involvement of Husband-Wife in Toothpaste Purchase

(N=105, n_1=61, n_2 = 44)

Stages in Purchase	*Type of Family*	*Level of Involvement %* W>H	H = W	H > W	χ^2
Idea Initiation	Single Earning Family (n_1)	48.57	32.85	18.58	4.74*
	Dual Earning Family (n_2)	50.83	38.63	10.58	
Information Collection	Single Earning Family (n_1)	50	35.71	14.29	2.62*
	Dual Earning Family (n_2)	59.64	27.27	13.09	
Final Decision	Single Earning Family (n_1)	57.14	30	12.86	6.84*
	Dual Earning Family (n_2)	75	1.09	9.91	

* = Insignificant.

Tanenbein, 1977; Atkin, 1978; Bahn, 1987; Ward and Waekman, 1972; Khan, 2000).

(vi) Despite the breaking up of joint family system, still (old) parents continue to live with their married children and they have considerable say in many household affairs including major purchases. This study is silent on this count too.

(vii) The products under study may not be representative of all the the cross-sections of product categories. More products could have made the study more meaningful.

(viii) Though moderating effect of type of family has been observed in this study, yet, some other moderating variables like education, age, family background and duration of marriage, if taken into consideration, could have made the study more practical and meaningful.

REFERENCES

Atkin, Charles, K. (1978), "Observations of Parent-child Interaction in Supermarket Decision Making", *Journal of Marketing*, 42, pp. 42-45.

Bahn, Kenneth (1987), "Do Mothers and Children Share Cereal and Beverage Preferences and Evaluative Criteria?" in *Advances in Consumer Research*, Wallendorf M. and Pau Anderson eds. Association for Consumer Research, pp. 281-86.

Baran R. (1981), "Pattern of Decision-Making Influence for Selected Products and Services", in *The Changing Marketing Environment: New Theories and Applications*, Bernhardt K. et al. eds. America Marketing Association; Chicago, pp. 139-42.

Bondfield E.H. (1978), "Perception of Marital Roles in Decision Process: Replication and Extension", in *Advances in Consumer Research*, Hunt K.H. eds. Association of Consumer Research, pp. 302-11.

Burns, Alvin (1976), "Spousal Involvement and Empathy in Jointly Resolved and Authoritatively Resolved Purchase Sub-decisions" in *Advances in Consumer Research*, Anderson, B.B. eds. Association for Consumer Research, pp. 199-207.

Burns, Alvin (1977), "Husband and Wife Purchase Decision Making Roles: Agreed, Presumed, Conceded and Disputed", in *Advances in Consumer Research*, Perreanlt W. eds. Association for Consumer Research, pp. 50-55.

Burns, Alvin and Donald Granbois H. (1977), "Factors Moderating the Resolution of Preference Conflict in Family Automobile Purchasing", *Journal of Marketing Research*, 14, pp. 77-86.

Burns, Alvin and Jo, A. Hopper (1986), "An Analysis of the Presence, Stability and Antecedents of Husband and Wife Purchase Decision Making Influence Assessment Agreement and Disagreement", in *Advances in Consumer Research*, Lutz R. eds. Association for Consumer Research, pp. 15-18.

Burns, Alvin and S. Devere (1981), "Four Situations and their Perceived Effects on Husband and Wife Purchase Decision Making" in *Advances in Consumer Research*, Monroe K. eds. Association for Consumer Research, pp. 736-41.

Cunningham Isabella C.M. and Robnert T. Green (1974), "Purchasing Roles in US Family, 1955 and 1973", *Journal of Marketing*, 30, pp. 61-64.

Davis Harry L. (1970), "Dimensions of Marital Roles in Consumer Decision Making", *Journal of Marketing Research*, 7, pp. 168-77.

Davis Harry L. (1971), "Measurement of Husband-Wife Influence in Consumer Decision Process", *Journal of Marketing Research*, 8, pp. 305-12.

Davis Harry L. (1976), "Decision Making Within the Household", *Journal of Consumer Research*, 2, Behavior", *Journal of Consumer Research*, 1, pp. 43-50.

Davis Harry L. and Benny P. Rigaux (1974), "Perception of Marital Roles in Decision Processes", *Journal of Consumer Research*, 1, pp. 51-62.

Filiatrault and Brent J.R. (1980), "Joint Purchasing Decisions: A Comparison of Influence Structure in Family and Couple Decision Making Units", *Journal of Consumer Research*, 7, pp. 141-14.

Foxman Ellen and Alvin Burns (1987), "Role Loan in the Household", *Advances in Consumer Research*, Wallendorf M. and P. Anderson, eds. Association for Consumer Research, pp. 458-462.

Green T. Robert et. al. (1983), "Societal Development and Family Purchasing Roles: A Cross-National Study", *Journal of Consumer Research*, 9, pp. 436-42.

Grashof F. John and Donald F. Dixon (1980), "The Household: The 'Proper' Model for Research into Purchasing and Consumption Behavior", in *Advances in Consumer Research*, Olson Jerry eds. Association for Consumer Research, pp. 525-31.

Gupta Sunil, Michael R. Hagerty and John G. Myers (18\982), "New Directions in Family Decision Making Research" in *Advances in Consumer Research*, Bogozzi R.P. and A.M. Tybout eds., pp. 445-50.

Haley, Russel, Overholser C.C. and Associates (1975), *Purchase Influence:*

Measures of Husband Wife Influence on Buying Decisions, New Cannon Corp. Haley, Overholser and Associates. Inc.

Imperia Giovanna, Thomas C. O'Guinn and Elizabeth A. Mac Adams (1984), "Family Decision Making Role Perceptions Among Mexican–American and Anglo Wives: A Cross Cultural Comparison" in *Advances in Consumer Research*, Hirschman E.C. and Holbrook M.B. eds. Association for Consumer Research, pp. 329-33.

Khan, M. Naved (2000), *Dimensions of Family Decision Making in the Purchase of Consumer Products*, Ph. D. Thesis, Department of Business Administration, Faculty of Management Studies & Research, Aligarh Muslim University, Aligarh, India.

Lavin M. (1985), "Husband-Wife Decision Making" in *1985 AMA Educators' Proceedings*, Lusch R.F. eds. American Marketing Association.

Moore-Shay Elizabeth and William Wilkie (1988), "Recent Developments in Research on Family Decisions", in *Advances in Consumer Research*, Houston M. eds. Association for Consumer Research, pp. 454-460.

Munsinger Gary M., Jean Webe and Richard Hansen (1975), "Joint Home Purchasing Decisions by Husband and Wives", *Journal of Consumer Research*, 1, pp. 60-66.

Nathan S. V. (1997), "Dimensions of Marital Roles in Consumer Decision Making", *Vikalpa*, Vol. 22, No. 1, pp. 11-21.

Nelson Margaret (1988), "The Resolution of Conflict in Joint Purchase Decisions by Decisions by Husbands and Wives: A Review and Empirical Test", in *Advances in Consumer Research*, Houston M. eds. Association for Consumer Research, pp. 436-442.

Park Whan C. (1982), "Joint Decisions in Home Purchasing: A Muddling-Through Process", *Journal of Consumer Research*, 9, pp. 151-162.

Park Whan C. and Richard J. Lutz (1982), "Decision Plans and Consumer Choice Dynamics", *Journal of Marketing Research*, 19, pp. 108-115.

Qualls William, (1987), "Household Decision Behavior: The Impact of Husband and Wives' Sex Role Orientation", *Journal of Consumer Research*, 14, pp. 264-279.

Rosen Dennis L. and Donald H. Granbois (1983), "Determinants of Role Structure in Family Financial Management", *Journal of Consumer Research*, 10, pp. 253-58.

Schaninger Charles M., W. Christian Buss and Rajiv Grover (1982), "The Effect of Sex Roles on Family Finance Handling and Decision Influence", in *An Assessment of Marketing Thoughts and Practice– 1982 Educator's Conference Proceedings*, Walker B.J. et. al., eds., American Marketing Association, pp. 43-47.

Seymour Daniel and Greg Lessne (1984), "Spousal Conflict Arousal: Scale Development", *Journal of Consumer Research*, 11, pp. 810-821.

Spiro Rosann L, (1983), "Persuasion in Family Decision Making", *Journal of Consumer Research*, 7, pp. 131-140.

Szybillo George J. and Aaron Tanebein (1977), "Should Children Be Seen But Not Heard?" *Journal of Advertising Research*, 17, pp. 7-13.

Szybillo George J. and Aaron Tanebein (1979), "Family Member Influence in Household Decision Making", *Journal of Consumer Research*, 6, pp. 312-17.

Szybillo George J. and Arlene Sosanie (1977), "Family Decision Making: Husband, Wife and Children", Advances in Consumer Research, Perreant W.D. eds. *Association for Consumer Research*, pp. 46-49.

Ward Scott and Daniel Wackman, (1972), "Children's Purchase Influence Attempts and Parental Yielding", *Journal of Marketing Research*, 9, pp. 316-319.

Woodside Arch G. and William H. Motes (1979), "Husband and Wife Perceptions of Marital Roles in Consumer Decision Processes for Six Products", in 1979 *Educators' Conference Proceedings,* Blackwell N. et al., eds. American Marketing Association, pp. 214-219.

15

A Study of Demographic and Psychographic Variables of Car Owners

INTRODUCTION

Of the various tools and techniques that are available to the marketer, off late, the psychographic variables have assumed great importance. This phenomenon can be attributed to the fact that consumers have become sophisticated in their approach towards purchase behaviour. Because of this reason, various segments and classes of consumers, each with its own unique taste and preferences, have emerged. To cater to the complexities of such a market, today's marketer has to study the subtle nuances in the behaviour of the consumers so as to fully satisfy their demands. Increasingly, the marketers are realizing that there exist differences in the nature and extent of purchases between any two groups of buyers despite similarities in demographic characteristics. Therefore, they are attempting to explain the significance of such differences by inquiring beyond demographics by delving into psychographics. Present study investigates the characteristics of the owners of cars, particularly three brands of cars, which have been introduced in India during the last decade. The researchers were also interested in finding out differences in psychographics, if any, among the owners of these cars, and to suggest appropriate marketing strategies.

The term psychographics was coined to describe a wide variety of psychological and behavioral descriptions of consumers in a specific market. The development of psychographics evolved from attempts by marketers to find measures more directly related to purchase and consumption than demographics alone. Perhaps the major thrust of psychographics is the recognition that buyers can be classified by a psychological state of readiness that results largely from their life style. This psychological readiness varies from individual to individual and may vary within the same individual buyer over a period of time.

Emanuel Denby (1989), one of the founders of psychographics, has described psychographics as:

> The use of psychological, sociological and anthropological factors, such as benefits desired (from the behaviour being studied), self-concept and lifestyle (or serving style) to determine how the market is segmented by the propensity of groups within the market–and their reasons–to take a particular decision about a product, person, ideology, or otherwise hold an attitude or use a medium. Demographics and socio-economics are also used as a constant check to see if psychographic marketing segmentation improves on other forms of segmentation, including user/non-user groupings.

Use of psychographics, both in market segmentation and promotions strategy formulation, has been gaining popularity in recent years. Its use sharpens the ability of marketers in searching the prospects not possible by merely relying on demographics. Lifestyle information gives the soul of a person, whereas, demographics alone gives only the skeleton and not a whole person. Knowledge of psychographics is essential as it enables advertisers to devise appropriate copy appeals to target segments based on lifestyles.

According to psychologists, values are a reflection of our needs adjusted for the realities of the world in which we live. Researchers have identified nine basic values that relate to purchase behavior (Kahle *et al.*, 1986). These are called the List of Values (LOV). These are: self-respect, self-fulfillment, security, sense of belonging, excitement, sense of accomplishment, fun and enjoyment in life, being well respected and having warm relationships. While most people would view all of these as desirable, their relative importance differs among people, and their importance changes over a person's life. For example, people who value fun and enjoyment like skiing, dancing, bicycling, and backpacking; and people who value warm relationships give gifts for no particular reason. Thus, the relative strength of values could be the basis for segmenting a specific market.

Probably the best-known psychographic segmentation tool is VALS, developed in 1978 by the research firm SRI International of US. The VALS system was developed from a large study of the US population that divided adults into nine segments based on similarities in their *values* (belief, desires, and prejudices) and their *lifestyles*–hence, the VALS acronym (Atlas, 1984). In 1990, SRI introduced VALS2 to reflect changes in how we live and make decisions. The two primary dimensions used to segment the population in VALS2 are an individual's resources and self-orientation. Resources are broadly defined to include not only income but also other factors such as health, education and self-confidence. Self-orientation reflects a person's self-image and the behaviour used to communicate that oriented image to others, Three self-orientation patterns are included in VALS2 i.e. principle-oriented, status oriented, and action oriented. Resources range from abundant to minimal. Based on a representative sample of the US population, and using resources and self-orientation, eight consumer segments of approximately equal size have been identified. These are *actualizers, fulfilled, achievers, experiencers, strivers, makers,* and *strugglers.* These groups widely differ in their demographic and personality traits. For example, *actualizers*, exhibit wide intellectual interests, engage in varied leisure activities, are well informed and are politically active. In contrast, *experiencers* are unconventional, active, impetuous, and energetic. They like new and offbeat things, are concerned about image, admire wealth and fame, and are uninterested in political issues (Wilkie, 1990; Schiffman and Kanuk, 2000).

Several organizations have used VALS2 to develop or refine their marketing strategies. For example, Transport Canada, the agency that operates major Canadian airports, used VALS2 to study the flying public passing through Vancouver, British Columbia. Though actualizers make up about 12 per cent of the general population, the study found that 37 per cent of the travelers belonged to this group. Since actualizers are a good market for quality arts and crafts, the results suggested that stores such as Sharper Image or Nature Company could do well at the airport (Rebecca, 1991).

Psychographic research has been used in the West by Colgate-Palmolive's Irish Spring soap, Jack Daniel's Whiskey, Peter Paul's Mounds, TUMS, AT&T phone services, Los Angeles Times, Lava Soap, Union 76 gasoline, Kentucky Fried Chicken, Nescafe coffee, People, and Dewar's White Label Scotch (Schiffman and Kanuk, 1995).

Many marketers of goods and services conduct psychographic research to capture insights and create profiles of the consumers they wish to target. The appeal of psychographic research lies in the frequently vivid and practical profiles of consumer segments that it can produce.

In its most common form, psychographic studies employ a battery of statements designed to identify relevant aspects of a consumer's personality, buying motives, interests, attitudes, beliefs, and values. Respondents are asked to evaluate such statements in terms of their degree of agreement (e.g. strongly agree, moderately agree, neither agree nor disagree, moderately disagree, strongly disagree etc.). For some statements, the respondent may be asked to indicate the degree of importance (e.g. very important, important, not important etc.). In addition to reflecting either personal or family activities, interests, and opinions, psychographic statements can be designed to be either *general* or *product-specific*. In a psychographic study of a specific product category, consumer researchers are likely to include both general and product-specific statements.

Today, trying the *shotgun approach* of reaching out to each and every possible potential consumer with the same offering and message is an exercise in futility. It is best to carve out a niche, a segment so to say, and work extensively on it. Psychographics because of its very nature of delving deep into the customer's psyche is a lethal tool that when exploited fully gives great results. A psychographic profile helps the marketer know the personality profile of his target market. Premising that similar personality individuals would in future, patronize the product, the marketer sends out messages that reinforce and elicit similar personality attributes.

The process calls for taking the product and weaving around it a ***personality net*** that enshrouds the product in a particular personality type. This has the effect of the ***personality net*** rubbing off on the product. This product will then provide the desired reinforcement to the user who sees himself in similar light. The process, therefore, calls for assigning a personality to the product—a personality that will strike a similar chord in the minds of those potential consumers who are of the similar make-up (or who desire to be of the similar make-up). Today psychographics is picking up wide acceptability amongst marketers—all because of its immense convincing powers. A psychographic rendition of a product adds vitality and life to it, something that demographics does not.

Three important marketing areas in which psychographic analysis has found wide applications today are given below:

Market Segmentation

Psychographic research is an especially useful tool in segmenting markets. Psychographic profile is useful in providing direction as to which segments to target, what to say to them, and even as to which advertising media might best be used to reach them.

Product Positioning and Repositioning

If a company is not certain which segment should be the target for new product development, it can use psychographic analysis to identify those consumers who seem to be least satisfied with existing products, and thus more likely to respond favourably to a new product. On the basis of its findings, the company can design a product and marketing strategy that specifically appeals to this market.

Promotional Campaigns

Psychographic analysis has been widely used in the development of advertising campaigns to answer three questions: "Whom should we target?" "What should we say"? "Where should we say it"? To help advertisers answer the third question, most mass media vehicles sponsor psychographic and demographic research as the basis for building detailed audience profile. By offering media buyers psychographic studies of their audience, in addition to traditional demographic profiles, mass media publishers and broadcasters make it possible for advertisers to select media that have audience most closely resembling their target markets.

In the present study an attempt has been made to identify the dominant demographics and psychographic variables of the owners of three cars i.e. Zen, Esteem and Cielo. After identifying these variables one will be able to suggest how the manufacturers of these cars can use these in devising various marketing strategies.

Rationale for Selecting Cars

Off late, in India a number of foreign and domestic players have introduced their cars in the premium segment. Their numerical presence was not significant enough to justify a study encompassing all the cars introduced. Only Maruti Udyog Ltd. and comparatively new entrant DCM-Daewoo had a significant numerical presence in the premium segment when this study was undertaken in the last quarter of 1997. Since both these companies were targeting the same category of the premium segment, a comparative study of the demographic and psychographic variables of owners of Maruti Esteem, Cielo and Zen was expected to yield interesting results.

The study of psychographics gains greater significance owing to the fact that the make of a car determines a person's status in the society. *In fact the car he owns tells about his personality, attitude and life style.*

METHODOLOGY

Objectives of Research

The following were the objectives of the study:

- To identify the dominant demographic variables of car owners.
- To measure the psychographic variables of these car owners.
- To measure the relationship, if any, between the demographic and psychographic variables.
- To suggest marketing strategies to marketers based on the findings of the study.

Research Instrument

In order to carry out the present study an appropriate research instrument was needed. After careful considerations of possible instruments, the researchers decided to use a modified version Edwards Personal Preference Test (EPPT). One reason of using this instrument was its earlier use in a similar type of study done in the late 1950s by Evans (1959). He used this instrument to find out the personality differences between the owners of Ford and Chevrolet in US.

In its original form EPPT was difficult to administer because of two reasons. Firstly, Edwards prepared this instrument for the measurement of 15 personality traits, each having nine dimensions. Thus, the final scale comprised 225 statements. Responding to 225 statements may have been a very time consuming and at times irritating experience. Secondly, the method of choosing the statement and scoring pattern, as proposed by Edwards, was difficult for the respondents. Particularly, choosing the responses from among the statements was very complicated and confusing. This was revealed by a pilot study done on a small sample of 20 car owners.

Therefore, it was decided to modify the original scale to make it more simple and usable so that the respondents would be able to understand it easily without spending much time. In the final modified form, this instrument incorporated, only six personality traits and the response pattern was converted to Likert type format. The respondents now had to indicate only their degree of agreement or disagreement for each statement on a five point scale. In all, 54 statements for six personality traits were used for the present study. One may argue that by simplifying the original scale developed by Edwards, the validity might have been sacrificed. However, keeping in mind the prevailing conditions and constraints, the researchers were of the opinion that a *satisficing* instrument is better suited to collect the relevant primary data in certain conditions than *optimum* one which may lead to spurious primary data. The same has been advocated by Weirs (1984).

The six personality traits, which were finally chosen from the EPPT, were *autonomy*, *affiliation*, *nurturance*, *deference* and *achievement*. These personality traits were selected on the basis of the considered opinion of five marketing managers. Initially they were asked to select eight personality traits out of the 15 used by Edwards in his original instrument, which in their opinion were relevant in the purchase of a car. Of these eight traits, there was unanimity on 6 traits which were finally included in the research instrument used in the study.

As far as the demographic variables of the respondents were concerned three variables, namely, income, age and profession were incorporated in the questionnaire. The respondents were required to provide these demographic variables along with their degree of agreement or disagreement on the 54 statements related to six personality traits as mentioned earlier.

Sampling Plan

In order to collect the data for the present study, mailing as a method of administering the instrument was considered to be inappropriate because of low response rate experienced by earlier researchers. Therefore, it was decided to contact the owners of these three cars on a personal basis. Meeting them and getting the questionnaire filled up was a difficult task. Contacting them even on the telephone was found to be difficult. Therefore, as a final measure, the field workers were asked to administer the research instrument, at the parking sites located in prime locations and commercial complexes in New Delhi. Those who obliged were explained the dimensions of the study and the rules for filling up the instrument. In case of any difficulty, the field workers cleared their doubts immediately so that they could properly fill up the questionnaire. Though this method is not based upon the probability sampling, yet, it was the only way one could get the cooperation of the respondents under the prevailing situation. However, care has been taken to inculcate representativeness by taking into considerations all prominent parking sites in New Delhi. The survey was carried out in the scorching heat of the summer month of June (1997). The reason for choosing the three cars was that the other brands such as Ford Escort, Opel Astra, Ford Ikon etc. had either not been launched or even if some of them were launched, their presence on the roads was insignificant. In this way the researchers were able to elicit responses from 50 respondents for each brand of car resulting into a total of 150 respondents.

Limitations of the Study

Though care has been taken to select the sample, which may be representative of the population, yet this study may suffer from the following limitations:

- Due to obvious time and resource constraints the sample size was not sufficiently large and neither was it geographically dispersed to truly represent the universe.
- Certain statements in the questionnaire were socially desirable and thus the respondents' response may not reflect their true feelings.
- Use of statistical tools in social sciences has its own limitations and this study is no exception.
- As mentioned earlier, after the data collection was completed some new cars in this segment have entered the market but the demographic and psychographic variables of the owners of these cars have not been identified. So the results may not be applicable to all the players in this segment.

RESULTS AND DISCUSSION

The data provided by the respondents in terms of three demographics variables i.e. age, occupation and income and six personality variables i.e. achievement, affiliation, deference, autonomy, nurturance and dominance were analysed with respect to the three brands of cars under study. In the first phase of the analysis, the demographic variables were taken and in the second phase the six personality variables were analysed. In case of demographic variables chi-square analysis was applied to find out significant differences, if any, among the respondents. As far as the psychographic variables were concerned, for each personality variable, the mean scores for each of the nine statements were calculated and then Analysis of Variance (ANOVA) was applied to find out the significant differences.

Analysis of Demographic Variables

The results of demographic profile of respondents are shown in Table 15.1. The table shows the three demographic variables as possessed by three car owners. As far as profession was concerned predominantly the businessmen and private sector executives went for Cielo (84%). In case of Esteem also, businessmen and private sector executives constituted the major segment (74%). The distribution of profession among the Zen owners was much more wider as compared to the other two car owners. Chi-square analysis also showed significant differences.

In case of second demographic variable i.e. age, Cielo and Esteem car owners were from the higher age bracket. The modal age group for Cielo was between 40 to 49 years, whereas, for Esteem it was above 50 years. In case of Zen, the modal age group was 30 to 39 year. This showed that owners of Zen were relatively younger in age as compared to the other car owners. The age difference was also found to be significant through chi-square analysis.

The last demographic variable studied was the monthly income. Here also one finds marked differences in the income distribution. In case of Zen, 72% belonged to the income category which ranged between Rs 15,000-Rs 24,999. Whereas, in this range there were only 6% Cielo owners and 12% Esteem owners. From the results, it is evident that proportionately larger number of Esteem owners were from the highest income group category i.e. Rs. 35,000 and above followed by Cielo owners. The income differences were also found significant.

Analysis of Psychographic Variables

The results of psychographic variables of the car owners for six personality variables under study are shown in Tables 15.2 to 15.7. As mentioned earlier, each personality variable contains nine dimensions, which were measured in the form of separate statements reflecting that particular dimension. In analyzing the results of psychographic variables a number of factors were considered. Firstly, the results were analysed in terms of whether there exist significant differences *vis-a-vis* the different dimensions of each variable. Secondly, the mean scores on each dimension have been analysed in terms of whether they represent high or low possession of a specific dimension among the car owners. For this purpose the following rating scale was used:

1.00–2.49	Low
2.50–3.49	Medium

3.51–3.99	High
4.00–5.00	Very High

This scale was used because in certain cases the results did not show any significant differences among various dimensions of a psychographic variable, yet, their relative presence among car owners could be of value in developing certain marketing strategies.

Thirdly, in addition to observing the significant differences on a particular dimension, significance was also determined in context of overall personality variable. Each personality trait has been discussed in the following section:

Autonomy

The results and the mean scores for the nine dimensions of this personality trait and the aggregate scores of the variable, combining all dimensions, are presented in Table 15.2. On dimensions 1, 4, 6, 7 & 9, there was significant variation amongst the respondents. Cielo and Zen owners ranked them *high* to *very high*. On dimensions 2 & 3, there was insignificant variation, yet, all the respondents ranked it *very high*. On dimension 5, (I like to do things that other people regard as unconventional) there was insignificant variation, but it was an important consideration for respondents as they ranked it *very high*. On dimension 6 (I like to avoid situations where I am expected to do things in a conventional manner), there was significant variation with greater number of Cielo and Zen owners being risk takers as compared to Esteem owners who appeared to being conformists. On dimension 7 (I like to do things in my own way) there was significant variation with Esteem respondents coming up as being more innovative. On dimension 8 (I like to criticize people who are in a position of authority), there was insignificant variation with all the respondents being averse to the idea of criticizing people in position of authority. On dimension 9, (I like to avoid responsibilities and obligations), there was significant variation with Zen owners coming up as least responsible.

As far as the overall trait was concerned, results show significant differences. Here, Zen owners were found to be more autonomy seekers as compared to Cielo and Esteem owners. No significant differences were found, however, between Cielo and Esteem owners on this personality trait.

Affiliation

The mean scores of car owners on the nine dimensions of affiliation as well as aggregate scores are shown in Table 15.3.

Interestingly, results on this personality variable showed mixed trend. In case of five out of the nine dimensions i.e. 1, 2, 3, 6

Table 15.1
Demographic Variables of Car Owners

	Percentage (%)		
Brands	*Ceilo*	*Esteem*	*Zen*
Profession			
Businessmen	64	44	30
Public Sector Executives	00	04	16
Private Sector Executives	20	30	32
Professionals	10	12	16
Consultants	06	10	06
Total	100	100	100
Age			
Between 30-39	16	10	68
40-49	58	42	22
50 & above	26	48	10
Total	100	100	100
Income			
Rs 15000-24999	06	12	72
Rs 25000-34999	62	40	20
Rs 35000 & above	32	48	08
Total	100	100	100

and 7, no significant differences were found. On dimensions 4, 5, 8 and 9, the results show significant differences. Even on those dimensions where the results were insignificant, the mean scores were *very high*. This indicates that all of them gave high importance to certain dimensions of *affiliation* such as loyalty to friends, active participation in friendly groups and sharing things with friends.

In case of forming new friendships, Zen owners showed marked differences. It is clear from the overall scores on this trait, that Zen owners showed high levels of affiliation trait as compared to others. This indicates gregarious nature of Zen owners. One possible reason may be that Zen owners are demographically younger in age and thus were more inclined towards cultivating friendships.

Nurturance

The mean scores on the 9 dimensions of nurturance as well as aggregate means are presented in Table 15.4.

Out of the 9 dimensions of this trait, only on four dimensions the results showed significant differences. These dimensions were 2, 4, 6 and 8. Interestingly, Zen owners had the highest mean scores on these 4 dimensions. This indicates that the incidence of nurturance in the Zen owners was high. They seemed to be more helpful, kind, generous and had a great deal of affection towards their friends. On the remaining dimensions of this personality trait i.e. 1, 3, 5, 7 and 9, though the differences were not significant, yet, all the groups scored *very high*. These dimensions are related with helping the friends when they are in trouble, treating people with kindness and sympathy, providing small favours to friends, to be generous with friends and confiding in many friends. Though all groups have shown high levels of nurturance but Zen owners were found to be more nurturance oriented.

Dominance

The findings and the mean scores on various dimensions of dominance trait are arranged in Table 15.5. On the first seven dimensions the differences were found to be insignificant. On dimensions 1, 2, 3, 5, 6 and 7, the differences were not only insignificant but they were considered by the respondents as of medium importance. On dimension 4 (When serving on a committee, I like to be appointed or elected chairperson), though the results showed insignificant differences, yet, all the owners scored high on this dimension. On the remaining two dimensions i.e. dimensions 8 & 9, the respondents showed variations. In case of dimension 8 (i.e. I like to supervise and direct the actions of other people whenever I can) Cielo and Esteem owners gave

Table 15.2
Relationship Between Ownership and Autonomy

S.No.	STATEMENT	MEAN SCORES				
		CIELO	ESTEEM	ZEN	F	P-value
1.	I like to be able to come and go as I want to	4.3	3.76	4.32	6.96	0.0012
2.	I like to say what I think about things	4.04	4.00	4.02	0.02	0.97
3.	I like to be independent of others in deciding what I want to do	4.66	4.52	4.36	2.79	0.0642
4.	I like to feel free to do what I want to do	4.52	4.04	4.56	9.5	0.0001
5.	I like to do things that other people regard as unconventional	4.66	4.38	4.52	1.68	0.18
6.	I like to avoid situations where I am expected to do things in a conventional manner	3.64	2.92	3.96	7.16	0.001
7.	I like to do things in my own way	4.32	4.72	4.46	3.46	0.033
8.	I like to criticize people who are in a position of authority	2.64	2.38	2.34	1.38	0.252
9.	I like to avoid responsibilities and obligations	2.02	1.5	3.28	8.08	.0004
	Aggregate Scores	3.87	3.58	3.98	4.56	0.046

more or less similar responses, whereas, Zen owners were found to be less dominating in nature. Finally, on dimension 9, Esteem owners were found to be comparatively less aggressive.

Deference

Table 15.6 shows the results obtained for the nine dimensions of deference. Significant differences were found among the car owners on dimensions 2, 3, 4, 5 and 6. In case of dimension 2 (i.e. I like to find out what great men and women have thought), Zen owners seemed to be more in awe of great men and women. In case of dimension 3, Zen owners scored *high* vis-à-vis others. They also scored *very high* on dimensions 4 & 5, which were related to admiring and complementing the superiors for their good work. Zen owners were found to be capable of accepting the leadership of people whom they admired as compared to the two remaining groups. Overall, the Zen owners were found to possess high level of deference vis-à-vis Esteem and Ceilo owners.

Achievement

Generally, when people are asked whether they want to achieve things in their life or not, most of them show that they are high achievers. It is an obvious human tendency to get something worthwhile or to do their best in a particular field or accomplish tasks, which require skills and efforts, or to become a recognised authority in one's profession. The mean scores, F-values and p-values of the three group of car owners are presented in Table 15.7. All the car owners scored *high* to *very high* on all the 9 dimensions. However, the results showed significant differences on four dimensions only. These were dimensions 4, 6, 7 and 9. In case of dimension 4, which is related with becoming a recognised authority in one's profession, Ceilo owners were found to be having the highest level of urge in this regard followed by Esteem and Zen owners. In case of dimension 6 (i.e. I like to be able to say that I have done a difficult job well) Zen owners showed high level of possession on this dimension. On the remaining two dimensions, on which results showed significant differences, again, Zen owners had very high scores. Though, on overall achievement trait no significant difference were found, yet, one may conclude that Zen owners, being young in age, had much to achieve in life and thus exhibited higher levels of achievement motive vis-à-vis the other two groups.

Table 15.3
Relationship Between Ownership and Affiliation

S.No.	*STATEMENT*	*MEAN SCORES*				
		CIELO	*ESTEEM*	*ZEN*	*F*	*P-value*
1.	I like to be loyal to my friends	4.64	4.58	4.42	1.58	0.2079
2.	I like to participate in groups in which the members have warm and friendly feelings towards one another	4.66	4.58	4.6	0.29	0.746
3.	I like to do things for my friends	4.06	4.2	4.3	1.16	0.313
4.	I like to form new friendships	3.82	4.04	4.58	15.7	6.00E-07
5.	I like to make as many friends as I can	1.52	1.72	2.9	32.2	3.00E-12
6.	I like to share things with my friends	4.18	4.28	4.56	2.85	0.0606
7.	I like to do things with my friends rather than by myself	2.58	2.74	2.66	0.21	0.808
8.	I like to have strong attachments with my friends	3.68	4.24	4.18	5.54	0.0048
9.	I like to write letters to my friends	2.62	3.34	3.5	14.5	2.00E-06
	Aggregate Scores	3.53	3.74	3.97	8.22	.237

PSYCHOGRAPHIC PROFILES AND MARKETING IMPLICATIONS

On the basis of the results discussed in the previous section, the following are the possible marketing implications for each brand under study.

Cielo

A typical Cielo owner is high on *autonomy*, *dominance* and *achievement*. This means that they are successful, sophisticated, active, take charge people with high self esteem and abundant resources. They are interested in growth, seek to develop, explore and express themselves in a variety of ways–sometimes guided by principle and sometimes by a desire to have an effect, to make a change. Image is important as evidence of status and power.

The marketer of Cielo should target the man who has arrived in the scene. The *business segment* forms the major chunk of the market for Cielo, and thus, the promotional campaigns should be sensitive to the aspirations of the business class. Since, Cielo owners are relatively price insensitive, as borne out by the research, emphasis should be placed on aesthetics and attributes even if it is at the cost of price.

Esteem

Esteem owners came high on *nurturance*, *achievement* and *affiliation*. They are successful, sophisticated, mature, satisfied, comfortable and reflective people who value order, knowledge and responsibility. Most are well educated and in professional occupations. They are well informed about national and world events, content with their careers, family and station in life. Esteem owners have a moderate respect for status quo, institution of authority, and social decorum, but are open-minded about new ideas and social change.

Though Esteem and Cielo cater to the same income group, yet, Esteem was found to be more popular with senior professionals. Thus, the promotional campaigns should emphasize the vehicle as a symbol of power and status. Since they are professionals, Esteem owners tend to be price sensitive and the marketer should not lose sight of this fact.

Zen

Zen owners are successful career and work oriented people who

Table 15.4
Relationship Between Ownership and Nurturance

S.No.	*STATEMENT*	*MEAN SCORES*				
		CIELO	*ESTEEM*	*ZEN*	*F*	*P-value*
1.	I like to help my friends when they are in trouble	4.08	4.22	4.36	2.06	0.1305
2.	I like to help other people who are less fortunate than I am	4	4.32	4.44	5.05	0.0075
3.	I like to treat other people with kindness and sympathy	4.52	4.5	4.46	0.18	0.832
4.	I like to forgive my friends who may sometimes hurt me	3.76	4.1	4.36	5.4	0.0054
5.	I like to do small favours for my friends	4.06	4.3	4.4	2.97	0.0538
6.	I like to be generous with my friends	4.02	4.32	4.42	4.57	0.01212
7.	I like to sympathize with my friends when they are hurt or sick	4.3	4.42	4.54	2.16	0.119
8.	I like to show great deal of affection towards my friends	3.96	4.3	4.42	6.1	0.0028
9.	I like my friends to confide in me	4.4	4.3	4.44	0.59	0.556
	Aggregate Scores	4.12	4.31	4.41	3.23	0.191

Table 15.5
Relationship Between Ownership and Dominance

S.No.	STATEMENT	MEAN SCORES				
		CIELO	ESTEEM	ZEN	F	P-value
1.	I like to argue for my point of view when it is challenged by others	3.08	3.28	2.9	1.06	0.348
2.	I like to be one of the leaders in the organisation and group to which I belong	3.26	3.28	3.38	0.12	0.8845
3.	I like to be regarded by others as a leader	3.44	3.14	3.46	0.79	0.457
4.	When serving on a committee, I like to be appointed or elected chairperson	3.82	3.72	4.02	0.92	0.4008
5.	When with a group of people, I like to make the decision about what we are going to do	3.6	3.32	3.04	2.19	0.1552
6.	I like to be called upon to settle arguements and disputes between others	3.58	3.56	3.96	1.63	0.1985
7.	I like to be able to persuade and influence others to do what I want to do	3.7	3.52	3.12	2.45	0.0896
8.	I like to supervise and direct the actions of other people whenever I can	3.7	3.7	3.08	4.51	0.0125
9.	I like to tell other people how to do their jobs	3.12	2.38	3.24	5.99	0.0031
	Aggregate Scores	3.49	3.32	3.35	.34	0.758

Table 15.6
Relationship Between Ownership and Deference

S.No.	STATEMENT	MEAN SCORES				
		CIELO	*ESTEEM*	*ZEN*	*F*	*P-value*
1.	When planning something, I like to get suggestions from other people whose opinions I respect	3.06	3.12	3.52	1.638	0.1978
2.	I like to find out what great men and women have thought	3.18	3.34	3.9	4.752	0.01
3.	I like to follow instructions and to do what is expected of me about various problems in which I am interested	2.76	2.78	3.54	8.252	0.004
4.	I like to praise someone I admire	3.36	3.54	4.2	9.103	0.0002
5.	I like to tell my superiors that they have done. a good job on something which I think they have	3.3	3.56	4.12	5.811	0.0037
6.	I like to accept the leadership of people I admire	2.4	2.56	3.04	3.511	0.0324
7.	I like to read about the lives of great men and women	4.38	4.52	4.52	1.124	0.3279
8.	I like to conform to customs and avoid doing things that people I respect might consider unconventional.	3.08	3.52	3.12	1.546	0.2165
9.	When I am in a groupie like to accept the leadership of someone else in deciding what the group is going to do	2.8	2.54	2.74	0.553	0.576
	Aggregate Scores	3.15	3.27	3.63	4.03	0.15

Table 15.7
Relationship Between Ownership and Achievement

S.No.	STATEMENT	MEAN SCORES				
		CIELO	ESTEEM	ZEN	F	P-value
1.	I like to do my very best in whatever I undertake	4.72	4.68	4.8	0.83	0.437
2.	I like to be succesful in things undertaken	4.72	4.84	4.9	1.85	0.1602
3.	I would like to accomplish tasks that others recognise as requiring skill and efforts	4.48	4.56	4.52	0.19	0.8306
4.	I would like to be recognised authority in some job, profession or field of specialization	4.72	4.48	4.22	7.52	0.0008
5.	I would like to accomplish something of great significance	4.82	4.76	4.72	0.65	0.5223
6.	I like to be able to say that I have done a difficult job well	3.92	3.98	4.46	4.15	0.0176
7.	I like to solve puzzles and problems that other people have difficulty with	3.72	4.1	4.06	3.04	0.0508
8.	I like to be able to do things better than other people can	4.48	4.44	4.7	2.28	0.1063
9.	I would like to write a great novel or play	3.08	3.52	4.12	17.05	2.20E-07
	Aggregate Scores	4.29	4.37	4.50	1.25	0.682

like to–and generally do–feel in control of their lives. They are deeply committed to their work and their families. Work provides them with a sense of duty, material rewards and prestige. They seek motivation, self definition and approval from the world around them. Their energy finds an outlet in sports, exercise and outdoor recreation. They are young and enjoy driving.

The marketer should target the young, upwardly mobile professionals and businessmen. Their promotional campaigns should highlight aesthetics and the fact that the product compliments their lifestyle in terms of values, attitudes and beliefs.

Zen owners came out as people who may graduate to owning a mid-sized car in future, of course at an affordable price. This should give marketers ample clues regarding the pricing strategy to be adopted in future.

REFERENCES

Atlas, James (1984), "Beyond Demographics", *Atlantic Monthly*, Oct., pp. 49-58.

Evans, Franklin B. (1959), "Psychological and Objective Factors in the Prediction of Brand Choice: Ford Vs. Chevrolet", *Journal of Business*, 32, pp. 340-369.

Kahle, Lynn R.; Sharon E. Beaty, and Pamela Homer (1986), "Alternative Measurement Approaches to Consumer Values: The List of Values (LOV) and Values and Lifestyle (VALS)", *Journal of Consumer Research*, 13, Dec., pp. 405-409.

Kotler, Philip (1999), *Marketing Management: Analysis, Planning, Implementation, and Control*, 9th Edition, New Delhi, Prentice-Hall.

Levin, Richard I., and Davis S. Rubin (1995), *Statistics for Managemen*, Sixth Edition, New Delhi, Prentice-Hall, pp. 516-547.

Pande, Bhanu, and Prasanth Prabhakaran (1996), "Once the Fumes Settle", *A&M*, 15 April, pp. 38-40.

Piirto, Rebecca (1991), "VALS the Second Time", *American Demographics*, July, p. 6.

Schiffman, Leon G., and Leslie Lazar Kanuk (1995), *Consumer Behaviour*, Fifth Edition, New Delhi, Prentice-Hall.

Schiffman, Leon G., and Leslie Lazar Kanuk (2000), *Consumer Behaviour*, Sixth Edition, New Delhi, Prentice-Hall.

Weirs, Ronald M. (1984), *Marketing Research*, New Jersey, Prentice-Hall, pp. 212-254.

Wilkie, William L. (1990), *Consumer Behaviour*, Second Edition, New York, John Wiley and Sons.

16

Measuring Consumer Satisfaction Through Importance Performance Analysis*

INTRODUCTION

Consumer satisfaction is a substantive domain in the field of marketing management because of two reasons. Firstly, it is a significant determinant of repeat purchase and consumer loyalty in case of convenience goods, and secondly, it generates positive word of mouth publicity for infrequently purchased high ticket-items and services. For individual consumer it is important because it reflects a positive outcome from the outlay of scarce resources and/or the fulfillment of unmet needs (Bearden and Teel, 1983). Word of mouth (WOM) about the product or company by a satisfied consumer is considered to be the best advertisement by many marketing oriented companies (Barry, 1980).

Marketing Concept as basic philosophy of business has been accepted as rule in developed countries of the world since 1970s. However, this philosophy gained acceptance in developing countries a bit late. With the advent of competition in the 1980s, Indian firms have realised the significance of marketing concept and gradually started adopting it (Khan and Patel, 1987). In the West, companies subscribing to this philosophy are paying increased attention to assess their current level of consumer satisfaction/ dissatisfaction associated with their products and services since more than three decades (Anderson, 1973). Researchers in this

* This study has been jointly conducted by Prof. Kaleem Mohammed Khan and Dr.Valeed A. Ansari, Reader, Department of Business Administration, AMU, Aligarh.

area also tried to examine the process through which consumers arrive at value judgment (Anderson and Arthus, 1977). These value judgements or evaluations are based primarily on product attributes because consumer sees a given product as a bundle of attributes. Consumer will pay the most attention to those attributes that are connected with their needs (Kotler, 2000). Consumers are found to apply different evaluative processes before coming to a brand choice on the basis of importance they attach to the different product attributes. According to Hunt (1977) consumer satisfaction with a product refers to the quality of individuals subjective evaluation of various outcomes and experiences associated with using or consuming it. Though, this definition was developed around 1970s based on the *expectation disconfirmation model* predominant at that time, yet, with the coming up of more theoretical approaches in the 1980s a revised definition was needed. Mowen (1990) has given the following definition:

> Consumer satisfaction/dissatisfaction consists of general feelings that a consumer has developed about a product or service after its purchase.

As such satisfaction is a type of consumer attitude which may result from expectancy confirmation as well as from other processes such as equity, attribution, performance evaluation and effect formation (Oliver and DeSarbo, 1980).

A question that arises frequently in the mind of a researcher is how and in what way one can measure the various dimensions of consumer satisfaction?. Consumer behaviour specialists believe that the evaluation process can be thought of as a cognitive process in which consumers compare prior expectations of product outcomes (i.e. with performance and other important attributes) to those actually experienced from the use of a product. The expectation prior to purchase and their realization has a direct bearing on the level of satisfaction (Engel, Kollat and Blackwell, 1973). Therefore, the consumer satisfaction/dissatisfaction is a function of the closeness between the buyers' product expectations and the products' perceived performance. If actual product performance equals or exceeds than those expected, satisfaction results. If, however, product performances are perceived below the expectations, dissatisfaction occurs (Priscilla and Nazursky,

1983). Swan and Comb (1976) has provided empirical support for these propositions.

It is felt, the phenomenon of consumer satisfaction/dissatisfaction can not be measured effectively if firms engage only in attribute importance research or attribute performance research separately. Correct picture of consumer satisfaction/dissatisfaction of a product or brand can only emerge when the research is directed towards both these dimensions simultaneously i.e. attribute importance and attribute performance. In the past, attempts were made by researchers to develop methods to measure product/service satisfaction/dissatisfaction. One such attempt is of using the delighted-terrible (DT) scale. Having been originally developed in the field of sociology, Westbrook (1980) suggests that this scale may also be applied appropriately to research on consumer satisfaction/ dissatisfaction. Martilla and James (1977) have proposed another technique for measuring attribute importance and performance, which can help a firm in the effective development of marketing programme. Owing to its versatility, this technique can be used for measuring various constructs. For instance, Leong and Tan (1992) have employed this approach for assessing the competitive standing of one nation – Singapore – with its key foreign investors. In the present study, the authors have used this approach in measuring the consumer satisfaction by finding the gap between the importance attached to each attribute by the consumers and their subsequent ratings of these attributes in terms of products performance as perceived by them. If both importance and performance matches each other, one may conclude that the consumer experienced satisfaction on the specific attribute. In this way the aggregate satisfaction level can also be measured by summing up the various important attributes and their respective perceived performances for a specific product/brand or a service.

The present study is an attempt to measure indirectly the consumer satisfaction/dissatisfaction by obtaining the importance attached to each attribute by consumers and then obtaining respective attribute performances using *importance performance analysis* for 100 cc motorcycles. Before we discuss the analysis and results, a brief description of the techniques used in the present study and the rationale of selecting 100 cc motorcycles as representative product is in order (It may be mentioned here that this technique can also be used for measuring the attribute importance and performance for any product or service).

THE TECHNIQUE: IMPORTANCE–PERFORMANCE GRID

In order to use this technique, the first step is the identification of attributes of a product/service, which are generally considered by consumer before they make a final brand choice. Identification of attributes can be done by different ways. Firstly, help can be taken from literature search. Secondly, the content analysis of advertisements of different brands appearing in various media can be performed. Thirdly, the consumers, dealers and knowledgeable persons can be asked to enumerate the important attributes of a product or service. In this connection, aided and unaided recall techniques can also be employed. Once the attributes are identified, the next step is arranging these attributes for importance and performance ratings by the users. Rating can be done on a four point scale ranging from of *extremely important* to *not important*. In the same way, attribute performance can also be rated by the same users on the four point scale ranging from *excellent performance* to *poor performance*. After the rating is done by the users, the mean importance and performance of each attribute can be calculated and compared for each brand. In comparing the mean importance and mean performance of an attribute, the deviation is taken into consideration. If, for example, the mean importance is higher than mean performance of an attribute and this difference proves to be statistically significant then one can infer that the consumer might have experienced some amount of dissatisfaction on that particular attribute. Whenever, one finds the mean performance exceeding the mean importance on a particular attribute then satisfaction will result. The extent of satisfaction or dissatisfaction depends on the magnitude of deviation on the one hand and the degree of importance attached to that attribute on the other. This means that for a highly important attribute, a slight fall in the performance may lead to high amount of dissatisfaction and vice versa.

An attractive feature of importance performance approach is that the results can be graphically displayed on an easily interpreted two-dimensional grid with four quadrants as given in Fig. 16.1.

Fig. 16.1: Importance Performance Grid

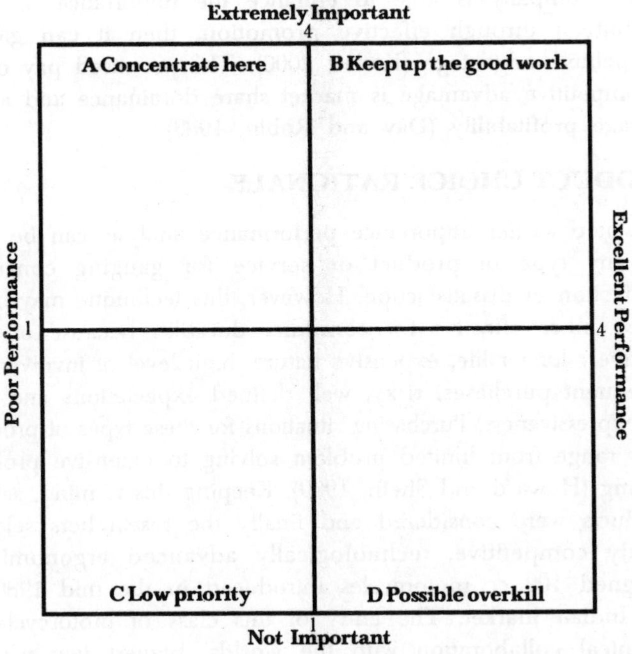

In analysing importance performance grid, particular attention should be given to those attributes falling in the *Quadrant A* which requires maximum concentration on the part of the company. Any attribute falling in this quadrant indicates that this attribute is extremely important to users but the concomitant perceived performance of this attribute is less than satisfactory and consequently may lead to considerable dissatisfaction.

Attributes falling in *Quadrant B* indicate that more or less the importance and performance are matched on the higher side. The company can keep the good work and try to move the attribute towards the right side of the grid. Attributes falling in *Quadrant C* are generally of low priority, because both from importance and performance point of view these attributes do not warrant much of company's efforts. In the *Quadrant D,* the company has managed to generate high performance for a particular attribute. However, consumers presently do not perceive attribute falling in quadrant D as important, though the company is an advantageous position vis-à-vis its competitors on these attributes. If the company is able to enhance the importance of these attribute(s) through effective promotion, then it can gain a competitive advantage (Kotler, 2000). The promised pay off of a competitive advantage is market share dominance and above average profitability (Day and Robin, 1988).

PRODUCT CHOICE RATIONALE

As stated earlier importance performance analysis can be used for any type of product or service for gauging consumer satisfaction or dissatisfaction. However, this technique may prove to be more effective for consumer durables because of their relatively longer life, expensive nature, high level of involvement, infrequent purchases, risky, well defined expectations and high self-expressiveness. Purchasing situations for these types of products may range from limited problem solving to extensive problem solving (Howard and Sheth, 1969). Keeping this is mind, several products were considered and finally the researchers selected highly competitive, technologically advanced ergonomically designed 100 cc motorcycles introduced in the mid 1980s in the Indian market. The entry of this class of motorcycles in technical collaboration with the worlds' biggest two wheeler companies Honda, Suzuki, Yamaha and Kawasaki, has brought a great shake up and metamorphosis in the Indian two wheeler market. Fifteen years ago there were barely few well-known names in this market. With the introduction of these motorcycles, the competition has become very keen and companies have begun poaching on each other territories. One of the indicators of the keen competition is the frequent use of comparative advertising by some of the motorcycle manufacturers. These manufactures are not competing on price and price-cutting is rare. Predominately the competition is on non-price factors, such as fuel efficiency, power, looks, acceleration, toughness etc. Therefore, these attributes are invariably highlighted by the companies in their advertising and promotional compaigns. Naturally, consumers must have formed certain expectations and started attaching different importance weights to these attributes. In order to avoid any inadvertent adverse publicity, of any particular brand, the researchers concealed the real brand names and instead have used fictitious brand names, such as A, B, C and D.

DATA BASE

The data for the present study were collected from the owners of four brands of 100 cc motorcycles in Aligarh city, which has a population around 1 million and is situated in Northern India, through a structured questionnaire. In the first part of questionnaire, respondents were asked to rate the importance they attached to different attributes of motorcycles before they made a final brand choice. In the second part of the questionnaire, again, they were asked to rate the performance of the same attributes. Attribute identification was accomplished through a pilot survey of the owners and also through the content analysis of advertisements appearing in different media. In all, the following nine attributes of motorcycles were finally selected for importance performance analysis.

1. Fuel economy
2. Acceleration
3. Power
4. Looks (style)
5. Toughness
6. Handling
7. Riding comfort
8. Maintenance cost
9. After sale service

For importance rating, respondents were provided four response categories and were asked to assign 4 for *extremely important*, 3 for *important*, 2 for *slightly important* and 1 for *not important*. In the same way, for performance also four response categories were provided and respondents were asked to assign 4 for *excellent* 3 for *good*, 2 for *fair* and 1 for *poor*. Thus, the rating of each respondent, for both importance and performance, was summated and aggregate mean rating for each attribute was calculated separately for each brand. For the database the dealers of these of these brands were contacted and the addresses of those who had purchased these motorcycles during the last two years were obtained. From the list of each brand users, sixty owners were selected for each brand on a random basis and later they were contacted on telephone and the rating were obtained from those who agree to participate in the study. In this way the responses of a total number of 205 respondents, for all the motorcycles, were analysed.

RESULTS

The mean importance and mean performance rating for all the nine attributes for each brand of motorcycles are arranged and presented in Tables 16.1, 16.2, 16.3 and 16.4 and the same information has been displayed in the graphical form by constructing *importance performance girds* in Figures 16.2, 16.3, 16.4 and 16.5 respectively. As mentioned earlier while discussing the technique,

Fig. 16.2: Importance Performance Grid for Brand A

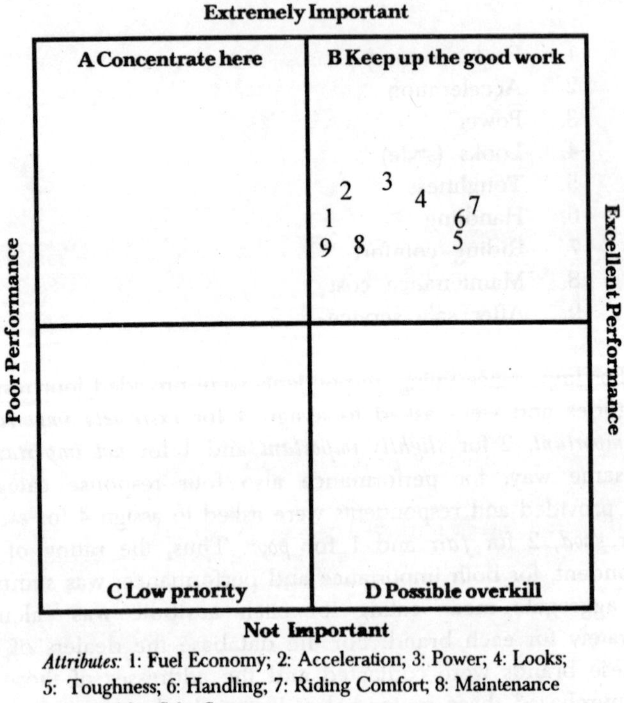

Attributes: 1: Fuel Economy; 2: Acceleration; 3: Power; 4: Looks; 5: Toughness; 6: Handling; 7: Riding Comfort; 8: Maintenance Cost; 9: After Sales Service

each grid has been divided into four quadrants. In dividing the grid, 2.5 mean has been taken as the cut-off point for high and low dimensions both for mean importance and mean performance. We have chosen this as mid point, which means that if the mean importance or mean performance for an attribute is more than 2.5, then it was considered to be on the higher side and a mean score of less than 2.5 was considered to be on the lower side. Though, the mid point selection seems to be an arbitrary one, yet, the researchers feel that approximately it demarcates the higher and lower side of scale.

Examining Fig. 16.2 for brand A, one can easily discern that all the attributes fall in the quadrant B i.e. "Keep up the good work" quadrant. However, when we examine the same results in Table 16.1, some disturbing trends seem to emerge as there is a noticeable gap between the importance and performance means of certain attributes. Notably, among them are fuel economy (1) power (3) after sales services (9) and acceleration (2). For all these attributes the users have assigned more importance and the concomitant performances are less than desired, thereby generating some amount of dissatisfaction. Therefore, company must pay attention to improve the performance of these attributes. In terms of toughness (5) handling (6) and riding comfort (7), the company should continue to "keep up the good work". These are the attributes in which the firm has some degree of competitive advantage. Naturally, the users must be experiencing high level of satisfaction on these attributes.

Table 16.1: Importance Performance Rating for Brand A

Attribute No.	*Attribute description*	*Mean importance*	*Mean performance*	*Deviation*
1.	Fuel Economy	3.00	2.60	-0.40
2.	Acceleration	3.24	2.68	-0.56
3.	Power	3.28	2.92	-0.36
4.	Looks	3.16	3.12	-0.04
5.	Toughness	2.92	3.20	+0.28
6.	Handling	3.00	3.20	+0.20
7.	Riding comfort	3.16	3.24	+0.08
8.	Maintenance cost	2.88	2.80	-0.08
9.	After sales services	2.84	2.52	-0.32

Fig. 16.3: Importance Performance Grid for Brand B

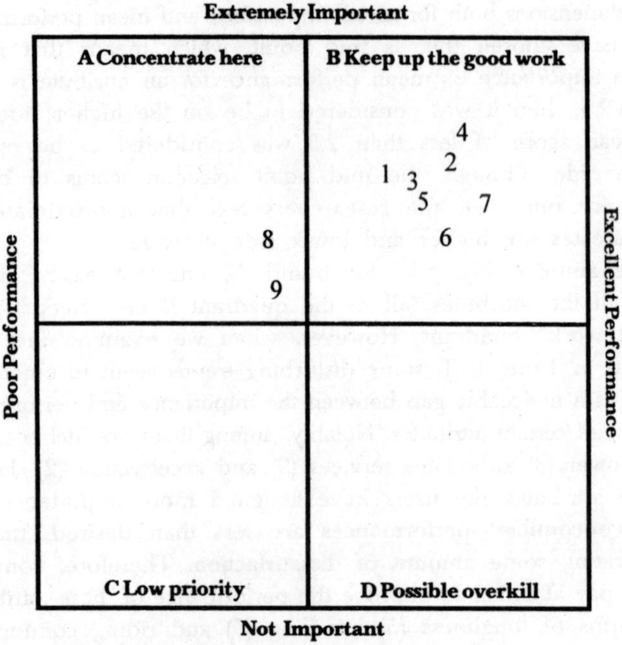

Attributes: 1: Fuel Economy; 2: Acceleration; 3: Power; 4: Looks; 5: Toughness; 6: Handling; 7: Riding Comfort; 8: Maintenance Cost; 9: After Sales Service

Table 16.2: Importance Performance Rating for Brand B

Attribute No.	*Attribute description*	*Mean importance*	*Mean performance*	*Deviation*
1.	Fuel Economy	3.36	2.92	- 0.44
2.	Acceleration	3.44	3.24	- 0.20
3.	Power	3.32	3.12	- 0.20
4.	Looks	3.52	3.28	- 0.04
5.	Toughness	3.20	3.08	- 0.12
6.	Handling	2.92	3.24	+0.32
7.	Riding comfort	3.20	3.48	+0.28
8.	Maintenance cost	2.92	2.29	- 0.63
9.	After sales services	2.60	2.39	- 0.24

Observing importance performance rating in Fig. 16.3, one finds out that all the attributes, except attributes 8 and 9, fall in quadrant B. In addition, to improve the performance of attributes 8 and 9, firm should also pay attention to improve the performances of four other attributes falling in quadrant B, particularly, fuel economy (1) because the gap between the importance and performance rating means is quite large. Other attributes which require some efforts on the part of the firm are acceleration (2) power (3) and looks (4).

For brand C one can observe from Fig. 16.4 that all the attributes again fall in "keep up the good work" quadrant. This indicates that, relatively speaking the owners of this brand are pleased

Fig. 16.4: Importance Performance Grid for Brand C

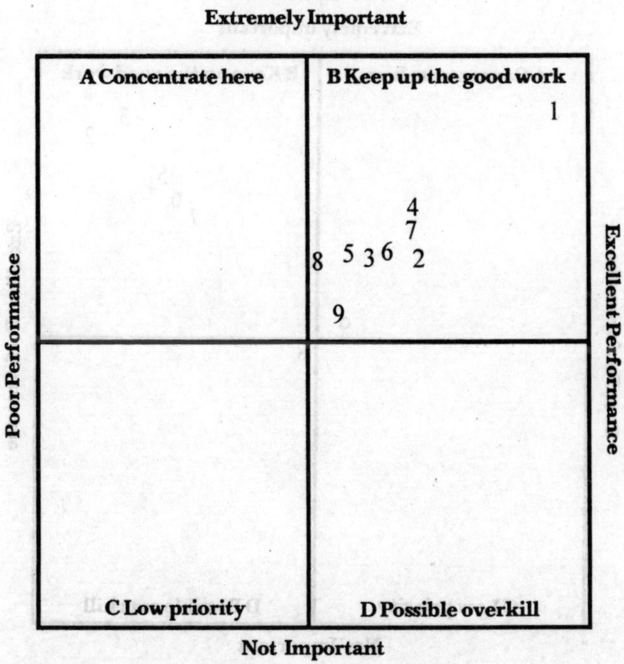

Attributes: 1: Fuel Economy; 2: Acceleration; 3: Power; 4: Looks; 5: Toughness; 6: Handling; 7: Riding Comfort; 8: Maintenance Cost; 9: After Sales Service

Table 16.3: Importance Performance Rating for Brand C

Attribute No.	*Attribute description*	*Mean importance*	*Mean performance*	*Deviation*
1.	Fuel Economy	3.88	3.92	+0.04
2.	Acceleration	2.88	3.16	+0.28
3.	Power	2.88	2.80	- 0.08
4.	Looks	3.20	3.12	- 0.08
5.	Toughness	2.92	2.68	- 0.24
6.	Handling	2.92	2.88	- 0.04
7.	Riding comfort	3.12	3.04	- 0.08
8.	Maintenance cost	2.84	2.56	- 0.28
9.	After sales services	2.60	2.64	+0.04

Fig. 16.5: Importance Performance Grid for Brand D

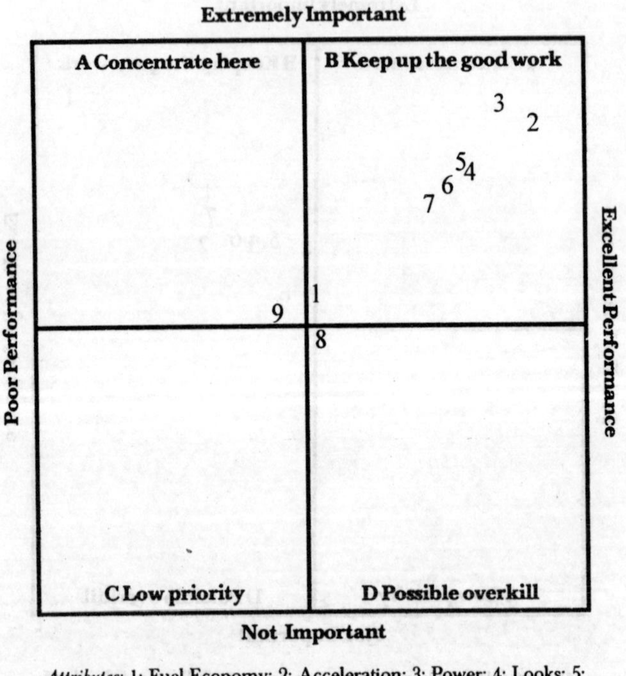

Attributes: 1: Fuel Economy; 2: Acceleration; 3: Power; 4: Looks; 5: Toughness; 6: Handling; 7: Riding Comfort; 8: Maintenance Cost; 9: After Sales Service

with the performances on all the attributes. However, the overall satisfaction can be enhanced further if the firm concentrate to improve the performances and image of toughness (attribute 5) and maintenance cost (8). Nevertheless, this brand had proved to be highly satisfactory to the owners vis-à-vis the other three brands.

The importance performance results for brand D are shown in Table 16.4 and Fig. 16.5 indicate that except attribute 8 and 9, all the remaining attributes fall in quadrant B. The level of dissatisfaction with seven attributes that are in the quadrant B seems to be rather low because the gap between the importance and performance rating is insignificant and may be attributed to sampling variations. As far as maintenance cost (8) is concerned the owners of this brand are experiencing high level of satisfaction because mean performance of this attribute is much higher than the mean importance. To a great extent this attributes can be used by the brand D firm as competitive advantage and highlight it in its promotional and marketing communication programme. The firm's real worry lies in after sales service (9) because it lies in quadrant A. Firm should take measures to improve after sales service by streamlining its customer service department on the one hand and motivating the channel members to increase after sales service performance on the other.

Table 16.4: Importance Performance Rating for Brand D

Attribute No.	*Attribute description*	*Mean importance*	*Mean performance*	*Deviation*
1.	Fuel Economy	2.60	2.52	- 0.08
2.	Acceleration	3.56	3.88	+0.32
3.	Power	3.72	3.64	- 0.08
4.	Looks	3.32	3.48	+.016
5.	Toughness	3.36	3.44	+0.08
6.	Handling	3.28	3.36	+0.08
7.	Riding comfort	3.16	3.20	+0.04
8.	Maintenance cost	2.48	2.64	+0.16
9.	After sales services	2.52	2.32	- 0.20

DISCUSSION

The forgoing analysis has shown that it is a versatile, easy to use technique not only for measuring importance and performance of an attribute but also can be used in finding out the extent of satisfaction/dissatisfaction related with a specific attribute in particular and with the product in general. Another important dimension of this analysis is that consumer groups attach different importance weights to different product attributes and then accordingly they select a specific brand. For example, one group of consumers may attach importance to a particular attribute and then try to match this importance with the perceived or potential performance of that attribute in the brand of its choice. Another group of consumers may attach high importance to some other attribute and accordingly it chooses that brand which it feels will give high performance on that attribute. This is what we witnessed in the results of importance performance analysis of four brands of motorcycles. For instance, in case of brand A, the first three most important attributes were power, acceleration and riding comfort. However, in the first two attributes the performance was considerably lower as compared to importance attached by users. For the third important attribute the performance exceeded the importance. This means that consumers experienced disconfirmed expectations leading to some amount of dissatisfaction with regard to first two attributes and simultaneously they experienced high level of satisfaction for third important attribute. To what extent the high satisfaction on one attribute compensates the dissatisfaction on other attributes depends largely on the importance weight consumers assign to different attributes for reaching towards a global attitude for the brand (Fishebein, Martin, 1967) and the consumers coping style to magnify or minimize the gap between the product performance and expectations (Day, 1984).

For the other brands again, we find that attribute importance mix is slightly different. For instance, in case of brand B the first three important attributes were looks, fuel, economy and power. The company manufacturing brand B has to do something drastically different to improve the performance on all three attributes because it is less than the mean performance rating (see Table 16.2). Owners of brand C have somewhat different attribute importance mix. Here maximum importance was assigned by the owners to fuel economy, followed by looks and riding comfort. Interestingly, this brand's performance closely matches with the importance on these three attributes. Because of these findings one may surmise that the satisfaction level of consumers must be highest for this brand. As far as brand D is concerned the owners have attached maximum importance to power, acceleration and toughness in order of descendence. Again, we find the performance of these attributes in brand D as being higher or equal to the importance assigned, thus leading to considerable satisfaction.

This discussion has clearly shown that this technique can be used for identifying the different segments of the market on the basis of importance attached to different attributes. As far as market of 100 cc motorcycle is concerned, it can conveniently be segmented on the basis of different benefits sought by consumers from the product. Studies have shown that in a highly competitive market, benefit segmentation could prove to be powerful market strategy (Haley, 1963 and Yankelovich, 1984).

CONCLUDING NOTE

This study has an applied research bias. Firms can use importance performance analysis not only to find the relative importance assigned to different product attributes but can also measure concomitant performance of these attributes in a particular brand. In addition to this, they can also measure the level of consumer satisfaction/dissatisfaction on the basis of gap between importance and performance. Companies can use this technique on a periodic basis to see the changes that are taking place in both the importance attached to different attributes by the users and the concomitant perceived performance. This technique can be used both as a planning and control tool. As a planning tool, importance performance analysis provides management with a useful focus for development marketing strategies and as a control device, it provides a firm a clear picture of its strengths and weaknesses. By taking prompt steps and rectifying the deficiencies and taking advantage of strengths, a particular firm can occupy a dominant and strong position in a market or in a particular segment of the market.

REFERENCES

Anderson Alen R. and Best Arthus (1977), "Consumer Complain–Does Business Listen?" *Harvard Business Review*, pp. 93-101.

Anderson, Ralph E. (1973) "Consumer Dissatisfaction: The Effect of Disconfirmed Expectancy on Perceived Product Performance", *Journal of Marketing Research*, Vol. 10, pp. 38-44.

Bayes L. Barry (1980), "Word of Mouth: The Indirect Effects of Marketing Efforts", *Journal of Advertising Research*, June/July, pp. 31-39.

Bearden William O. and Jeese Teel (1983), "Selected Determinants of Consumer Satisfaction and Complaint Reports", *Journal of Marketing Research*, 19, November, pp. 321-328.

Day S. George and Wensley Robin (1988), "Assessing Advantage: A Framework for Diagnosing Competitive Superiority", *Journal of Marketing*, Vol. 52, April, pp. 1-20.

Day L. Ralph (1984), "Modelling Choices Among Alternative Responses to Dissatisfaction", in *Advances in Consumer Research*, ed. Thomas C. Kinnear, XI, pp. 496-99.

Engel James F. Kollat, David T. and Blackwell Roger D. (1973), *Consumer Behaviour*, Holt Rinehart and Winston, New York, pp. 534-43.

Fishbein Martin (1967), "Attitude and Prediction of Behaviour", in *Readings in Attitude Theory and Measurement*, ed. Martin Fishbein, New York, John Wiley, pp. 477-92.

Howard A. John and Sheth N. Jagdish (1969), *The Theory of Buyer Behavior*, John Wiley & Sons, New York, pp. 27-28.

Hunt H. Keity (1977), "Consumer Satisfaction, Dissatisfaction: An Overview and Research Directions", in *Conceptualisation and Measurement of Consumer Satisfaction and Dissatisfaction* ed. H. Keith Hunt, Marketing Science Institute, Cambridge, pp. 455-88.

Khan Kaleem M. and Naresh Patel (1987), "Has Marketing Concept Been Adopted in India?" *Marketology Quarterly*, Vol. 19, July-December, pp. 5-9.

Khan Kaleem M. and Aijaaz Mohd (1988), "Comparative Advertising: Content Analysis of Magazine Advertisements", *Indian Management*, Vol. 27, December, pp. 4-10.

Kotler Philips (2000), *Marketing Management*, Prentice Hall India Pvt. Limited., New Delhi.

La Barbera A. Priscilla and Nazursky David (1983), "A Longitudinal Assessment of Consumer Satisfaction/Dissatisfaction: A Dynamic Aspect of the Cognitive Process", *Journal of Marketing Research*, November, pp. 393-404.

Leong S.M. and Chin Tiong Tan (1991), "Assessing National Competitive Superiority: An Importance-Performance Matrix Approach", *Asia*

Pacific International Journal of Marketing, Vol. 3, No. 2, pp. 26-37.

Martilla A. John and James C. John (1977), "Importance Performance Analysis", *Journal of Marketing*, Vol. 2, April, pp. 38-40.

Mowen John C, (1990), *Consumer Behaviour*, McMillan Publishing Company, New York, p. 345.

Oliver and DeSarbo (1980), "Response Determinants in Satisfaction Judgements", *Journal of Consumer Research*, Vol. 15, pp. 455-488.

Swan John E. and Coms Linda J. (1976), "Product Performance and Consumer Satisfaction: A New Concept", *Journal of Marketing*, 40, pp. 25-33.

Westbrook Robert A. (1980), "A Rating Scale for Measuring Product/ Service Satisfaction", *Journal of Marketing*, Vol. 44, pp. 69-72.

Yankelovich Daniel (1984), "New Criteria for Marketing Segmentation", *Harvard Business Review*, March-April, pp. 83-90.

Haley J. Russel (1963), "Benefit Segmentation: A Decision Oriented Research Tool", *Journal of Marketing*, July, pp. 30-35.

Index